Historical Problems:
Studies and Documents

Edited by
PROFESSOR G. R. ELTON
University of Cambridge

22

THE TREASURY 1660–1870

In the same series

THE TREASURY 1660-1870

The Foundations of Control

Henry Roseveare

King's College, London

LONDON: GEORGE ALLEN & UNWIN LTD
NEW YORK: BARNES AND NOBLE BOOKS
(A division of Harper & Row Publishers, Inc.)

First published in 1973

© George Allen & Unwin Ltd 1973

Published in the USA 1973 by Harper & Row Publishers, Inc.
Barnes and Noble Import Division

BRITISH ISBN 0 04 942114 x hardback
          0 04 942115 8 paperback

AMERICAN ISBN 06-495984-8

Printed in Great Britain
in 10 point Plantin type
by The Aldine Press, Letchworth

GENERAL INTRODUCTION

The reader and the teacher of history might be forgiven for thinking that there are now too many series of historical documents in existence, all claiming to offer light on particular problems and all able to fulfil their claims. At any rate, the general editor of yet another series feels obliged to explain why he is helping one more collection of such volumes into existence.

One purpose of this series is to put at the disposal of the student original materials illustrating historical problems, but this is no longer anything out of the way. A little less usual is the decision to admit every sort of historical question: there are no barriers of time or place or theme. However, what really distinguishes this enterprise is the fact that it combines generous collections of documents with introductory essays long enough to explore the theme widely and deeply. In the doctrine of educationalists, it is the original documents that should be given to the student; in the experience of teachers, documents thrown naked before the untrained mind turn from pearls to paste. The study of history cannot be confined either to the learning up of results without a consideration of the foundations, or to a review of those foundations without the assistance of the expert mind. The task of teaching involves explanation and instruction, and these volumes recognize this possibly unfashionable fact. Beyond that, they enable the writers to say new and important things about their subject matter: to write history of an exploratory kind, which is the only important historical writing there is.

As a result, each volume will be a historical monograph worth the attention which all such monographs deserve, and each volume will stand on its own. While the format of the series is uniform, the contents will vary according to need. Some problems require the reconsideration which makes the known enlighteningly new; others need the attention of original research; yet others will have to enter controversy because the prevailing notions on many historical questions are demonstrably wrong. The authors of this series are free to treat their subject in whatever manner it seems to them to require. They will present some of their evidence for inspection and help the learner to see how history is written, but they will themselves also write history.

G.R.E.

For Iris

PREFACE

The terminal dates of this study require some explanation. They have not been chosen arbitrarily, or for convenience: a shorter period could have been more comfortably handled. Rather, 1660 and 1870 impose themselves, marking out boundaries for any study which seeks to examine the Treasury's early evolution.[1] On the one hand, the 1660s witness the very striking emergence of the Treasury as a department of state, exercising a new degree of authority through some novel means. At the other end, the conclusion of one era and the beginning of another are emphatically defined by a whole row of landmarks – with the completion of 'the circle of control' by the Exchequer and Audit Departments Act of 1866 and the consequent Treasury Minute of 1868 (Docs. 18 and 19), with the inauguration of Open Competition in the Civil Service and a major reorganization of the Treasury in 1870 (Doc. 27). While there is always something artificial about the historian's demarcation of boundaries, I hope to show that there can be no mistaking the reality of these.

However, the reader can judge this for himself. At several points in the Introduction I shall argue that some valuable interpretations of the Treasury's history have been flawed by narrow or incorrect perspectives, suggesting uniqueness or special importance in developments which take on a quite different significance when seen in the larger context. The object of this book is to provide that context and some of the documentation on which an opinion can be formed.

Likewise, the reader must judge whether the aspects I have chosen to discuss are the really important ones. Here again, although selection was essential in a book of this scale, it is not solely convenience which has determined the choice. I have tried to define something about the nature of Treasury control which is more important than the superficial characteristics of its day-to-day enforcement. My theme is, rather, the creation of the administrative, political and constitutional base from which such enforcement could begin. Part of this foundation was certainly composed of immemorial powers antedating the 1660s, and the significance of the late-seventeenth-century Treasury (discussed in Section One) lies precisely in the way in which traditional authority was consolidated with such vigour, consistency and originality that it was never again in danger of eclipse. But effective Treasury control

[1] For reasons which will become apparent in Section 3, the same dates provided the obvious limits for the Institute of Historical Research's recent publication, *Officeholders in Modern Britain: Treasury Officials, 1660–1870*, ed. J. C. Sainty.

really needed effective parliamentary control for its logical completion, and for this reason crucial stages in the evolution of the Treasury's authority are closely linked to the steps by which the House of Commons made itself competent to control public expenditure. This is a theme to be traced through parliamentary inquiries, debates and legislation as much as through Treasury minutes, and it is as much concerned with the Exchequer and its anomalies as with the senior institution which so strikingly failed to reform it. Section Two, therefore, carries an account of this problem past the abolition of the Exchequer in 1834 to the sequence of mid-nineteenth-century reforms which left the Treasury under a heavy but healthy responsibility to the watchdogs of the House of Commons.

The autonomy of the Treasury reasserts itself in Section Three, which deals with the evolution of its internal organization. This was never very elaborate at any point before the Second World War, but even at the earliest date human problems of organization and methods were vital to its institutional efficiency. The development of its hierarchy was an important achievement of the late-seventeenth-century Treasury and, by the second half of the eighteenth century, questions of training and specialization are being earnestly considered. By the early nineteenth century problems of discipline and recruitment are acute, and even Treasury clerks begin to ask themselves 'what are we doing, and is this the best way of doing it?'. This unusual degree of self-awareness about the professional shortcomings of the department only narrowly anticipated the moment at which public concern focussed on the question of civil service reform in general and the Treasury's role in particular. As a result, the collision between the criticisms of those outside the Treasury and the views of those inside was more painful than it might otherwise have been. The Treasury was reformed, but it was also demoralized, and the history of the department up to 1870 is one of slow reconstruction. In the process, the professional self-sufficiency of the department was largely recovered, with results which have shaped its character until modern times.

These are the complementary themes which I have chosen to document, and they will seem to leave little room for many traditional features of the Treasury's image – patronage and parliamentary management, fiscal policy and high finance. This is partly owing to the limitations of space, but I hope it is also because I have correctly identified what was fundamental rather than incidental to the Treasury's development – its 'problem' rather than its problems. Clearly there is room for argument about this and I shall be happy if this book stimulates it.

H. ROSEVEARE

ACKNOWLEDGEMENTS

It would have been impossible to compile this book without the resources of the Public Record Office and the British Museum's Manuscript and State Paper Rooms. I am greatly indebted to them and to the staffs of the London Library and Institute of Historical Research for their assistance. I have a particular debt to Mr John Sainty of the Institute of Historical Research for discussion and advice on the selection of documents, and I am most grateful to him for drawing attention to Document 20. Manuscript material from the Public Record Office is Crown Copyright, and is published here with the permission of the Controller of Her Majesty's Stationery Office.

Material from the British Museum is published with the kind permission of the Trustees.

ABBREVIATIONS

Add. MSS.	Additional Manuscripts, British Museum
BIHR	*Bulletin of the Institute of Historical Research*
BM	British Museum
CTB	*Calendar of Treasury Books*
CTB & P	*Calendar of Treasury Books and Papers*
CSPD	*Calendar of State Papers Domestic*
EHR	*English Historical Review*
HMC	Historical Manuscripts Commission
PP	*Parliamentary Papers*
PRO	Public Record Office
SPDom	State Papers Domestic, Public Record Office
SPFor	State Papers Foreign, Public Record Office

Unless stated otherwise, I have modernized the spelling, capitalization and punctuation of all documents, whether from manuscript or printed sources.

CONTENTS

INTRODUCTION

The Treasury Commission of 1667 and its legacy

WRITING of 'the Treasury' at almost any point in the last three hundred years of its history, one could find it troublesome to explain precisely what one means by the term. Bricks and mortar in Whitehall? A quorum of 'My Lords'? The permanent officials? A legal abstraction? The answers will differ according to time and circumstance, but at least answers can be given in terms of an institution, with institutional characteristics – physical location, established hierarchy, acknowledged authority. For nearly three hundred years 'the Treasury' has been, in that sense, a distinct administrative entity with a permanent and well-defined presence in the machinery of English government.

It is much less easy to think in such terms of 'the Treasury' in the early 1660s. There was indeed a Lord Treasurer, the fourth earl of Southampton, who conducted business in his quarters at Whitehall with the help of a secretary, a solicitor, a serjeant-at-arms and a small group of messengers. He held one of the most senior and ancient offices of state, with defined duties and explicit authority, and in his character as Treasurer of the Exchequer presided over an organization which possessed in superabundance all the attributes of an institution. The Exchequer was not only ancient, it was reformed. Its medieval origins had rooted it firmly in the law and custom of the realm. Its sixteenth-century evolution had left it undisputed master of the Crown's finances. It possessed a very large staff with complex but exactly-defined functions. The Exchequer, to all appearances, was formidably equipped as the central institution of English finance.

How and why, then, did a distinct institution called 'the Treasury' emerge as the dominant arbiter of financial administration? How does one measure, let alone explain, the development of its authority and autonomy in relation to the sovereign institutions of government – to the Crown, to the Privy Council and to the other great departments of state? Is the development of the Treasury a reflection of constitutional change, or of administrative innovation? Is it an optical illusion caused by the decline of the Exchequer? At what point did the process reach maturity? To whom belongs the credit? The questions can be multiplied.

The only detailed study of the process[1] has shown itself sensitive to the difficulties. It acknowledges the inadequacy of an investigation confined to the years 1660 to 1702, for this is not the only fertile period of Treasury evolution. Long before the earl of Danby mastered the twin worlds of parliament and finance, Lord Treasurers like Burghley, Robert Cecil or Juxon had exercised a similar dominance of political and administrative power, and it still remained for Walpole and the Younger Pitt to complete the identification of the Treasury with the premiership. Equally, we are reminded, the King remained master in his own house until the end of the seventeenth century. The Treasury's independence of the sovereign's will, or wilfulness, cannot be taken for granted before, or even after, 1688.[2] And, even if the Privy Council ceased to superintend the Treasury before the death of Charles II, it was still likely that financial decisions – which are often political decisions – would be subject to the collective verdict of the Cabinet. Indeed, the late seventeenth-century Treasury was peculiarly vulnerable to political cross-currents. While single Lord Treasurers were uniquely exposed to assaults, a Treasury Commission was often stultified by its internal divisions.[3] The clearest conclusions of the book are, therefore, that 'in the period between 1660 and 1702 the tendency was for the authority of the Treasury to increase', and that 'if the Treasury was a great office in 1660 it was a greater one in 1702.'[4] During the process 'the Treasury office grew from something approaching the personal retinue of a magnate into a professional body of civil servants. The process had begun before 1660 and it continued after 1702.' 'One cannot describe it as the invention of any one man.'[5]

With these broad and cautious generalizations one may safely agree. However, the author attempted some bolder assertions. He was dissatisfied with the traditional view, associated with W. A. Shaw and D. M. Gill,[6] that the significant turning-point in the Treasury's history was the death of the earl of Southampton in 1667 and the appointment of a Treasury Commission with Sir George Downing as its secretary. Downing, he argues, was a social and political nonentity

---

[1] S. B. Baxter, *The Development of the Treasury 1660–1702* (London, 1957).

[2] Baxter, *Treasury*, p. 260, cf. p. 55.

[3] Ibid., pp. 60–1, cf. pp. 35, 262.

[4] Ibid., pp. 3–4.

[5] Ibid., p. 257, cf. p. 169.

[6] W. A. Shaw expounded his views of Treasury evolution in his editorial prefaces to the *Calendar of Treasury Books*, and, notably, in his preface to the *Calendar of Treasury Books and Papers, 1729–30*, London, 1897. D. M. Gill's essay, 'The Treasury, 1660–1714', *EHR*, xlvi (1931), 600 retains value as an interpretation.

whose financial ideas were unoriginal and not always successful. He did much to establish the Treasury's book-keeping but the incentive was negative, a response to the decline of Exchequer records.[7] If the development of the Treasury office under Downing was 'great' and 'important', nevertheless 'the place of Secretary was less important between 1667 and 1671 than it was before or after'.[8] Similarly, although the Treasury Commission of 1667 was an active and expert body which successfully asserted its authority against the Secretaries of State, it found that in trying to enforce retrenchments in government expenditure by means of Orders in Council it got 'caught in its own web', unable to alter the Council's mandate.[9] Lord Treasurer Danby did not make the same mistake: a proviso was written into his retrenchment scheme of 1676 which allowed alterations without reference to the Council. To this point great significance is attached. It leads to the suggestion that 'if one is to choose a particular year in which the Treasury reached maturity, it would be 1676'. 'If one must have a turning point, let it be 1676 rather than 1667.' 'By 1676 then, the Treasury had emerged as a department of state.'[10]

One can sympathize with this attempt to give a novel shape to the story of Treasury evolution. W. A. Shaw and D. M. Gill are not wholly reliable guides. If it has ever been asserted that the Treasury 'sprang fully armed from the head of Charles II on a day in May 1667', or that 'Downing made up the Treasury office out of whole cloth' and 'was responsible for the virtual creation of a department of State' then the critic is right to deny it.[11] But with the accompanying arguments and assertions one must largely disagree. The views summarized in the preceding paragraph are either unfair, misjudged or demonstrably incorrect, and in debating these points I believe one can best serve the purpose of this section, which is designed to illustrate the way in which the Treasury established its authority in a comparatively short period after 1667. They are years which have a quite disproportionate significance for the later evolution of the Treasury.

Any attempt to re-assess the significance of 1667 must first take account of all the evidence that the Treasury Commission appointed on the earl of Southampton's death on 16 May was intended by the king and recognized by contemporaries to mark a radical new departure.

---

[7] Baxter, *Treasury*, p. 217.
[8] Ibid., pp. 168, 181, cf. pp. 127, 217.
[9] Ibid., p. 62.
[10] Ibid., pp. 62, 63, 65, 66, 262.
[11] Some such claims are indeed made by W. A. Shaw in his introduction to the *CTB & P 1729-30*, p. lii and by John Beresford in *The Godfather of Downing Street: Sir George Downing, 1623-1684* (London, 1925), p. 202.

Speculation before the event had anticipated another conventional Lord Treasurer chosen from among senior courtiers – perhaps Lord Arlington or Lord Sandwich.[12] Then the talk was of a Commission which, like those of the early seventeenth century, would be temporary and include great officers of state such as the Lord Chancellor and the two Secretaries of State. But it was the Lord Chancellor, the earl of Clarendon, who had to bear the initial shock of the king's uncounselled decision – a decision which, although taken amid the debts and disasters of the second Dutch war, was not a hasty one. Evidently Charles and his brother had been pondering the merits of Cromwellian administration which they knew to have been, characteristically, government by committee, and had decided that they preferred this republican style of managerial control to the courtly deference of some superannuated peer. The Ordnance Office was being satisfactorily run by a board of Commissioners, and it was already the king's intention to put the Scottish Treasury into Commission.[13] Thus, in naming Sir Thomas Clifford, Sir William Coventry and Sir John Duncombe as a Treasury board of tough-minded young men who could be relied upon to say 'No!' Charles II was not lightly breaking with tradition, nor was he making a temporary disposition. 'He would never make another Treasurer,' Charles had told the scandalized Lord Chancellor. It needed all Clarendon's remonstrances to persuade the king that the surviving Chancellor of the Exchequer, Lord Ashley, who held his place on life tenure, must be a member of the board, if not of the quorum, and that a dignified figure like the Duke of Albemarle should be added to give weight to a department which 'had much to do with the Nobility and chief gentry of the Kingdom'. And he must at least make the obscure Duncombe a Privy Councillor. Charles acquiesced, but he had secured his essential purpose. The legal authority of a quorum could be exercised by the 'rougher hands' of his original choice.

Even in its enlarged form, the announcement of the Treasury Commission was startling enough. 'All the Court is disturbed,' noted

---

[12] For rumours about the succession to the Treasurership before Southampton's death see the *Diary of Samuel Pepys* for 18 March, 24, 26, 29 April, 1 May 1667. (Pending the appearance of the later volumes in R. C. Latham's definitive edition of the Diary the Wheatley edition must be consulted, but further footnote references will be by the date only.)

[13] For clues to the king's motives in making this decision we must rely largely upon Clarendon's censorious account, *The Life of Edward Earl of Clarendon* (Oxford, 1760), ii, 354–8. However, A. L. Murray, in 'The Scottish Treasury, 1667–1708', *Scottish Historical Review* (1966), xlv, 89–104, has shed further light by citing Sir R. Moray's remark to the earl of Rothes, that the king had 'intended the change in the Thesaurary of Scotland to precede that of England . . . as a leading case to the rest'.

Pepys. Observers were struck by the Commissioners' youthfulness and surprised by the king's originality. Bets were taken that the experiment would not last long.[14] But the sceptics were soon disabused. Nothing in the history of Restoration administration is more remarkable, or was more heartening to contemporaries, than the manner in which this able group of men established their mastery of the Treasury. Their impact was immediate and impressive. Pepys, Joseph Williamson and other observers carefully put on record their admiration for the speed and dexterity of the Commissioners' proceedings, and by October 1667 even the House of Commons was eager to underwrite their efforts with its own authority.[15] Indeed, by December, Members of Parliament had begun to fear that the Treasury's remarkably good husbandry would 'bring the King to be out of debt and to save money and so will not be in need of the Parliament' – a fear which proved groundless, but Charles could soon afford to boast to the Court of France of his Treasury's new mastery, and in time the Danish envoy was to report home that the king's credit in the business community had been transformed by the Treasury's careful administration.[16] The ultimate parliamentary verdict on the 1667 Treasury Commission, and the two Lord Treasurers who followed it, was that 'the Treasury is better managed by Commissioners than by a Lord Treasurer'.[17]

How did the Treasury Commission earn this remarkable contemporary reputation? More important, how did they succeed in leaving such a deep mark on the subsequent history of the department? It would require a lengthier monograph than this to answer satisfactorily, but it is possible to illustrate, from the extensive range of the Treasury's activities, two fundamental themes of achievement. The first is the basic matter of *authority* and the steps by which the Treasury Commission established its status and powers within the structure of Restoration government. This involved defining its relationship with the Secretaries of State, the Privy Council and, above all, with the king, an achievement upon which depended the whole character of 'Treasury control' not only in its own day but for its successors.

[14] Pepys, *Diary*, 31 May, 3 June 1667; Arlington to the duke of Ormonde, 22 May 1667 (Bodleian, Carte MSS. 46 f. 478).

[15] Pepys, *Diary*, 3 June 1667, 20 January 1668; Sir Joseph Williamson's Journal, 31 May 1667 (PRO SP 29/231 p. 22); Sir Allen Brodrick to the duke of Ormonde, 8 June 1667 (Bodleian, Carte MSS. 35 f. 465b); Sir John Hobart to John Hobart, 10 October 1667 (Bodleian, Tanner MSS. 45 f. 227).

[16] Pepys, *Diary*, 6 December 1667 (cf. 2 December 1667); C. H. Hartmann, *The King My Brother* (London, 1954), p. 212; Christopher Lindenov to the Danish Chancery, 15 January 1669, in *The First Triple Alliance*, ed. W. Westergaard (New Haven, 1947), p. 70.

[17] Sir Thomas Meres, 17 April 1679; Anchitel Grey, *Debates of the House of Commons* (London, 1769), vii, 120.

The second theme of achievement can be defined, in modern terms, as a matter of *organization and methods*, and relates to the remarkable fertility of innovation by which the Commission and its secretary evolved the routines and records of their office and imposed the disciplines of regularity and exactness upon subordinate departments.

From these two achievements everything else followed. The deceptively modest objectives of the Treasury's work at this time, as at others, were (*a*) a revenue accurately assessed, efficiently collected and punctually paid; and (*b*) an expenditure carefully regulated, honestly disbursed and promptly accounted for. To these ends, authority and discipline were vital, and they were even more important for a third and perhaps most crucial concern, (*c*) the Crown's borrowing. Borrowing, it need hardly be stressed, was not necessarily a symptom of debt, a mark of failure in reconciling (*a*) with (*b*). Borrowing was a normal requirement, inevitable in an unsophisticated monetary system closely linked to an agricultural economy. The king, like anyone else, needed cash in advance of his receipts, and he needed it quickly and cheaply. Unfortunately, he needed it on a scale which posed unique technical problems for which the English money market was not yet well adapted. And the distinctive feature of Charles II's dilemma, which marks him off from his needy predecessors, is that the privileged vantage-point of the Crown as a borrower had been gravely damaged by the constitutional upheavals of the seventeenth century.[18] There was no longer much hope for 'forced loans' exacted under the threat of the prerogative courts. The time had come, at last, for the Crown to offer purely businesslike inducements to its lenders, to build up its credit as a marketable commodity founded upon the probity and punctuality, as well as the profitability, of its dealings. Here was a special incentive to administrative efficiency which did much to stimulate the Treasury's evolution after 1660.

At this point it is appropriate to re-introduce Sir George Downing and consider some misconceptions about his importance which are betrayed, for example, in the statement that 'Downing never had to work under the wretched conditions of 1665, when the Exchequer was split between Westminster and Nonsuch'.[19] This seems plausible enough. Downing was not yet Secretary to the Treasury: he was the king's representative at The Hague for much of 1665 and his functions as a Teller of the Exchequer were being performed by a deputy. And yet it can be shown that before, during, as well as after 1665, Downing

---

[18] For a detailed account of the sanctions which the early Stuarts employed against recalcitrant creditors, see R. Ashton, *The Crown and the Money Market, 1603–40* (Oxford, 1960), particularly pp. 10, 69, 155.

[19] Baxter, *Treasury*, p. 178.

was almost the sole source of initiative making for a solution of the Crown's financial problems. His diplomatic duties did not prevent him attending Parliament and setting his mark on the mercantilist legislation of 1660 and 1663. Likewise his position in Holland made him peculiarly sensitive to England's fiscal and administrative shortcomings. On the eve of a trade war with the United Provinces it was a matter of concern to him that the Dutch had a low and well-informed opinion of the Crown's financial resources. England, they believed, could not sustain a conflict for 'you are not so good husbands of your money nor do lay it out so carefully and with that advantage as they'.[20] Underlying this incapacity was a defective system of Treasury management: Crown revenues were laxly administered. Instead of being paid into the Exchequer and then issued under the Treasurer's supervision they were too often diverted at source, transferred by the semi-independent revenue 'farmers' direct to government creditors and officials. Of course, this was a traditional expedient, authorized by successive Treasurers, which had the specious advantage of circumventing the cumbersome machinery of the Exchequer, but it created dangerous opportunities for collusion, misappropriation and delay which cost the king dear. It was an abdication of 'Treasury control', and, writing to a Secretary of State, Downing pointed out the subtler consequences – that the diversion of royal revenues undermined the credit of the Exchequer, and that it was not the king's lack of money but this lack of credit which was ruining him. In Holland too they lacked money but were rich in reputation which was based on the punctuality and good order of their dealings.[21] Preaching the same theme to the Lord Chancellor, he urged that England should set itself to out-strip the creditworthiness of the Dutch by reviving the proverbial integrity of the Exchequer and bringing all revenues under its control. Until this happened the king could not expect to have either money or credit, and 'my Lord I would lose all I have if it might not very easily be brought to this in England, and my Lord I know what I say'.[22]

This was the confident passion which made Downing the author of one of the earliest and certainly the most significant of steps in the evolution of parliamentary and Treasury control of government finance – the appropriation and borrowing clauses in the Additional Aid of 1665. Back in England by the beginning of September, Downing vigorously promoted his scheme with the king and the Commons against the fiercest ministerial objections and had the satisfaction of

[20] Downing to Sir H. Bennet, 17 January 1665 (SPFor 84/174 f. 20).
[21] Downing to Sir. E. Nicholas, 29 August 1662 (BM Egerton MSS. 2538 f. 120).
[22] Downing to the earl of Clarendon, 27 January 1663 (Bodleian, Clarendon MSS. 106 ff. 68b–69).

seeing it enacted by the end of October.[23] The resulting Act, with its novel provisions, is not unfamiliar to students of constitutional history,[24] but its administrative details are important enough for the Treasury's evolution to bear summarizing once again.

1. The £1,250,000 tax, leviable in 24 monthly instalments, was to be paid directly into the Exchequer without any diversion.

2. The tax was appropriated to the expenses of the war, and the money was to be paid out solely for that purpose.

3. The receipts and the issues of the money were to be separately recorded in two registers, kept at the Exchequer but open to free public inspection.

4. In a third public register, the Lord Treasurer's instructions to issue the funds were to be listed 'in course', i.e. a numbered, chronological sequence which the Exchequer was strictly required to follow.

5. The Exchequer was also to draw up 'Treasury Orders' – foolscap documents, embodying the Treasurer's instructions to make an issue of funds, bearing his and the Chancellor of the Exchequer's signatures and the same number as the entry in the register. These Treasury Orders would be of three distinct types: (a) orders 'impresting', or allocating, funds to departmental officials, such as the Treasurer of the Navy or the Paymaster of the Forces; (b) orders to pay tradesmen and contractors for goods and services supplied for the war; and (c) orders to repay individuals for loans advanced to the king on the credit of this tax.

6. This last category of Treasury Orders was authorized to bear the written parliamentary guarantee of 6 per cent interest, payable half-yearly.

7. All three types of Treasury Orders (which were essentially promises-to-pay when, in the course of 24 months, the tax money became available) could be sold, and transferred from person to person by a written endorsement on the Order, notifiable to the Exchequer. Thus they were legally negotiable at a time when few other credit instruments enjoyed that status.[25]

8. Whatever the type of the Order, or the status of its bearer, whether Privy Councillor or needy tradesman, 'all and every person

[23] The hostile account in Clarendon, *Life*, ii, 190–203 is our principal source for this episode. Clarendon bitterly opposed Downing's innovations and stresses contemporary criticisms, with the unintended effect of making Downing's long-term vindication all the more striking.

[24] J. P. Kenyon, *The Stuart Constitution* (Cambridge, 1966), pp. 389–91 prints some of its more important clauses. For the full text of 17 Car. II, c. 1 see *Statutes of the Realm* (London, 1819), v, 570–4.

[25] For the significance of negotiability in seventeenth-century commercial law see J. Milnes Holden, *The History of Negotiable Instruments in English Law* (London, 1955).

and persons shall be paid in course according as their orders shall stand entered in the said register book.' This was the dangerously egalitarian principle which Clarendon most bitterly deplored, seeing it as a surrender of the Treasurer's discretion. For Downing, however, it was the essence of his scheme – a cast-iron parliamentary guarantee to the small investor that the Treasury would honour its obligations without favouritism. And it was the small investor whom Downing hoped to attract, anxious as he was to undercut the group of goldsmith-bankers who, since the Restoration, had monopolized government borrowing with a return of 10 or even 12 per cent.

Ultimately, the innovations of this Act were to become the standard devices of the so-called 'financial revolution',[26] but the immediately important point is that Downing had to work extremely hard to make his experiment succeed. He had to contend not only with the enmity of Clarendon and the misgivings of the king but with the active hostility of the Treasurer. For, rather than endorse Downing's scheme to raise loans, the earl of Southampton set about soliciting advance payments of the tax for which he offered to pay 6 per cent. This was a not unusual device for raising ready cash, but by the terms of this new Act any such payments of tax money were, of course, strictly appropriated to paying off the registered liabilities *immediately*. In other words, as fast as Downing was raising long-term credit for the king the Treasurer was liquidating it with money for which the king would still have to pay interest! This stupid, or malicious, piece of maladministration had to be rapidly countered by Downing and sympathetic Privy Councillors in a country-wide campaign of letters and in a remarkable pamphlet, *A State of the Case Between furnishing His Majesty with Money by way of Loan, or by way of Advance of the Tax*.[27] In this it was carefully explained to citizens, and country gentry in particular, why it was loans and not advances that were being solicited. The special attractions of Treasury Orders as gilt-edged negotiable securities were stressed: 'men do daily accommodate their occasions by buying or selling of them', and investors were urged to communicate with Sir George Downing at the Exchequer.

This must be the first loan-prospectus of its kind to stress economic as well as patriotic motivation, and Downing was certainly the first to spot the potential of another new form of communication in the

[26] See P. G. M. Dickson, *The Financial Revolution in England* (London, 1967). This study could have given more weight to pre-1688 experience of debt-management. The author is certainly mistaken in stating (p. 351) that it was only after 1688 that Treasury Orders were printed. By 1667, this and most other features of the post-Revolution Order system were fully developed. For examples of early printed Treasury Orders, see PRO E 407/119, 120.

[27] What appears to be the only known copy of this pamphlet in England is in the Goldsmiths' Library, University of London.

foundation of the *London Gazette* as the official news-sheet of government. Offering help in promoting its struggling circulation, he eventually secured space to advertise the progress of liabilities and loans being registered in course on the security of the Additional Aid. Henceforth, throughout the 'financial revolution' and into our own times, the *Gazette* was to carry public announcements of government loan operations[28] (Doc. 6).

All this time, it should be stressed, the Lord Treasurer and the Chancellor of the Exchequer were sheltering at Oxford, with the main Exchequer staff dispersed in Surrey. It was Sir George Downing who remained in plague-stricken Westminster, eventually drumming up nearly £200,000 in loans and sending a constant stream of suggestions to his chiefs. A single letter from the Treasurer to the Auditor of the Receipt gives striking testimony to the real source of initiative at this time. 'Downing complains ... Downing proposes ... Downing wants ... Downing conceives ... I know not how to gratify Downing in his desires.'[29]

So much for the idea that Downing never had to work under the wretched conditions of 1665, or 1666 for that matter, when the Exchequer was divided and the Treasurer demoralized. The important point is that, months before Southampton's death, the ideas and energies which were to do so much for the Treasury's regeneration had been mobilized on behalf of the king's credit. In choosing Downing as their Secretary, the 1667 Treasury Commissioners were shrewdly subscribing to a policy and the abilities which could implement it.

However, the problem which had a logical priority for the Treasury Commissioners was one which they had to solve for themselves. Somehow, they had to get their status and authority respected, not only by the two Secretaries of State and other Privy Councillors but by the king himself. This was a difficult business and had to be fought through a whole series of skirmishes which were brought to a climax by the historic Order in Council of 31 January 1668 (Docs. 1, 2(a) and (b)).

It has been rightly pointed out that this remarkable achievement did not represent an inflation of the Treasury's inherent powers. 'Southampton might easily have obtained such a set of rules had he wished for

[28] Downing to Joseph Williamson, 25 November, 14, 30 December 1665, 4, 6, 9, 13, 16, 20 January 1666 (*CSPD 1665–6*, pp. 72, 124, 190, 193, 195, 201, 203, 213, *CSPD 1670*, p. 704); P. M. Handover, *A History of the London Gazette, 1665–1965*, pp. 13, 20, 27. Initially, the editor of the *Gazette* was only prepared to help Downing through his handwritten, but widely-read, newsletter service (P. Fraser, *The Intelligence of the Secretaries of State, 1660–88*, Cambridge, 1955).

[29] The earl of Southampton to Sir Robert Long, 5 January 1666 (PRO T 51/XIII, f. 143), partially printed in *CTB 1660–7*, p. 712.

them'[30] but, in fact, he had not. On the contrary, he had explicitly abdicated his power to adjudicate on the crucial question of royal bounty, pleading ignorance of the claimants. The novelty of the achievement, in other words, lies in the fact that 'the position was defended after 1668, as an almost identical position had not been defended after 1660'[31] and it would be a mistake to minimize the importance of this for the sake of later assertions of Treasury authority. Such later assertions (Docs. 2(e), (f) and (g)) are essentially echoes of this fundamental Order of January 1668, so carefully recorded in the Privy Council register and inscribed, for all to see, on a board hung up in the Treasury Chambers. Not until 1868 (Doc. 19) shall we find a definition with equal claims as a new departure in the enforcement of Treasury control. Not until 1920 was the Treasury's place in the machinery of government to be more strikingly affirmed.[32]

The Order in Council of 31 January was designed primarily to guarantee the Treasury's discretionary authority over revenue and expenditure against the authority of the Secretaries of State, and coming at a time when the Secretaryship was acquiring renewed potency in the hands of Lord Arlington this was of considerable administrative importance. But the position was significantly strengthened on 12 February 1668 by a definition of the Treasury's relationship with the Privy Council (Doc. 2(c)) which went as far as it could in conferring practical autonomy on the Treasury. Of course, the Treasury Commissioners, in looking to the king, would also be looking to the Privy Council for support on more far-reaching questions of policy. They might collaborate with fellow privy councillors on specific matters referred to them. But it is certainly not the case that the 1667 Treasury Commissioners got themselves humiliatingly tied up by the proceedings of the joint Treasury–Privy Council retrenchment committee which Charles set up in July 1667.[33] This idea betrays a fundamental mis- understanding of the Treasury's power not only in the seventeenth century but at any time.

For at no time has the Treasury had the authority to fix, unilaterally, the establishments or expenditure levels of the independent depart- ments of government. That has always been a matter to be determined by the effective centre of authority, be it the king, or the king-in-council

---

[30] Baxter, *Treasury*, p. 14; cf. ibid., p. 10, *CTB 1660–7*, p. 104.

[31] Ibid., p. 61.

[32] In *The Treasury: the Evolution of a British Institution* (London, 1969), p. 248, I have argued for the significance of the measures of 1919–20 which consolidated the Treasury's control of civil establishments, and the Permanent Secretary's 'Headship' of the Civil Service.

[33] Baxter, *Treasury*, pp. 61–2. There is no reference to the Order of 12 February 1668 in this book, and its analysis of Treasury-Privy Council relations is badly flawed.

or the cabinet. The Treasury puts its case, and the departments put theirs; the decision is not the Treasury's although the Treasury must cope with the financial consequences. Its authority, as distinct from its influence, only begins at the point where it is left to decide how and when the financial implications are to be fulfilled – and this is precisely what was happening in 1667–8.

The retrenchment scheme of 22 July 1668, which made a detailed apportionment of the king's annual expenditure, totalling £746,475 15s 10d plus £250,000 for interest charges and contingencies,[34] was the product of a Privy Council sub-committee of five (later seven) senior ministers and the five Treasury Lords. In their proceedings the onus lay primarily on the ministers to make economies in the departments – the various branches of the royal household, the forces, the pension list, embassies, etc. Initially, they worked with pathetic timidity: 'the Cormorant Keeper to be taken away by which will be saved £84. Keeper of the Volary cut off, £30.'[35] In November 1667 Charles was presented with an estimate that, against revenue of less than £900,000 p.a. he must set an annual expenditure of £1,242,855 16s 8d.[36] Dismayed, he ordered the committee to try again, setting them an expenditure target of £700,000, which the report of July 1668 nearly achieved. But it did so only after the most painfully protracted negotiations which left the Treasury Lords thoroughly embittered by the lack of realism among their colleagues. The king prevaricated, courtiers obstructed, their enemies multiplied. Although economies had been imposed on the departments in March 1668, those embodied in the report of 22 July were merely notional targets, and when the king called upon the Treasury to enforce them the Commissioners had to roll up their sleeves for the really difficult work of making them effective. It is at this point that the Treasury minuted: 'The Order of Council for disposal of His Majesty's revenue according to the several branches of His Majesty's expense is to be considered and how far my Lords are tied up thereby.'[37] But this is simply a memorandum of Downing's, reflecting the Treasury in the process of seeing how far, if at all, the Order in Council committed them in the apportionment of *revenue*, which it must be stressed is a quite different thing from the apportionment of *expenditure*. Until the creation of the Consolidated Fund in 1787 it was a major task of financial administration to ensure

[34] PRO SPDom 29/243, f. 102.
[35] BM Egerton MSS. 2543, ff. 129–33; printed by W. A. Shaw in *CTB 1681–5* (Pt 3), pp. 1646–50.
[36] SPDom 29/236, f. 144; PC 2/60, p. 57.
[37] 2 September 1668 (*CTB 1667–8*, p. 429). It is the words 'tied up' which appear to have prompted Dr Baxter to come to the conclusions in his *Treasury*, pp. 61–2. W. A. Shaw's interpretation is in my opinion equally erroneous – *CTB 1689–92*, p. cxxi.

that individual sources of revenue were adequate to service those specific items of expenditure for which they were earmarked. This was the Treasury's peculiar responsibility (and one of its principal headaches) which could not be usurped by Privy Council or cabinet. Indeed, in July 1668 the Order in Council did *not* tie them up in the disposal of revenue, but in the process of reviewing the Order, Downing and the Auditor of the Receipt had to bring to the Treasury Lords' attention the complete unreality of the expenditure proposals. As the Privy Council ruefully admitted on 18 September, several branches of the king's expenses had been omitted and 'some other rules of the said Order are impracticable'. It had to be revised and reissued on 26 September.[38]

But there had yet to come the most important document in the series. Dated 20 October and addressed to the king, not the Privy Council, it is the Treasury's independent report on the painful realities of his financial position which made both the Orders in Council of 22 July and 26 September almost unworkable (Doc. 5). Its deferential language should not mask its real character. It is a masterful review which amply vindicated the Treasury's claim to be arbiter of what the king could, or could not, afford. It completely eclipsed the deliberations of the Privy Council committee and became the basis of the king's final dispositions on 23 November 1668.[39]

Thus in no derogatory sense was the Treasury 'bound' by the Orders in Council. It was its duty to try to enforce them, but the apportionment of the king's revenues to his expenses was the Treasury's own, presented independently and authoritatively. In no sense, therefore, was the Treasury acting in a 'subordinate capacity' in matters within its own jurisdiction, and the case for a significant difference between the Treasury's dependence in 1668 and independence in 1676, so far as it is based on the events of 1668, falls to the ground. Indeed, if one now turns to the Order in Council of 1676 (Doc. 2(d)), it may suggest an interpretation much less in the earl of Danby's favour than has been proposed. The discretion which the king was graciously prepared to exercise for Danby, if he saw fit, had been firmly commandeered by the 'rougher hands' of 1667.

The report of 20 October 1668 therefore marks one of the early high points in the Treasury Commission's achievement, only made possible by their continuous labours to impose order and regularity upon the king's financial affairs. The picture it presents was, admittedly, a bleak one which ominously foreshadows the bankruptcy of 1672. The Treasury Lords were under no illusions about their chances of

[38] PRO PC 2/61, pp. 17, 36–8.
[39] Ibid., p. 119. There is no evidence in Baxter, *Treasury*, that the author has consulted the Privy Council registers or knew of the report of 20 October 1668.

rescuing the king single-handed at this late date.[40] But their ability to apportion huge debts in an orderly way and to calculate the chronology of their redemption reflects an important new degree of discipline over the Exchequer, the revenue farms and the spending departments.

Of all these areas, the Exchequer posed fundamental problems which will be discussed later.[41] They were not solved by the 1667 Treasury Commission. Nevertheless, the prompt collaboration of the Exchequer was vital to the Treasury Lords' achievements, and one of the first things they did was to summon the officials of that department and order them to work harder (Doc. 10). The machinery of the Exchequer was to be set in motion against all delinquent revenue collectors and departmental accountants, and this meant punctual audit and rigorous pursuit by the officials of the Upper Exchequer. Recalcitrants were to be rounded up under arrest and *habeas corpus* was to be withheld from the king's debtors. Before long an observer could report that 'the commissioners of the Treasury bring a terror to all bankers, accomptants, patentees, etc. . . .'[42]

Fortunately, the key official in the Lower Exchequer, the Auditor of the Receipt, was a man upon whom the Treasury could rely. Sir Robert Long was exceptional among seventeenth-century Exchequer officials in having a conscientious devotion to the personal performance of his duties. He had warmly supported Downing's scheme for payment in course on the Additional Aid, and he proved fully responsive to the Treasury Commission. He was the Treasury's principal executive in the Exchequer of Receipt, receiving a steady flow of instructions and returning a regular sequence of information. In particular, it was to him that the Treasury gave its instructions for the issue of money; it was from him that they received reports of its receipt. If any man could work out the current Exchequer balance between income and expenditure it was the Auditor of the Receipt, and the Treasury was quick to ask him for a statement of current liabilities. Thereafter, their concern was to have regular reports. In addition to his conventional half-yearly balance-sheets, Long was instructed to provide those weekly cash statements of receipts and issues which were to be the working basis of the Treasury's day-to-day decisions on expenditure.

But there were limits to the Auditor's competence. He was essentially an executive official with no significant powers of initiative or discre-

---

[40] 'Had they come in two years ago they doubt not to have done what the king would by this time.' Sir William Coventry to Pepys, 27 December 1667 (Pepys, *Diary*); cf. ibid., 9 August 1667, 27 December 1668.

[41] See below, Section Two, pp. 48–50.

[42] Sir Allen Brodrick to the duke of Ormonde, 3 August 1667 (Bodleian, Carte MSS. 35, f. 595).

tion.[43] Furthermore, his jurisdiction did not extend to all areas of Crown finance. Numerous transactions took place beyond the immediate orbit of the Exchequer of Receipt – loans, transfers, drawbacks, diversions and assignments of funds, which did not immediately, if ever, come into the normal weekly cash records of the Lower Exchequer.

It is in this context that one must place the elaboration of the Treasury's records after 1667 and consider the assertion that the incentive was negative, a response to Exchequer decay.[44] I believe this to be quite mistaken. It can be shown that the situation was almost exactly the reverse of this; that the Treasury's records were positively evolved after 1667 as part of a deliberate campaign to exercise closer control of revenue and expenditure; that these records complemented, not supplanted, the records of the Exchequer, with lasting results. That there was a propensity to decay in the Exchequer cannot be denied; it had been ossifying for centuries, and Sir Robert Long's zeal was exceptional. Under any circumstances, the Treasury would have been forced to make good the shortcomings of the Exchequer if it wanted comprehensive information. But this should not obscure the fundamental point – that the diversification of special classes of Treasury records was the by-product of a deliberate initiative by Downing and the Treasury Lords which, by extending the system of Treasury Orders registered in course to the king's ordinary revenues, hoped to mobilize the king's credit on a basis of efficient book-keeping. This campaign is the key to almost everything the Treasury Commission did.

As we have seen, it had long been Downing's ambition that the king's ordinary revenues should pass into and out of the Exchequer under close Treasury supervision, and this immediately became the policy of the 1667 Commission. The fact that nearly all the sources were being administered by independent syndicates of businessmen and gentry was something of an obstacle but not an insuperable one. The real difficulty arose because the king was heavily indebted to these 'farmers' either for advances or for loans, or for compensation due to them for the war-time disruption of trade.[45] They had strong claims to recoup themselves by withholding their rents, and when the Treasury

---

[43] Under Southampton's treasurership, Sir Robert Long had often carried the responsibility of nominating the revenue fund from which a particular payment was to be made. It was an essential step in the Treasury Commission's assertion of control that they resumed this vital discretionary power for themselves.

[44] Baxter, *Treasury*, pp. 217–19; cf. pp. 180, 257.

[45] For an accurate and comprehensive picture of the revenue situation in the reign of Charles II, readers must await the publication of C. D. Chandaman's study of the English Public Revenue, 1660–88, a London University Ph.D. dissertation of 1954.

Commission took office it found most of its revenue-cupboards quite bare. Its first step was to impose some order on this situation by forbidding the farmers to make any further diversion of their revenue except on the Treasury's explicit instructions.[46] Its second step was to agree with the farmers upon a detailed schedule of repayments.[47] After that it was possible to plan ahead and apportion current expenditure among the future yields of revenues which were, henceforth, to be paid punctually into the Exchequer.

For this disciplined apportionment of past, present and future liabilities, the 1665 principle of 'payment in course' provided an ideal basis. But in extending Downing's system of Treasury Orders, numbered, registered and assignable, to the king's ordinary revenues, the Treasury lacked the statutory authority which had been the essence of the 1665 operations. However, this was made good in three distinct ways. Firstly, on 18 June 1667, the king issued his solemn promise that the Exchequer would always honour its obligations punctually, and 'that we will not upon any occasion whatsoever permit or suffer any alteration, anticipation or interruption to be made, of our said subjects' securities; but that they shall from time to time receive the moneys so secured unto them, in the same course and method, as they were charged. . . .' [48] This 'sacred' resolution was to apply particularly to loans made by individual investors on the credit of the king's revenues and it was precisely this promise which Charles II was to break with the 'Stop of the Exchequer' in January 1672.

Meanwhile, the second attribute of the 1665 system was reconstructed in the autumn of 1667 when Downing carried through parliament a Bill making Treasury Orders, registered in course on the king's ordinary revenues, legally transferable by endorsement in the same way as those created by the Additional Aid and its successors.[49] Extended in this way to the long-term incomes of the Crown, the system now had far-reaching possibilities for the creation of public credit which Downing found immensely exciting.[50] But for the rest of his system – the accurate book-keeping and efficient administration of the registers –

---

[46] Treasury letter, 30 May 1667; Treasury minutes, 31 May, 15, 24, 26 June, 1, 12 July, 8, 16 August 1667, *CTB 1667–8*, pp. 3, 12, 18, 19, 23, 35, 57, 65, 163. The Customs Farmers were severely reprimanded for a breach of these orders, 18 September 1667, PRO T 11/1, p. 22.

[47] Treasury minutes, 13, 16, 17, 23, 25 September, 2 October, 5, 19 November 1667; Treasury letter, 7 October 1667, *CTB 1667–8*, pp. 77, 82, 83, 85, 89, 92, 98, 115, 122, 192.

[48] PRO Printed Proclamations, Charles II, SPDom 45/12 No. 244a; printed by A. Browning, *English Historical Documents, 1660–1714* (London, 1953), pp. 350–1.

[49] 19 and 20 Car. II, c. 4.

[50] Pepys, *Diary*, 6 November 1667.

the public had no guarantee other than the professional integrity of the Exchequer. The Treasury Commissioners and their Secretary were determined that the public should not be disappointed. By the middle of September the Auditor of the Receipt had been warned to prepare separate registers for payment-in-course on the main royal revenues – Customs, Excise and Hearth Tax.[51] In January 1668 he was sternly reminded to see that all Treasury Orders were properly numbered in sequence so that their owners could fairly estimate their probable date of redemption.[52] By the spring of 1668 the list of Orders registered on the Customs was well advanced, and Downing could proudly advertise the achievement in the Gazette (Doc. 6(b)). By the summer of 1668, the main revenues – or what was left of them – were being passed through the Exchequer and disbursed under firm Treasury control.

The book-keeping implications of this system are important, and they will become clearer if one observes how the passage of a Treasury Order through all its stages from issue to redemption gave rise to a long sequence of records. To construct an imaginary case, let us suppose that the Treasury Lords have decided to make £1000 available to the Victualler of the Navy – part of a larger sum for which they already have the king's authority under the privy seal. Cash to that amount is not immediately available, but the Treasury's records of existing liabilities and their expectation of future revenues justify them in deciding that the payment could be made from the Customs revenue due in twelve months' time. The Secretary to the Treasury makes a brief note of the decision in (a) his Minute Book. He also addresses a warrant to the Auditor of the Receipt, instructing him to draw up a formal Order to authorize the issue of £1000 to the Victualler of the Navy from the Customs revenue of the specified month. The Secretary, or his clerks, record the warrant in (b) the Treasury Warrant Book, and at the Exchequer the Auditor, or his clerks, copy it into (c) the Auditor's Warrant Book. The Auditor then draws up the Order, allotting it a numbered place in the sequence of other Orders already registered on that month of the Customs revenue. He notes all this in (d) his Order Book, and sends the Order over to the Treasury. Validated there by the signature of three or more of the Treasury Lords, recorded in (e) the Treasury Order Book, the Order is now ready for issue to the Victualler. He, of course, wants ready cash and probably the first thing he does with the Order is sell it to a goldsmith-banker, transferring his title by an endorsement written on the Order. It is the banker who eventually presents it for encashment at the Exchequer when he learns from the Treasury advertisements in the Gazette that his Order is among those now due for redemption, and, although this type of

[51] Treasury minute, 13 September 1667 (CTB 1667–8, p. 82).
[52] Treasury minute, 21 January 1668 (CTB 1667–8, p. 253).

imprest Order is not interest-bearing he will claim, and eventually get, interest on his loan. Meanwhile, the Order is back in the hands of the Auditor of the Receipt who endorses it with his 'direction' to a specified Teller of the Exchequer, instructing him to pay the money from the Customs revenue in his hands. The Auditor will record the transaction in (f) his Issue Book, but the Order must first go to his colleague, the Clerk of the Pells, who acts as a check upon the Auditor's proceedings and keeps a duplicate set of records. The Clerk of the Pells enters the Order in (g) his Order Book, in English, and the payment in (h) his Issue Book, in Latin, and endorses the Order with his 'recordatur' which gives final authority for payment by the Teller, who takes the payee's receipt and keeps the Order.

Thus the Treasury Order could give rise to a long sequence of records (and this is to say nothing of the two Issue Rolls kept by the Auditor of the Receipt and the Clerk of the Pells as the ultimate legal record of payment!), most of which simply reflect its absorption by the 'ancient course' of the Exchequer. Cumbersome though it may seem, this routine duplication of every stage in the passage of Treasury instructions through the department was essential if the Exchequer was to discharge its traditional responsibilities for strict legality and infallible record. In addition, the Auditor's role in drawing up the Order, numbering and registering it in course, advertising its redemption and expediting its payment, was absolutely vital to the public credit of the system.

The Treasury's book-keeping, on the other hand, served a different purpose – of control. The initial decision to make the payment and the disposition of the liability among incoming revenues, based upon the information available in the Treasury, were crucial expressions of Treasury authority which could not be abdicated to Exchequer officials, however efficient. The Treasury's Minute Book, Warrant Book and Order Book should be thought of as *memoranda* – as distinct from the Exchequer's *records* – which enabled it to exercise its discretion promptly and independently. When it wanted formal statements, founded on meticulous book-keeping, it could always turn to the Auditor of the Receipt, and it often did. But for the purpose of day-to-day decisions it had nearly all it needed in the Treasury office. If this distinction of function is kept in mind there can be no risk of confusing the rise of Treasury book-keeping with a decline in the Exchequer. The Exchequer, on the contrary, was galvanized by the requirements of the Treasury Order system.[53]

This point also helps to place in perspective the physical separation between the two departments. The removal of the Treasurer's office from the Exchequer buildings in Palace Yard, Westminster had

53 See below, p. 49.

occurred under the earl of Southampton without any dramatic effect
on the Treasury's record-keeping. More influential were the heavier
clerical requirements of a commission of five for whom papers must
be circulated, copies made, decisions recorded, and to this one must
add the accident of personality which brought together at least three
men, Duncombe, Coventry and their Secretary, Downing, who had
pronounced appetites for methodical paperwork. Their determination
to make a business-like new start in the conduct of Treasury affairs
was enough to ensure some proliferation of its records wherever the
office was located. But, in the situation created by the quarter of a mile
separating the Exchequer from the Treasury in Whitehall, the decisive
factor was the administrative requirements of the Treasury Order
system. This can be seen clearly enough from entries in the Minute
Book itself, particularly for the spring of 1668 when the arrangement
of liabilities upon revenues was nearing completion (Doc. 8). What
could not be guessed is the extraordinary vitality which the system
was to display over the next two centuries. However, in 1842, when a
Public Record Office official first penetrated the rotting morass of
Treasury papers, it soon became clear to him that 1667 marked an
historic turning point. He could distinguish the earliest evolution of
Treasury, as distinct from Exchequer, records in the reign of Charles I.
There followed an intermediate stage from 1660 to 1667. But with
the Treasury Commission of 1667 'a new system began, which hath
subsisted, without essential variation, to the present time: the third
period, therefore, of Treasury Books, ought to be considered as yet
current. . . .'[54]

Among the series of volumes originating with the 1667 Commission
were Letter Books dealing with each branch of revenue administration,
the Warrant Books and Order Books already mentioned, a special class
of 'Irish Books' and an important series of 'Warrants not relating to
Money' which comprehend a wide range of Treasury instructions.[55]
However, pride of place must go to the Minute Book, or 'Journall
Book' as it called itself, which was the first and most lasting of the
innovations of 1667. From 27 May of that year (Doc. 8) the series
runs with only a few missing volumes until 1870 when Treasury
minutes ceased to be entered formally in separately bound books. In
the course of these two centuries its character was sometimes to
change in response to differing administrative styles. In the early
eighteenth century, for example, the Minute Book shrank to a mere
skeleton, one volume serving to record the perfunctory Board meetings
of several years. By the early nineteenth century, however, a pedantic

[54] *Seventh Report of the Deputy Keeper of the Public Records* (1846), Appendix
II, p. 11.
[55] See W. A. Shaw's introductory account in *CTB & P 1729–30*, pp. xvi–liv.

emphasis on the entry of all decisions, *and* the papers on which they were based, was filling the huge volumes at the rate of one a month. Surveying the whole range one can say that at no period was the Minute Book a more lively and expressive reflection of Treasury business than at its inception. Drawn up from rough notes taken by the Secretary and his clerks as the day's business was done, its entries are terse but sometimes eloquent records of a long series of reports, interviews, arguments and decisions.

The business of 22 July 1667 (Doc. 7) has been selected at random, not as a 'typical day' – there was no such thing – but at least as an ordinary day which just happens to contain several items of special interest. Items [3] and [25], for example, reveal the Treasury Commission at an early stage in the process of trying to master the total situation with which they were faced; and items [6] and [20] are important steps by which they imposed the discipline of routine upon the Exchequer and the spending departments. Many items, [1], [11], [12], [15], [16], [22], [24] and [27], are evidence of the Treasury Commission's desperate concern to bully the amateurish administration of the Crown lands, Royal Aids and Chimney tax into some semblance of efficiency. Their threats of arrest were not empty. Copinger and Rawleigh, the Bristol Chimney tax receivers of item [15], were taken into custody and came to blows on the Treasury premises. The tribulations of Cadwallader Jones, (item [27]) had only just commenced. Item [10], on the other hand, reveals the Board in a more humane guise, trying to mitigate the scandal which enabled money-lenders to discount seamen's pay-vouchers at a huge profit.[56]

However, it is items [2], [5] and [26] which are the most significant clues to the kind of work which distinguished the 1667 Commission. They reflect its closely-related efforts firstly to regulate the terms of government borrowing, and secondly to reconstruct the revenue-farm contracts on terms more favourable to the king. In the case of the Customs farmers they were attempting to clear up a situation largely of the king's own making. When they entered office they found that Charles had just struck a rather unsatisfactory bargain with a well-established syndicate of merchants and goldsmith-bankers, allowing them a three-year contract to collect the Customs in return for a £200,000 advance and a rent of £350,000 p.a., rising to £370,000 in the last year. But the Treasury Lords were sure that the king could have done better, and the conclusion of the war in July 1667 strengthened their case. In the course of the autumn they forced through a revocation of the contract and negotiated a new one based on a rental of £400,000 p.a. payable in a strict schedule of fortnightly instalments.

[56] This is a problem well illustrated in Pepys, *Diary*, 1, 6 April 1665, 13, 14, 15, 16 February, 12 March and, especially, 14 June, 13 November 1667.

As their report of 20 October 1668 makes clear, this steady flow of carefully earmarked funds was vital to the maintenance of the Treasury Order system.

It was much less easy to apply business-like disciplines to the great spending departments. They enjoyed a certain degree of autonomy. While they were obliged to wait upon the Treasury to know when and how they would get their funds, they possessed considerable discretion in deciding how and when they spent them. Departmental treasurers were called to account in the Exchequer at irregular intervals, and until they laid down office (or died) their affairs were usually free from detailed inquisition. It was within this privileged immunity that most of the characteristic abuses of seventeenth- and eighteenth-century English government – peculation, profiteering and waste – tended to arise. As we shall see,[57] the anomalies of the system were not cleared up before the nineteenth century. Meanwhile, however, the 1667 Treasury Commissioners were determined to exercise as much control as they could, and in this respect at least they were helped by the crisis in the king's affairs. Issued in a state of emergency, the Order in Council of 17 June 1667 (Doc. 3) clearly laid down the all-important Treasury rule of 'specific sanction' – i.e. that even though a Department may have a formal authorization to spend a sum of money under a royal warrant, or parliamentary provision, it must still submit to the Treasury's discretion for specific permission to do so. This is a fundamental rule of Treasury control which is exercised (and disputed) in our own times,[58] but in the circumstances of seventeenth-century stringency it was vital if the Treasury was to be anything more than a rubber stamp on payments from the Exchequer.

The weekly reports which the Order in Council enjoined were likewise essential to the Treasury's control. They were the counterpart of the weekly or fortnightly statements required from the revenue farmers and the Exchequer[59] and together made up a body of information from which the Treasury could take its measures, adjusting almost on a day-to-day basis the rate of expenditure to the flow of revenue. It was not always easy. 'Write the principal officers and Commissioners of the Navy,' the Secretary was instructed in June 1668, 'that my Lords are surprised to find in the Navy certificate ending the 7th instant, that orders have been signed by the said officers, &c., for the sum of £290,000 for tickets and seamen's wages, and that my Lords desire to

---

[57] Below, Section 2.
[58] Sixth Report from the Select Committee on Estimates, 1957–8, 'Treasury Control of Expenditure', pp. 46, 47, 58; Seventh Special Report from the Select Committee on Estimates, 1958–9, 'Observations of the Treasury', pp. 13–14; discussed in Roseveare, *Treasury*, pp. 287–96.
[59] Treasury minutes, 15 June, 3, 22 July 1667, *CTB 1667–8*, pp. 12, 26, 42.

be satisfied how this great sum doth arise.'[60] Indeed, in the case of the Navy, the biggest of the spending departments, the Treasury Lords were determined not to be mere spectators. As the diary of Pepys will testify, the 1667 Commission presented a real threat to the cosy inefficiencies of naval administration.[61] While the Treasury respected the managerial autonomy of the Navy Board and declined to interfere on behalf of petitioners in the particular payments it made, it was ready to superintend the general appropriation of naval funds. It demanded regular reports of the prices paid for naval stores and asserted a traditional power to make or break supply contracts.[62] In 1668 a new victualling contract was submitted to competitive tenders and painstakingly adjudicated by the Treasury in the face of powerful rival patrons.[63] In 1671 they strengthened their grip on expenditure by adding the post of Comptroller of Storekeepers' Accounts to those of Comptroller of Treasurer's Accounts and Comptroller of Victualler's Accounts created early in 1667.[64]

Similar outposts of Treasury control were created in other departments. In November 1667, for example, the Treasury secured the appointment of a Comptroller and Surveyor in the Great Wardrobe, a large and notoriously lax purchasing agency of the royal household.[65] It was the king's indifference to economies in the Wardrobe which led an exasperated Treasury Commissioner to remind him of the proverb that 'he that will not stoop for a pin will never be worth a pound'. The king turned on his heel.[66] Although Charles gave active and moral support to much of the Treasury's exertions, personally attending some crucial discussions at the Board, the Treasury's comparatively weak grip on departmental expenditure was too often broken by royal wilfulness, and it is no coincidence that this renaissance of Treasury

---

[60] Treasury minute, 17 June 1668 (*CTB 1667–8*, p. 355).

[61] Pepys, *Diary*, 22 May, 23 July, 3, 9, 20 August, 23 December 1667, 8 January, 3 April 1668, 12 February 1669. As Pepys was to note, 'the life of a virtuous Officer in the Navy is a continual war defensive, viz. against the Ministers of State, and in particular the Lord Treasurers ... grudging every penny of money almost that is spent, and so keeping it short and postponing it to all other occasions'. *Samuel Pepys's Naval Minutes*, ed. J. R. Tanner, Navy Records Society, 1926.

[62] Treasury minutes, 2 August, 5 December 1667, 17 January, 5 May, 5 June, 24 July 1668 (*CTB 1667–8*, pp. 52, 139, 232, 313, 346, 396); Downing to Navy Board, 9 March, 6 April 1668 (*CSPD 1667–8*, pp. 275, 330).

[63] Pepys, *Diary*, 26 August, 7, 10, 21, 23, 24 September 1668.

[64] J. Ehrman, *The Navy in the War of William III, 1689–1692* (Cambridge, 1953), p. 181; *A Descriptive Catalogue of the Naval Manuscripts in the Pepys Library*, ed. J. R. Tanner (4 vols. 1903–23), i, 17. In 1677, Danby was instructed by the king to consolidate Treasury superintendence by appointing an inspector of navy accounts (*CTB 1676–9*, pp. 455, 673, 683–4). See also Doc. 4.

[65] Treasury minutes, 18 November 1667 (*CTB 1667–8*, p. 121).

[66] Pepys, *Diary*, 2 January 1668.

control occurred in conditions of exceptional financial stringency. It is difficult to imagine Charles and his court acquiescing in the Treasury's constraints unless this had been so.

Unfortunately, the same shortage of funds which brought the departments as suppliants to the Treasury's weekly distribution also embarrassed the Treasury's efforts to control the terms of government borrowing. When the 1667 Commission took office there can be little doubt that they shared Downing's ambition to cheapen the rates of Crown loans and out-manœuvre the goldsmith-bankers by appealing to the general public for funds – but they could hardly have chosen a worse time to do so. The early summer of 1667 marked the lowest point of a costly war. In July the Dutch were in the Thames and there was a run on the banks. The Treasury was immediately forced into the closest dependence on Lombard Street, promising the bankers 'all kindness', prompt payments and a guaranteed bonus of 4 per cent above the legal 6 per cent rate of interest.[67] But departmental treasurers, hawking their Treasury Orders round the money market, found it impossible to discount them for cash and by September 1667 the Treasury was obliged to seek formal sanction for an allowance of the 4 per cent gratuity to *any* persons willing to advance money – an offer repeatedly renewed, without much success, until March 1669.[68] Not until January 1669 was the Treasury able to reassert itself with an ambitious scheme to bring down interest rates by marshalling Crown lands as collateral security for 8 per cent loans on the Customs revenue, but the project was hardly a success. The fundamental inadequacy of royal revenues as a basis for large-scale credit operations, so cogently demonstrated in the Treasury's report of October 1668, ultimately prevailed. The report's ominous speculation on 'any other means' of freeing the king of his accumulated debts took concrete form in the 'Stop of the Exchequer' of 5 January 1672, when repayments and interest on the registered liabilities of the Treasury Orders were suspended. By then, however, the original membership of the Treasury Commission had suffered changes,[69] and it can hardly be held responsible for an act of bad faith by the king and the Privy Council

[67] Treasury minutes, 30 May, 1, 3 June, 19 July 1667; Treasury letter, 16 August 1667 (*CTB 1667–8*, pp. 2, 5, 6, 41).

[68] Treasury minutes, 17, 19, 25 September, 23 October, 18 November 1667 (*CTB 1667–8*, pp. 84, 86, 93, 110, 121; PRO PC 2/59, pp. 587–8, PC 2/60, p. 63, PC 2/61, pp. 74, 223).

[69] Sir William Coventry was dismissed in April 1669 and the duke of Albemarle died in January 1670. Sir George Downing was replaced as Secretary by Sir Robert Howard at the end of September 1671. Sir John Duncombe, Lord Ashley and Sir Thomas Clifford continued to serve together until November 1672, and the disputed responsibility for advising the Stop is generally accorded to Clifford, who was appointed Lord Treasurer in December 1672.

which its members had feared and struggled to avert. As long ago as February 1669, Sir William Coventry had warned Pepys of the earl of Southampton's prophecy 'that impossible would be found impossible at last; meaning that the King would run himself out, beyond all his credit and his funds, and then we should too late find it impossible; which is, he says, now come to pass.'[70]

Inevitably, the Stop did lasting damage to the personal credit of the Crown, and its consequences were to haunt the Treasury long after 1688. But it did not impair the administrative legacy of the Treasury Commission. The system of registered Orders and payment in course was not discredited, let alone destroyed. Its techniques remained the routine basis of the government's financial operations well into the eighteenth century, and it must take its place, with the establishment of Treasury authority and Treasury book-keeping, as one of the 1667 Commission's most important achievements.

Nevertheless, the legacy had to be transmitted and its machinery maintained, and it is important to consider how much some subsequent rulers of the seventeenth-century Treasury had to contribute to the work of 1667–72. I have already indicated that the case for the significance of the 1676 retrenchment scheme, as a momentous stage in the maturity of Treasury control, is marred by misconceptions about the events of 1668. But this is not to question Danby's real contribution to the evolution of the Treasury. A strong case could be made for him if one examined Danby's skilful and toughminded settlement of the post-'Stop' debt and his equally impressive consolidation of revenue administration. For example, by an ingenious reconstruction of the Excise-collection contracts he brought that revenue (now flourishing in a much kinder economic climate) under closer Treasury control without sacrificing the advantages of 'farming', which had traditionally been the competitive bidding for the contract and the guarantee of a fixed rental for the Crown. He created a powerful credit agency in the Excise which supplied large loans at 8 per cent, and in 1677 he ensured that the profits of the farming contract accrued in larger measure to the king.[71] This shrewd step, from 'farming' to 'management' shortly foreshadowed the decision of 1683 to make the Excise entirely a salaried, government undertaking. The Customs had already been taken over as a government department in 1671, under Sir George Downing's chairmanship, and henceforth collaboration with the Customs Commissioners became a regular Treasury responsibility.

---

[70] Pepys, *Diary*, 14 February 1669; cf. Downing's gloomy assessment, ibid., 27 December 1668.

[71] A. Browning, *Thomas Osborne, Earl of Danby, Duke of Leeds, 1632–1712* (3 vols., Glasgow, 1944–51), i, 129–37; 208–11; E. Hughes, *Studies in Administration and Finance, 1558–1825* (Manchester, 1934), pp. 150–9.

Every week now found the Treasury dealing with problems arising from the enforcement of the Navigation Acts in England and the colonies, or superintending the appointment, promotion and chivvying of the regional Customs executive.[72] This important extension of the Treasury's administrative responsibilities is bound up with another distinctive feature of the Treasury under Danby – its enhanced political significance. In 1667 the Commission had been quite deliberately apolitical in character, its members standing self-consciously detached from faction and loyal to an ideal of professional integrity.[73] This was admirable, but dangerously unrealistic. Coventry's dismissal in 1669, the prize for an unscrupulous court intrigue, indicated what subsequent history has often proved, that mere professionalism is never enough. Other courtiers had been quick to discern that the growth of the Treasury's status after 1667 had made it infinitely more attractive as a post from which to command power. In May 1667 it had been shrewdly observed of Arlington that he considered himself more influential as Secretary of State than he could be at the Treasury,[74] and measured against the earl of Southampton's modest stature this seemed plausible. But it is significant that after the Treasury's victories of January and February 1668 (most of them at the expense of the Secretaries of State) Arlington's name regularly crops up as a contender for the Lord Treasurer's white staff.[75] He was still contending against Danby in 1674. The Treasury held its dangers, as Danby, Godolphin and Harley were later to learn. But it also conferred exceptional opportunities for self-advancement. Danby was a second-rank figure in June 1673; by early 1675 he was the Crown's principal minister, standing on a solid base of financial achievement.[76]

Danby had the merit of bringing to the Treasury a sophisticated sense of the nature of politics as a practical science in which financial management was one, though only one, important ingredient. In one of his early memoranda (tentatively dated October 1673), the objectives of Treasury control take second place to the promotion of a Protestant foreign policy and an elaborate recipe for parliamentary management as the cardinal points of his political programme.[77] It is not surprising,

[72] See, for example, Treasury letters, 23 March, 5 May 1676, 16 November 1677 (*CTB 1676–9*, pp. 170–2, 205–6, 784–5).
[73] Pepys, *Diary*, 2 September, 30 December 1667, 29 January, 19 May 1668.
[74] Ibid., 1 May 1667.
[75] Ibid., 28 September 1668; *CSPD 1667–68*, p.259 ; Add. MSS. 36916, ff. 115, 221; *Letters to Sir Joseph Williamson* (Camden Society, 1874), i, 6; *Hatton Correspondence* (Camden Society, 1878), i, 102–3; V. Barbour, *Henry Bennet, Earl of Arlington* (Washington, 1914), 110n., 204–5.
[76] Browning, *Danby*, i, 107, 109, 146.
[77] Browning, *Danby*, ii, 63, 64.

therefore, that under Danby the Treasury emerged as the centre of 'court party' organization, taking over from the Secretaries of State a parliamentary role which, through the Junior Lords of the Treasury, it still nominally performs today. It was under Danby, too, that the political implications of Treasury control became fully apparent as the revenue administration grew more and more heavily charged with pensions, sinecures and downright bribes.[78] By 1675, opponents of Danby had begun the long sequence of attempts to drive from House of Commons the tainted beneficiaries of Treasury largesse. They were defeated, and with a view to the stable character of eighteenth-century politics, with its court party of 'king's friends' obediently marching and counter-marching under the Treasury's eye, this has seemed one of the most notable of Danby's achievements.

Yet, while the organization of a short-lived court party may be placed to Danby's credit as a politician, it is important to note that an administrative price had to be paid which did lasting damage to the true interests of the Treasury. The clue to this lies in the pattern of office-holding before, during and after the Treasury Commission of 1667.

Briefly, despite some half-hearted attempts at reform under the early Stuarts, the characteristic tenure on which offices were held in much of seventeenth-century English administration had come to be 'tenure for life', a status conferred by letters patent and virtually unassailable except by attainder for treason. Death could vacate an office, of course, but the increasing number of reversions granted to offices of life tenure ensured that they could pass out of administrative control for some generations ahead. Even officials holding their places 'during good behaviour' were legally secure from dismissal for anything short of proved criminality – the only tenure really susceptible to dismissal for incompetence being tenure 'during pleasure'.[79]

However, it is clear from a succession of Treasury minutes in 1667 and 1668 (Docs. 1 and 10) that the Treasury Commissioners were determined to redress this situation in the interests of efficiency by ending reversions, curtailing life tenures and bringing as many offices as possible back to tenure 'during pleasure'. At least one minute suggests that they were also pressing on the king a complete break with the traditional style of remuneration (based on early medieval or, at best, Tudor valuations, supplemented by fee-taking and perquisites) and recommending a new system of salaries for the great officers of state.[80] Had they succeeded, the character of eighteenth-century English

---

[78] Browning, *Danby*, i, 192–3, 205–7.

[79] J. Sainty, 'A Reform in the Tenure of Offices during the reign of Charles II,' *Bulletin of the Institute of Historical Research* (1968), 150–71. The following paragraphs are heavily indebted to this study.

[80] Treasury minute, 14 July 1668 (*CTB 1667–8*, p. 383); Sir John Nicholas to Sir Edward Nicholas, 18 November 1668 (BM Egerton MSS. 2539, f. 281).

politics might have been significantly different. As it is, a detailed analysis of the tenure of office in the late seventeenth century reveals beyond doubt that between 1667 and 1672 the Treasury succeeded in altering the pattern of tenures in several departments of government – the Office of Works, the Mint, the Ordnance Office, the Privy Council staff and certain branches of the royal household.[81] As a demonstration of the Treasury's unrivalled capacity to reform the character of English government the achievement was precocious – and shortlived. After 1672, under the Treasurerships of Clifford and Danby, the achievement was reversed. 'An attitude of indifference and even hostility towards the principles of the reform of tenure' allowed many of these offices to fall back into the hands of life-interests and reversions which, in some cases, were not extinguished until the reigns of Queen Anne and the Hanoverians.[82] To that extent, the Treasury's efforts to create conditions for efficient managerial control in government were retarded, for more than a century, until the initiative of the House of Commons launched a new era of economical and administrative reform.[83] It was a heavy price to pay for Danby's political ascendancy.

Indeed, the full administrative costs of Danby's Treasurership cannot be readily assessed because the informality of his proceedings has left inadequate evidence for a judgment. Sitting in his house near Whitehall, Danby sent for the Chancellor of the Exchequer on the infrequent occasions when he needed him,[84] but there was no formal Board holding organized discussions and coming to recorded decisions. The Treasury Minute Book went into a sharp decline under Downing's two successors, as did other aspects of the Treasury's book-keeping. With Danby's brother-in-law, Charles Bertie, as Secretary to the Treasury, and Danby's bitterest enemy, Sir Robert Howard, as Auditor of the Receipt, a situation arose which proved extremely damaging to the efficiency and morale of the whole system.[85] The legacy of the 1667 Treasury Commission was placed in jeopardy.

However, it was rescued, consolidated and transmitted to the future by the Treasury Commissions which sat between 1679 and 1684. Dominated for most of these years by the Earl of Rochester (who became Lord Treasurer in 1685) the Treasury proved fully alive to its inheritance. Like the Commissioners of 1667, those of 1679 made a brisk start, calling for immediate and regular reports from all the revenue collecting and disbursing officers.[86] They re-registered the

---

[81] Sainty, *BIHR* (1968), 159–60.
[82] Sainty, *BIHR* (1968), 160–1.
[83] See below, pp. 65–6.
[84] Baxter, *Treasury*, p. 22.
[85] Ibid., p. 183; Browning, *Danby*, i, 110, and below, pp. 50–1.
[86] *CTB 1679–80*, pp. 5–12, 37, 62.

Treasury's authority over revenue and expenditure with another Order
in Council, and made a particular point of asserting their jurisdiction
over Irish finance (Doc. 2(f)). They held the departments to the
authorized limits of their expenditure and establishments, and dis-
allowed breaches of the rule of specific Treasury sanction.[87] They
revived the effort to regulate office-holding and administered the
absorption of the Excise executive as a salaried and highly professional
government department. They exerted themselves across the whole
range of Treasury responsibilities with the characteristic vigour of
'new brooms', and their achievement was notable.

However, it was not unique; its features were not original. The
phenomenon of new brooms makes frequent appearances in the history
of the Treasury, as of most other institutions. Indeed, the working of
the party-political system, from the late seventeenth century onwards,
made it particularly likely that with every major turn in the wheel of
parliamentary fortune a new administration would enter the Treasury
resolved to discredit its predecessor by the superior efficiency of its
proceedings. There was invariably some abuse, some laxity or degeneration of authority which could be made good with a flourish, and the
entry of a new Treasury Commission in the Minute Book is not
infrequently the prelude to an ostentatious flurry of resolutions on
organization and authority. This was the case in 1679, a year of acute
political crisis in which it was particularly important to efface the
legacy of a Lord Treasurer who for long had been accused of administrative malpractice. It was to be similarly the case in 1714-15, in 1782
and in 1830 – each instance producing resolutions which are of importance in this collection of documents.[88]

This is not to question the value of their achievement; later rulers
of the Treasury, including Danby and the Commission of 1679,
exercised a combination of political and administrative power much
superior to anything available to the Commissioners of 1667, and they
used it to good effect; but it is to indicate a qualitative, administrative
distinction which should not be obscured by political considerations of
patronage and power. It is to assert that at no other period in Treasury
history can one find quite so creative or comprehensive a resurrection
of Treasury authority as in the months after May 1667. This work was
fundamental and proved enduring, laying a permanent basis which
later Treasury Boards could take for granted. In the eighteenth century,
when precedents for the range of Treasury authority had to be con-

---

[87] *CTB 1681-5*, pp. 39-40, 137, 263-9, 311, 352, 455, 753-4; *CSPD 1679-80*,
p. 390.
[88] See below, Doc. 21(a) the regulation of Treasury business, 18 November
1714; Doc. 21(o) the reorganization of 30 November 1782; and pp. 93-4 for
the Whig reforms of 1830-4.

sulted, it was not to 1676 or 1679 that ministers looked; it was to 1667 and 1668 – to the Orders in Council of November 1667 and January 1668, and to the retrenchment schemes of March to November 1668.[89] These were the historic corner-stones of Treasury control, and they allow one to say of the Treasury in particular what Professor Edward Hughes once wrote of fiscal developments in general: 'the significance of the administrative changes in Charles II's time is that the work was never gone back upon.'[90]

[89] PRO SP 44/72, pp. 89–95; 99–161; this volume is a compilation entitled 'Precedents Chas. II to Geo. II'.
[90] Edward Hughes, *Studies in Administration and Finance, 1558–1825* (Manchester, 1934), p. 138.

2

Parliament and the Treasury: the Problem of Accountability

THE Treasury emerged from the reign of Charles II with its institutional character greatly enhanced. Its authority had been unmistakably registered by formal statements and by daily enforcement. Precedents, routines and records of business had built up patterns of control over revenue and expenditure which would serve their purpose for some generations to come. At the very least, 'the Treasury' was now literally and metaphorically on the map of Whitehall,[1] a permanent institution which was unlikely to be eclipsed as easily as Lord Treasurers had been in the generations before 1667.

However, the Treasury had yet to face some of its severest challenges. The wars of William III and Queen Anne posed acute financial problems which called for fiscal innovation and credit management of exceptional ingenuity. And these problems had their political as well as their administrative aspect. The Treasury and its rulers were drawn more deeply than ever into the parliamentary world, forced to evolve techniques of collaboration with a recalcitrant and inquisitorial House of Commons. In William III they found a master whose legitimate anxiety about his resources, their disposal and the complex patronage which went with them, threatened to impair the practising self-sufficiency which the Treasury had only recently evolved.[2] The autonomy of the Treasury could not yet be taken for granted.

The manner in which the Treasury responded to all these challenges would have to be thoroughly assessed in any narrative history of the department, but it could be dealt with here only at the price of obscuring a profounder and more lasting problem which, although earnestly debated in the reigns of William and Anne, was scarcely resolved before

[1] For the earliest location of 'the Treasury', ca. 1670, see 'A Survey and Ground Plot of the Royal Palace of Whitehall,' attributed to John Fisher, illustrated and discussed by G. S. Dugdale, *Whitehall through the Centuries* (London, 1950), pp. 64–6.

[2] S. B. Baxter, *The Development of the Treasury 1660–1702* (London, 1957), pp. 49–50, 53, 60, 75, 76, 98–100, 137–8. Note also the implications of Doc. 2(h) below.

the second half of the nineteenth century. This is the problem of 'accountability' – ostensibly a technical and very arid question, yet one whose solution was absolutely fundamental to the evolution of the Treasury.

'Accountability', in this context of Treasury history, is a problem which one might risk defining simply as the task of enforcing the prompt, accurate and honest discharge of responsibility by those handling public money. Unfortunately, however, the task was in no way simple, nor was it one which the Treasury could perform alone. It was to prove in large part a parliamentary, and hence a political and constitutional, problem of considerable technical complexity, and to appreciate this at the outset it may be helpful to take advantage of hindsight and review the six distinct features of the system by which it was ultimately solved. By the second half of the nineteenth century we shall find at work a logical sequence of (theoretically) watertight stages requiring (a) a technique of estimate, by which the annual requirements of forthcoming public expenditure could be accurately assessed, and (b) a convention of parliamentary appropriation, by which funds could be strictly allocated to these needs. It also required (c) an independent agency (the reformed Exchequer) empowered to issue these appropriated funds to (d) responsible, non-political paymasters, disbursing funds on behalf of government departments. Finally, it required (e) effective machinery for the independent audit of this expenditure and (f) the submission of the balanced, annual account to the scrutinizing committee of the House of Commons. This brought the process of public expenditure full circle, laying before parliament the means of checking that its estimates and appropriations had been adhered to.

But although, by modern criteria of accountability, these stages appear logically interdependent, the important historical fact is that the logic was only slowly perceived, the interdependence only belatedly created. Each feature of the system of estimate, appropriation, issue and audit was the product of separate lines of evolution and the history of the system is therefore not one theme but several, peculiarly difficult to narrate. However, the essence of the process is the discovery by parliament of the basis on which the Treasury and the House of Commons could collaborate to enforce public accountability – something vital to the character of the Treasury and fundamental to the growth of responsible government. It is this which I want to illustrate.

At the commencement of our period the problem was not so obviously a parliamentary one as it was later to appear. It was an administrative one, entirely within the jurisdiction of the Crown. Although there were fifteenth-century precedents, and at least one seventeenth-century instance, of the appropriation and retrospective audit of government expenditure, these precocious experiments had been eclipsed by two centuries of quiescence.[3] In the 1660s the problem of accountability could be regarded from the Treasury's point of view as the deceptively simple one of making the Exchequer do its job. After all, it was the Exchequer – in particular the Upper Exchequer or Exchequer of Account – which carried the primary responsibility for the audit of accounts and the prosecution of defaulters, things which it could be expected to do without prompting and only the minimum of Treasury intervention. The King's Remembrancer, with a wide range of revenue and expenditure accounts under his jurisdiction, seemed amply equipped to ensure regularity of audit with his formidable powers of enforcement (Doc. 9). Who could resist successive attacks from his armoury of writs – *fieri facias, capias ad satisfaciendum, extent, diem clausit extremum, melius inquirendum, levari facias, venditioni exponas,* to say nothing of a Commission of Rebellion?[4] Not surprisingly, whenever their competence was challenged, Exchequer officials responded with defiant confidence in the infallibility of the 'ancient course' – a complex but versatile array of procedures which were no longer susceptible to improvement.[5]

Yet, measured against the simplest criteria of effective accountability, such as promptness, honesty and accuracy, the Exchequer had long been found wanting. Honest by very negative standards, Exchequer audit was never, ever prompt. And by what criterion could it be judged to be accurate? The essence of Exchequer audit, throughout the centuries, had been a judicial process by which accountants were formally examined about their registered liabilities and, if they could produce evidence that they had discharged them, were legally acquitted of further responsibility. But not all liabilities were accurately recorded, and not all the evidence was properly tested. The delays characteristic of the 'ancient course' created profitable opportunities for malversation which never came within the Exchequer's narrow scrutiny. Tardy, piecemeal, archaic, the processes of Exchequer audit were not designed to produce an accurate or comprehensive account of what was really happening to public funds.[6]

[3] For a commentary upon this theme see J. S. Roskell, 'Perspectives in English Parliamentary History', *Bulletin of the John Rylands Library* (1963–4), xlvi, 468–74.

[4] 'The Course of Proceedings for Getting in the King's Debts' in the Office of the King's Remembrancer – BM Add. MSS. 36108, f. 10v – lists this array of processes. For examples of their issue, 18 March 1676 see *CTB 1676–9*, p. 159.

[5] See for example the defensive treatise of 1670 (PRO E 369/117), cited below, p. 50.

[6] For the Exchequer's shortcomings in the early modern period see an incisive account by Professor G. R. Elton, *The Tudor Revolution in Government* (Cambridge, 1953), pp. 20–5; or, in considerable technical detail, A. Steel, *The*

It was to take more than one hundred and fifty years to eliminate evils which were fully apparent in the 1660s. The obstacles were partly conceptual ones – a failure to perceive precisely what the problem required. In larger part they were institutional obstacles – the fiercely conservative resistance of officials with a vested interest in anachronisms. Needless to say, they presented their case in highminded terms as guardians of a sacred and immemorial trust,[7] but the material, and very comfortable, foundation of their position lay simply in their security of tenure. Nearly all the major officials of the Exchequer (including the Chancellor, until 1672) held their places for life. Some officers, such as the King's Remembrancer, the Lord Treasurer's Remembrancer and the Clerk of the Pells, were virtually hereditary. They were immune to displacement for mere inefficiency and remarkably resistant to charges of dishonesty. Performing their duties only through deputies they pocketed their fees and defied the administrative sanctions of the Treasury.[8]

It should come as no surprise to learn that the Treasury Commissioners of 1667 were not prepared to acquiesce in this situation. They did not content themselves with merely urging the officials of the Exchequer to work harder – they intervened repeatedly to see that they did so, paying particular attention to those departments of the Upper Exchequer which were responsible for audit (Doc. 10). Later, in their concern for the efficiency of the Treasury Order system, they concentrated on the Lower Exchequer, stressing the public interest and condemning, with remarkable asperity, its habit of observing holy-days quite unknown to other departments.[9] The Lord Keeper and Master of the Rolls were likewise jolted – told that ten years of negligence in the court of Chancery was obstructing the prosecution of innumerable accounts to the king's great damage.[10] But perhaps their most daring step was to address a challenge to the heart of the whole archaic system. Of what use, they asked, are the tallies – those notched,

Receipt of the Exchequer, 1377–1485 (Cambridge, 1954), pp. vii–xx, xxix–xl, 1–36, 371–406. The functions of the Exchequer in the seventeenth and eighteenth centuries are summarized by Baxter, *Treasury*, pp. 109–66 and J. E. D. Binney, *British Public Finance and Administration, 1774–92* (Oxford, 1958), pp. 189–232.

[7] It was axiomatic among its officials that the Exchequer antedated the Conquest, if not the Flood. The damaging role of this dogmatic antiquarianism is well illustrated in G. R. Elton, 'The Elizabethan Exchequer: War in the Receipt', *Elizabethan Government and Society: Essays presented to Sir John Neale*, ed. S. T. Bindoff, J. Hurstfield and C. H. Williams (London, 1961), pp. 213–48.

[8] J. C. Sainty, 'The Tenure of Office in the Exchequer', *EHR* (1965), pp. 457–8, 460–5; Baxter, *Treasury*, pp. 113, 124–5, 165.

[9] Treasury letter, 13 May 1670 (*CTB 1669–72*), pp. 568–9.

[10] Treasury letter, 16 March 1670 (*CTB 1669–72*), pp. 539–40.

wooden instruments, split on the receipt of money and, if the 'ancient course' were strictly observed, rejoined to prove their authenticity at audit? The fact that the rejoining of foil and counterfoil was rarely bothered with made it reasonable to ask, of what value were the tallies to the king in point of profit or security?[11]

In reply they received a notable treatise, composed by Sir Robert Crooke, Clerk of the Pipe. It was full of fabulous lore, asserting the immemorial origins of the Exchequer and the infallibility of its procedures. More pointedly, it stressed its capacity for survival in the face of all 'turnings and changings' and of innovations attempted for 'private and sinister ends', a barbed innuendo which surely missed its mark. But the confident conservatism behind it was amply vindicated. The tally-sticks survived the Commission of 1667, and they survived the reformers of the 1780s. They were still being notched and split in the 1820s.

The Treasury Commission of 1667 was no more successful in reforming Exchequer tenures. They did what they could to ensure that the deputies who actually undertook the work were properly sworn in and gave security for their good behaviour, but the main life interests in Exchequer posts were perpetuated when vacancies arose.[12] The penalties for this were to become clear after the death of the admirable Sir Robert Long in 1673 and his succession as Auditor of the Receipt by Sir Robert Howard. Holding this key position on life tenure until 1698, Howard contributed more than most to the degeneration of the late seventeenth-century Exchequer. He not only neglected his official responsibilities to check on the propriety of transactions in the Lower Exchequer, he actively connived at misappropriation. The first of a series of scandals was exposed in 1677 when a suspicious Danby ordered a check on the four Tellers – the men who actually held the cash balances of the Exchequer. This revealed a deficiency of £12,508 9s 3d in the office of only one Teller, Sir William Doyly, but it could be inferred from the story that emerged that there had been malpractices among all the Tellers and that Howard had been a party to them.[13] The Attorney General alleged, '1. Sir Robert knew that several Tellers and their clerks made use of the King's money to their private accounts, and that it was not revealed by him, nay, was indus-

---

[11] The Treasury's questions, of 5 May 1670, can be deduced from the Exchequer's reply, 'A Narrative of the Antiquity, Institution, Dignity and Authority of his Majesty's Court of Exchequer and of the right use of Tallies there leavied for the King's Treasure in order to the King's Security and the Subjects Indempnity,' (PRO E 369/117). It is significant that this treatise of 1670 proved invaluable to A. Steel's account of the fifteenth-century Exchequer. It is discussed by H. Jenkinson in *Proceedings of the Society of Antiquaries*, xxv.

[12] Sainty, *BIHR* (1968), pp. 160, 162–3.

[13] Baxter, *Treasury*, pp. 151–6.

triously concealed by him. 2. He not only did so, but for his private occasions borrowed the King's money from the Tellers, and to repay it borrowed from other Tellers.'[14]

Eventually, Doyly was suspended and his property attached to make good the debt. Howard remained unscathed, however, secure in his tenure and free to contribute to another major scandal in 1697 when a deficiency of £27,000 came to light. The culprit, Guy Palmes, was an incompetent Teller who had bungled some improper but not wholly criminal dealings, and the Treasury, anxious to safeguard public confidence at a difficult time, were ready to smooth the business over.[15] But the investigation concluded that part of the blame had to be laid upon Sir Robert Howard for not observing the ancient course of the Exchequer, by entering records of payments without ensuring that they had really been made. And the really depressing aspect of this case was that it came within a month of the Treasury's most constructive effort to solve its problems in the Exchequer – the *Act for the better observation of the course anciently used in the Exchequer*.[16] The Act had not only restated the correct procedures for the issue and receipt of money in the Exchequer, it had ratified some useful innovations, such as the practice, inaugurated by Downing, of advertising the course of loan repayments on Treasury Orders. Furthermore, it had provided for Treasury control over those Exchequer officials who actually performed the duties of the Receipt – the chief clerks of the patent officers. Not only were they to be put on oath for the proper performance of their tasks but they could only be appointed with Treasury approval. This still left the titular incumbents untouched, but it was the best that could be done until the piecemeal demolition of Exchequer sinecures in the late eighteenth century.

The initiative for this Act of 1696 had come from the Treasury, in particular from the Secretary William Lowndes. It belongs, however, to a context of growing concern among members of parliament about the wider problems of accountability. Although they failed to conceive an appropriate solution they succeeded in exposing the fact that there *was* a problem and in revealing some of its complexities. Already in the reign of Charles II the fruitless expenditure of the second Dutch war had raised questions about the efficiency, as well as the integrity, of public expenditure. Why had the fleet not been equipped for the campaign of 1667? What had happened to the millions voted for the

[14] *CSPD 1677–8*, p. 448.
[15] Baxter, *Treasury*, pp. 157–62; *CSPD 1697*, pp. 176–7 – 'Part of this blame was laid on Sir Robert Howard for not observing the ancient rules of the Exchequer, though they are enforced by a late act of Parliament; but he continued to certify the payments made ... without examining the vouchers, to ascertain whether the money were paid or not, as he ought to do every week.'
[16] 8 & 9 William III, c. 28; *Statutes of the Realm*, vii, 275–9.

war? Why were our seamen starving in the streets? The attempt to enforce a retrospective audit of these vast sums, £2½ million of which had not been explicitly appropriated to the war, raised a prolonged political storm from which a compromise eventually emerged. But the Act setting up a commission of inquiry into accounts embodied a notable advance on the degree of public accountability imposed on the Crown at any time since the early fifteenth century.[17] In its retrospective character it was a more striking expression of distrust than the precautionary provisions for accounts which had been written into the Subsidy Act of 1624,[18] and in its detailed provisions went further than many later measures were to venture. It authorized the commissioners to examine the propriety of the expenditure not only of the parliamentary grants but of the ordinary Customs revenue and of the receipts accruing from prizes. They could call upon departmental treasurers, receivers, cashiers, pursers, tradesmen and seamen to give evidence under oath and imprison them if they refused. They were empowered to reform 'the manner and method' of public accounts as well as certify their authenticity to the Exchequer. And the report of the nine commissioners – all laymen without parliamentary or official positions – could be presented independently to both Houses of Parliament as well as to the king. There were features of this Act which later parliamentary Accounts Commissions were to envy.

Yet it could hardly have been less effective. The commission's findings, reported in the winter of 1669-70, were trampled underfoot by an angry Court and lost sight of in the press of other parliamentary business.[19] No immediate legislative or administrative reform can be directly traced to their findings. But while it held the floor of the House of Commons in November and December 1669 the Commission's report taught some useful lessons at the expense of the Treasurer of the Navy, Sir George Carteret. Inevitably, he was accountable for the largest share of war expenditure, estimated by the commission to be over £3,600,000, and his handling of it led the commission to make a significant series of charges. He was alleged to have misapplied large amounts appropriated to specific services, recording payments in one

[17] 19 & 20 Car. II, c. 1, *Statutes of the Realm*, v, 624-7; partially printed in J. P. Kenyon, *The Stuart Constitution*, pp. 392-5, and A. Browning, *English Historical Documents, 1660-1714*, pp. 176-8.

[18] 21 Jac. I, c. 33, ss. 37, 39, *Statutes of the Realm*, iv, 1247-62; Kenyon, *Stuart Constitution*, pp. 76-80. These accounts were eventually submitted to Parliament, but without significant repercussions – HMC, *Manuscripts of the House of Lords* (new series), xi (1962), p. 207; J. Rushworth, (ed.) *Historical Collections of Private Passages of State* (London, 1721), i, pp. 208, 213 (I am indebted to Mr C. S. R. Russell for these two references).

[19] D. T. Witcombe, *Charles II and the Cavalier House of Commons, 1663-1674* (Manchester, 1966), pp. 93-4.

year although not making them until the next. He had credited bankers with loans at dates long before the money had been received and was believed to have paid 9 per cent on them while claiming 10 per cent from the Exchequer. Bills had been paid for naval stores about whose actual existence no evidence could be produced and, most aggravating of all, he appeared to have held large cash balances when seamen were starving for lack of pay. As for the Navy Board, it appeared guilty of the grossest negligence. It had condoned dishonest supply contracts, had approved the Navy treasurer's bookkeeping without investigating-its accuracy, and, by failing to submit the accounts of a host of minor officials to searching, annual investigation, had encouraged every imaginable type of malpractice – embezzlement, dead-pays, extortion and delay.[20]

The House of Commons found most of these charges proved; the House of Lords did not. Carteret (and Pepys) made a plausible defence, and although this is not the place to pursue the question of guilt it can be said that several technical malpractices were consistent with an honest discharge of duty. The whole system of 'impresting' departmental treasurers with large but notional sums of money in the form of Treasury Orders conferred on them a dangerously inconsistent mixture of independence and responsibility. It was up to them to raise cash on their paper credits as best they could and dispose of it to a number of competing claims. The right hand, which disbursed money for naval stores, could not for ever deny itself the resources of the left hand, intended for seamen's pay; the palms of the bankers, offering ready cash in advance of the tardy Exchequer, had to be reasonably greased. Under the stringent credit conditions of 1666 it is extremely likely that Carteret, as he claimed, pledged his personal fortune to get the fleet to sea.[21] This anomalous confusion of public and personal credit was a fundamental evil of the unreformed system.

But beyond these points, to which the House of Commons gave scant sympathy, they were forced to recognize some of the profounder problems of public accountability. They learned, for example, that whatever their statutes might say they had no adequate sanctions to enforce the Executive's obedience to a parliamentary appropriation.[22] It was also clear that there was no coherent system of departmental or national bookkeeping.[23] And, at bottom, it was evident that the Exchequer was simply not competent to deal with fraudulent accountants,

---

[20] *Eighth Report of the Royal Commission on Historical Manuscripts* (London, 1881), Part I, Appendix (Manuscripts of the House of Lords), pp. 128–33; A. Grey, *Debates of the House of Commons* (London, 1769), i, 157–9, 163–74.
[21] Grey, *Debates*, i, 170.
[22] Ibid., 172.
[23] Ibid., 181.

for it accepted at face value the vouchers for expenditure which were presented to it. As the chairman of the Accounts Commission summed up: 'they think the Exchequer as much to blame as Sir George Carteret'.[24]

This lesson had to be repeated again and again. Nevertheless, although the 1667–9 accounts inquiry was comparatively sterile, it can be placed at the source of attitudes which had an important role to play in the parliamentary life of the next fifty years. Distrust of the Executive's competence and moral integrity was not peculiar to the late seventeenth century, but rarely has the sentiment contributed so largely to the character of opposition politics. At the very heart of 'country party' aspirations, antedating and transcending Whig or Tory divisions, this sentiment was to express itself in a connected series of demands – for strict appropriation of supply, parliamentary audit of accounts, the control of government credit, and the exclusion from the House of Commons of the main beneficiaries of public funds.[25] Carteret's expulsion from the House was an early symptom. Henceforth the politics of finance were to be as fiercely fought as the politics of religion.

Already by 1668 opinion in the Commons had advanced beyond the appropriation of extraordinary supply, which the Crown had conceded in 1665, to a demand for the appropriation of the ordinary revenues – in particular, the Customs.[26] It was argued that this simply made explicit what had always been implicit in the Crown's annual revenues – an obligation to use them for the protection of the commonwealth. But it was a sharp encroachment upon the Crown's discretionary prerogative which was successfully resisted at every turn until 1688. Instead, the House of Commons found means to enforce internal controls, evolving within a few years no less than three of the four classic rules which still govern the financial procedures of that House.[27] Firstly, in 1667, they resolved that financial proposals should be given a preliminary debate in the Committee of the Whole House before being put to any formal vote. This guaranteed full and free discussion outside the constricting conditions of a formal debate where government influence could be brought to bear through the Speaker. The second part of the

[24] Grey, *Debates*, i, 181.

[25] For the political exploitation of these attitudes, see J. H. Plumb, *The Growth of Political Stability in England, 1675–1725* (London, 1967), pp. 47–9, 117, 127–8, 138, 140–8; or G. Holmes, *British Politics in the Age of Anne* (London, 1967), pp. 116–47.

[26] 1 May 1668, Grey, *Debates*, i, 148–56; note the similar attempt in October 1675, Grey, *Debates*, iii, 317–20, 446–59.

[27] The 'rules' were given this helpful classification by Lord Campion's edition of Erskine May's *Parliamentary Practice*, 1946. For a recent historical survey of their evolution see G. Reid, *The Politics of Financial Control* (London, 1966), pp. 33–61.

resolution provided further insurance against sinister pressures by requiring an interval to elapse between the proposal and its debate. No government proposal for a money bill could be sprung upon a thin House of Commons, henceforth, without giving opportunity for critical deliberation.[28] The third principle was established soon after, in 1671 and 1678, when the House asserted and then consolidated its right, as against the House of Lords, to define the terms of financial grants to the Crown. These were claimed to be the sole gift of the Commons and they were to begin with the Commons. 'The ends, purposes, considerations and conditions, limitations and qualifications of such grants' were in no circumstances to be altered by the Upper House.[29]

It was also in 1671 that the House of Commons made a significant attempt to resolve the credit difficulties of the Crown by authorizing a preferential interest rate of 7 per cent for loans made to the Exchequer on the security of an additional parliamentary supply, the Subsidy Act of 1671.[30] This interference in their special province was not at all welcome to the Treasury Lords and it proved a conspicuous failure, but the House of Commons was henceforth prepared to intervene in those borrowing arrangements of the Crown which were seen to have a bearing on public policy. The Stop of the Exchequer was a timely demonstration of the irresponsibility with which government debts could be dishonoured. It was high time, argued Sir William Coventry – now an opposition spokesman – that the king's credit was recognized as a public trust: 'the subject's property is in the King's credit.'[31] Indeed, 1675 saw an attempt, extremely distressing to Sir George Downing, to transfer the custody of parliamentary credits from the Exchequer (and hence the Treasury) to the City of London,[32] and although this came to nothing the additional parliamentary supplies made available to Charles II between 1677 and 1679 were not only strictly appropriated but contained detailed provision for borrowing at rates of interest above the market rate. They closed a loophole in the Acts of 1665–71 by appropriating the loan money as well as the tax receipts; the Treasury's discretion was completely circumscribed and penalties were provided against disobedience by paymasters and laxity

[28] 18 February 1668, *Journals of the House of Commons*, ix, 52; also printed in W. C. Costin and J. S. Watson, *The Law and Working of the Constitution*, i, 153–4; Reid, *Financial Control*, p. 47.

[29] 13 April 1671, 3 July 1678, *Journals of the House of Commons*, ix, 235, 509; Costin and Watson, *Constitution*, i, 154; Browning, *English Historical Documents 1660–1714*, p. 227; Reid, *Financial Control*, pp. 55–6.

[30] 22 & 23 Car. II, c. 3, s. 6. As a further measure of interference in the money market, the Act levied a penal duty of 15s. in £100 against goldsmith-bankers or any other creditor of the king taking more than 6 per cent in interest.

[31] Grey, *Debates*, iii, 62–3.

[32] Ibid., 352–60.

by Exchequer officials.[33] The Auditor of the Receipt was given a statutory responsibility to report his accounts to the House of Commons, and the Act of 1679 for the urgent disbandment of troops went to the remarkable lengths of empowering the Treasury to apply its funds to this end without formal authorization from the king under the Privy Seal.[34] This invasion of the financial prerogative of the Crown must be seen in the context of the Popish plot, a crisis year in which the king's life and parliamentary security seemed equally endangered. Yet it would be a mistake to write off these developments as ephemeral, panic innovations. They demonstrate that the principles which were to govern the control of public credit in the eighteenth century had already been formulated, and disprove the assertion that it was only *after* 1688 that 'appropriation clauses in acts of supply go hand-in-hand with credit arrangements, with borrowing and repaying clauses. . . .'[35] On the contrary, the development of parliamentary controls of public finance in the reign of Charles II had very nearly kept pace with the development of autonomous Treasury control; and the two processes are not unrelated.

However, one of the developments which is distinctive in the post-Revolution period amply demonstrates that the relationship between Parliament and the Treasury was not yet one of trust and collaboration. Between 1691 and 1697, and from 1702 to 1703 and 1711 to 1713, a series of Parliamentary Accounts Commissions mounted searching inquiries into public expenditure. Embodying a deep distrust of the Executive's probity and competence, they differed from their precursor of 1667 in being composed (with only one exception) of Members of Parliament[36] and perhaps as a consequence they all too soon became vehicles for narrow political vendettas, hounding party rivals and the officeholding protégés of the Court. The Parliamentary Accounts Commissions have been described as 'the front bench of the country party' which 'directed opposition tactics generally'.[37] Yet it would be a mistake to write off completely the administrative significance of their work. Clearly their inquisitions exerted some positive influence on the quality of public life. Standards of official probity were asserted,

---

[33] See 29 Car. II, c. 1, ss. 39, 45; 29 & 30 Car. II, c. 1, ss. 62, 66, 67; 30 Car. II, c. 1, ss. 15, 19, 22–3. The appropriation clauses from the latter are printed by Kenyon, *Stuart Constitution*, p. 396.

[34] 31 Car. II, c. 1, s. 12.

[35] W. A. Shaw, *CTB 1689–92* (Pt 1), p. clxxvi.

[36] The background and membership of these Commissions is usefully summarized by W. A. Shaw in *CTB 1689–92*, pp. cli–clxxiv and *CTB 1695–1702* (Introduction volume), pp. clv–clxxvi. The isolated exception occurred in 1700.

[37] A. McInnes, *Robert Harley: Puritan Politician* (London, 1970), p. 44. See also Holmes, *British Politics*, pp. 136–40; D. Rubini, *Court and Country, 1688–1702* (London, 1967), pp. 69–81.

if not raised; victims were selected and examples made. Even if the Commissions did not venture to propound large schemes for administrative reform, they did at least bring into the open the less obvious deficiencies of public accountability which were being aggravated by war. Here and there in their reports and the minutes of their evidence one can find them face to face with fundamental anomalies – the immunity of large public spending departments to effective audit and the resulting inconsistencies of public accounts, the intransigence of Exchequer officials reluctant to do their duty and the remarkable impotence of the Treasury to deal with any of these situations.[38]

Indeed, the Treasury was very willing to discuss its dilemma, and the evidence which William Lowndes gave in 1703, as Secretary to the Treasury, is remarkable for its frank pessimism (Doc. 11(a)). His motives may have been mixed. In hinting that the two Auditors of the Imprests had been guilty of corruption and that the Exchequer had been better run under earlier Chancellors, Lowndes the Member of Parliament may have been contributing to the Tory vendetta against the earl of Halifax who had been Chancellor of the Exchequer, 1694–9, and Auditor of the Receipt since 1699. There was no mistaking the political bias of the case levelled against him.[39] But it was unquestionably Lowndes the outraged administrator, the disappointed architect of the 1696 Act for the better observation of the ancient course of the Exchequer, who deplored the continuing neglect of rules which, properly obeyed, should have been adequate to ensure public accountability. And the House of Commons seized the administrative as well as the political point. In its resolutions against Halifax it spelled out the negligences of the Auditor of the Receipt and called for his prosecution by the Crown.[40] On 11 February 1703, in an Address to the Queen, it went into even greater detail on the complex shortcomings of Exchequer audit.

Unfortunately, this promising campaign was thwarted by the House of Lords which, by intervening to defend Halifax, diverted energies into a jurisdictional wrangle which was ended only by a prorogation. It was therefore left to the Executive to put its own house in order. The prosecution of Halifax petered out in 1704 with a *nolle prosequi*, but at the Treasury Godolphin did his best to sort out professional rivalries in the Exchequer and reinforce the ancient course.[41] The

---

[38] See, for example, the debates of 3, 12 December 1691, 16 November 1692, 19, 23, 25 January 1695, 4, 7, 18, 19 January and 11 February 1703; W. Cobbett, *Parliamentary History of England*, v, 666–70, 681–2, 772, 779, 883–6; vi, 97–130, 135–43.

[39] Clayton Roberts, *The Growth of Responsible Government in Stuart England* (Cambridge, 1966), pp. 331–2; Holmes, *British Politics*, pp. 139–40, 236.

[40] Cobbett, *Parliamentary History*, vi, 133–5.

[41] *CTB 1703*, pp. 48–9, 53–4, 59, 62, 66, 67, 83, 266.

decision to appoint the Auditors of the Imprests on 'good behaviour' tenure when the opportunities arose in 1703 and 1705 seems to reflect an effort to control these key officials of the Upper Exchequer.[42] The Treasury's appointment of two comptrollers of army accounts in 1703 certainly represents a deliberate response to the scandals arising from the affairs of the earl of Ranelagh, the Paymaster of the Forces. Nothing conclusive was established by the Parliamentary Accounts Commission's inquiry into his accounts, which were far too complicated to unravel, but the reasonable suspicion that army expenditure overseas had involved flagrant profiteering could best be met by an extension of Treasury control, and this was duly secured.[43]

In these few instances, then, Parliamentary inquisitions were followed by some measure of administrative reform, but although the examples could be amplified they would give a misleading impression. The political conflicts of Queen Anne's reign did rather more to retard than promote the development of public accountability. Although the worst features of a spoils system were resisted, by Harley as much as by Godolphin, the purges of Whig officials after 1710 and of Tory officials after 1714 did significant damage to the professionalism of some revenue departments,[44] and although the Exchequer tenures were largely immune to political dismissals they could not escape the consequences of partisan appointments. Queen Anne's reign therefore saw another regression in the standards governing the tenures of Exchequer offices. Life grants and reversions began to reappear, and with the Masham family firmly rooted in the office of the King's Remembrancer, and a Harley and a Foley entrenched as Auditors of the Imprests, it is not difficult to understand why there was a reaction in the Whig interest after 1714. Sinecurism for the benefit of relatives and dependants of leading politicians had now become the dominant characteristic of the eighteenth-century Exchequer.[45]

However, most serious in its consequences was the discrediting of the Parliamentary Accounts Commissions as disinterested agencies for reform. No Whig Member of Parliament had been elected to any Commission since 1702, and the revived Commissions of 1711–13 were frankly partisan Tory inquisitions which, urged on by extremists, duly secured victims in the duke of Marlborough and Robert Walpole.[46] Objectivity of a kind sometimes emerged. The report of 1713, for example, was a conscientious indictment of real abuses (Doc. 12) and

[42] Sainty, *EHR* (1965), p. 468.
[43] R. E. Scouller, *The Armies of Queen Anne* (Oxford, 1966), pp. 8, 9, 33.
[44] W. R. Ward, *The English Land Tax in the Eighteenth Century* (Oxford, 1953), pp. 62, 63, 64–5; Edward Hughes, *Studies in Administration and Finance*, pp. 189–91.
[45] Sainty, *EHR* (1965), pp. 467–70.
[46] Holmes, *British Politics*, p. 140.

provides interesting material for comparison with the reports of the 1780s (Doc. 14). But, as a commissioner complained – 'severall matters which wou'd have been of great service and importance to the public had they been duly improv'd, were laid open. But ... such matters were entirely slighted, and no regard was shewn or notice taken of any thing which did not directly strike against the reputations of some considerable person of the opposite party.'[47]

Not surprisingly, therefore, parliamentary inquiries into accounts were allowed to lapse after 1714. The Whig oligarchy had no reason to relish them and Walpole, who had been sent to the Tower after the inquisition of 1712, vigorously resisted attempts at their revival. They were, he told the House of Commons in 1735, 'a very extraordinary method of proceeding, a method which has not been practised for many years, and never was often practised'; they would cause general alarm and undermine public credit.[48] Similar arguments were being used to good effect in 1775.[49] As a consequence, the routine supply procedures of the House of Commons exerted almost no pressure in the interests of accountability in the mid eighteenth century.[50] Estimates of annual defence expenditure were given only perfunctory scrutiny,[51] and accounts were not required. Pressure for inquiries was quickly stifled on the few occasions it emerged.[52] The appropriation clauses, written into supply bills as a matter of course, were with equal regularity flouted. The submissiveness of the House of Commons to the demands made upon it went to the remarkable lengths of acquiescing, with increasing frequency, in Votes of Credit, which were blank cheques for large amounts granted to the government without estimate or appropriation.

Yet the ideal of public accountability enforced by parliament was never entirely lost sight of. From the 1720s to the 1770s a critical tradition was kept alive by men of unequal merits and mixed motives, such as Sir William Wyndham, William Pulteney and David Hartley. It was still possible to embarrass the Treasury with well-informed probing. In 1727 there was the case of the Commissioners of Hawkers

[47] Ibid., p. 140–1, citing *Lockhart Papers*, ed. A. Aufrere (1817), i, 89.
[48] Cobbett, *Parliamentary History*, ix, 832. The speech, of 25 February 1735, is attributed to Walpole jointly with others, but may reasonably be assumed to express his sentiments.
[49] Cobbett, *Parliamentary History*, xviii, 840.
[50] P. D. G. Thomas, *The House of Commons in the Eighteenth Century* (Oxford, 1971), pp. 82, 87. The whole of Chapter III, 'The Business of the House: Finance' is relevant to this point.
[51] Thomas, *House of Commons*, p. 82; D. A. Baugh, *British Naval Administration in the Age of Walpole* (Princeton, 1965), pp. 454–70.
[52] See, for example, Cobbett, *Parliamentary History*, viii, 501; ix, 825, 835, 1005; A. Foord, *His Majesty's Opposition, 1714–1830* (Oxford, 1964), pp. 176, 183, 186–7.

and Pedlars, bankrupt defaulters for over £36,000; in 1741 the revelation that the accounts of the 4½ per cent duty on Barbados and the Leeward Isles had not been passed since 1684, and in 1753 the lottery peculations of Peter Leheup, a clerk in the Treasury.[53] Another, more celebrated, House of Commons inquiry into Treasury mismanagement was the Committee of Secrecy appointed to investigate Sir Robert Walpole's secret service expenditure which reported in 1742. Its attempt to uncover the routes by which the Crown's discretionary funds were used for electoral corruption reveals not only the servile role of certain Treasury clerks but also the ease with which Exchequer processes could be used to obscure the precise timing and destination of public expenditure (Doc. 13). The House of Commons were learning, once again, what their predecessors had been taught in the 1660s and 1690s – that the ancient course of the Exchequer was a practised vehicle for deception, not account.

Thwarted by the House of Lords, the Committee of Secrecy is also significant for its futility, but it served to consolidate some long-standing prejudices against the Crown's Civil List. At £700,000 per annum for William, Anne and George I, and £800,000 per annum for George II, the Civil List was a modest sum set amongst gross public expenditure averaging £6 million per annum, but as the vestigial area of the Crown's financial independence it had a quite disproportionate political significance.[54] While to some it seemed a conservative guarantee of the balance of the constitution, to others it appeared the key to its subversion. Voted once and for all at the beginning of a reign it was not subject to annual estimate or appropriation, and from it were financed the most sensitive operations of government – diplomacy, justice, intelligence, pensions, as well as the upkeep of the royal households and the salaries of departmental officials. Even setting aside the deep-rooted suspicion that the Privy Purse and secret service expenditure were being used to subvert the independence of Parliament, it was inevitable that hostility to the government's foreign or domestic politics would focus on the only means of pursuing them independently, the Crown's Civil List.

Consequently, it was the Civil List, where waste was unobtrusive, rather than military expenditure, where it was gross, which bore the

---

[53] 7 March 1727, Cobbett, *Parliamentary History*, viii, 552–3; *The Parliamentary Diary of Sir Edward Knatchbull 1722–30*, ed. A. Newman (Camden Society, Third Series, xcix, 1963), pp. 64, 66–7; *CTB 1737–44*, p. 486; Cobbett, *Parliamentary History*, xv, 227–8. For other examples of attacks on the inconsistencies of accounts and administrative abuses, see *Knatchbull Diary*, pp. 95, 125, 128.

[54] This important theme is valuably analysed by E. A. Reitan, 'The Civil List in Eighteenth-Century British Politics,' *Historical Journal* (1966), pp. 318–37.

brunt of parliamentary campaigns for accountability. The payment of Civil List debts in 1769 elicited the government's promise to give accounts to Parliament, and in 1777, with more arrears and a demand for £900,000 as the permanent annual provision for the Crown, Parliament was able to move another step nearer control. The crucial stage came in the winter of 1779–80 when influences outside as well as inside the House of Commons launched a comprehensive campaign for 'economical reform'.[55]

The context, as in the 1660s and the 1690s, was a costly war and an unpopular administration. But one of the distinctive features of the Economical Reform campaign is the success of the administration in making a constructive response. Rejecting the proposals of Barré and Burke in the Commons, of Richmond and Shelburne in the Lords, Lord North introduced his own scheme for a Commission of Accounts which, commentators have failed to appreciate, was intelligently modelled upon the precedent of 1667. It was to be a small committee of expert laymen, not politicians, empowered to take departmental evidence upon oath and to present recommendations for reform.[56] This was an entirely healthier conception than the Accounts Commissions of the 1690s which Shelburne and Barré had had in mind, and over the next few years Lord North was to be splendidly vindicated. Unlike the Commissions of Robert Harley's day, Lord North's stood clear of partisan politics, and unlike those of Charles II's reign, they were respectfully attended to. The fifteen reports of the Commissioners for examining, taking and stating the public accounts, presented between 1780 and 1786, permanently influenced the character of British government.[57]

The fact that they did so is not entirely due to the originality of their diagnosis. The student of the 1691–1713 reports will find in those of the 1780s much that is tediously familiar. Here again is the discovery that the accounts of defence expenditure were twenty years in arrears, that huge sums were being detained by public officials[58] and that Exchequer procedures were a sham and its audits a fiction, costly, inaccurate and inconsistent. What is original about these reports is the

[55] For the political background to the campaign, see I. R. Christie, *Wilkes, Wyvill and Reform* (London 1962); Reitan, *Historical Journal* (1966), p. 329.
[56] 20 Geo. III, c. 54; *Statutes at Large* (London, 1780), xiii, 590–2; Binney, *Public Finance*, pp. 7–14. The resemblance to the measure of 1667 would have been clearer if Lord North had persevered in his intention to appoint nine, instead of seven, commissioners – cf. Binney, *Public Finance*, p. 13.
[57] Binney, *Public Finance*, pp. 14–15 helpfully summarizes the main recommendations of the reports.
[58] The most celebrated instance is that of Henry Fox, Lord Holland, discussed in 'Henry Fox as Paymaster-General of the Forces' by L. S. Sutherland and J. E. D. Binney, *EHR* (1955), lxx, 229; Binney, *Public Finance*, p. 151.

forcefulness and clarity of their recommendations which, as they worked their way from one abuse to another, gradually developed a comprehensive and quite radical philosophy of the public interest (Doc. 14). Its logic was remorseless. The public interest demanded economy, and economy meant simplicity. Simplicity in public administration could only be achieved by sweeping away anomalies and anachronistic procedures, replacing them with machinery that was uniform, impartial, speedy and cheap. With this razor-sharp utilitarian formula at hand the possibilities of reform seemed limitless.

Indeed, the Commissioners raised more issues than could be settled in the 1780s; the far-reaching implications of their reports took eighty years to work out. But on the fundamental theme of accountability for public money under Treasury control, the Commissioners contributed some immediately helpful criticism. In dealing with public accountants, whether collecting or disbursing public money, they roundly condemned the tardy system of audit which allowed them to retain large balances for long periods to their personal advantage. This could be stopped simply enough: let the accounts be consolidated, drawn on only when required and placed in the custody of the Bank of England. Then, turning to the audit machinery of the Exchequer, they bluntly recommended its replacement. It was not now a matter of making the Exchequer do its job, as in 1667 or 1696; it was time to sweep it aside, abolishing the redundant rituals of the tally court, paring down the Tellers' department and superseding the Auditors of the Imprests. The wooden tallies, the Exchequer-Latin and unique hieroglyphics could be left to the antiquarians, clearing the way for speedy and intelligible accounting.[59] Only on one crucial point did the Commissioners betray something like timidity. For, in reviewing the whole revenue-collecting and money-disbursing system, it must have become obvious to them that the Treasury was exercising a very limited control. Indeed, at several points in their reports they drew attention to the Treasury's ignorance of the requirements of the great spending departments which obliged them to sanction large payments without knowing if they were really necessary.[60] They urged – let the Treasury be given the means of exercising an informed control. But beyond this, they did not venture to level criticism at the central administration of public finance.

Instead, it was Edmund Burke who, in 1780, captured the credit for discerning that the Legislature must take upon itself the active responsibility for reforming the Executive, and that the best guarantee of a permanently reformed Executive would be a more powerful Treasury

[59] Eighth Report of the Commissioners, *Commons Journal*, xxxix, 56–7.
[60] Note particularly the comments in the Fifth and Twelfth Reports, printed below, Doc. 14(d) and (f).

exercising comprehensive control.[61] In his great speech on Economical Reform of 11 February 1780 he made it one of his cardinal requirements that the Treasury should be assured of an unfettered superintendence of public income and expenditure. As things were, its control was obstructed by 'subordinate treasuries' – the independent empires of the departmental paymasters – and by an anachronistic Exchequer. 'This much is certain, that neither the present nor any other first lord of the treasury has ever been able to take a survey, or to make even a tolerable guess, of the expenses of government for any one year, so as to enable him with the least degree of certainty, or even probability, to bring his affairs within compass. ... As things are circumstanced, the first lord of the treasury cannot make an estimate.'[62]

Yet of all the hares started by the economical reformers, the idea of reinforcing Treasury suzerainty proved the least attractive. Objectives better suited to the reduction of the influence of the Crown were more vigorously pursued, and such steps as were taken to invigorate Treasury control were taken from within.[63] But measures such as Burke's Civil Establishment Act and the Act regulating the office of Paymaster-General of the Forces, of 1782 and 1781 respectively,[64] mark the beginning of a long process by which public money in general and the Civil List in particular were brought under parliamentary control. The principle was now established that departmental balances, such as the huge sums held by the Treasurer of the Navy or the Paymaster of the Forces, were to be kept as small as possible in Bank of England custody, and that Civil List expenditure should conform to a schedule ordained by Parliament and regulated by the Treasury. More promising still was William Pitt's inauguration of Exchequer reform. His Act of 1785 implemented the recommendations of the Commissioners of Accounts by abolishing the Exchequer's two Auditors of Imprests and replacing them with a professional board of auditors working under Treasury supervision.[65] It was one of several celebrated measures taken by Pitt – the reform of the Sinking Fund, the reinvigoration of fiscal

[61] Burke's objectives are succinctly presented in his 'Memoranda for Consideration' of March 1782: '1st the *Principle* of oeconomy by the appropriation of the Civil List – which is the *great* point. The 2d – the suppression of Offices – which is a detached part rather than a member. 3dly the destruction of *all* subordinate Treasuries, by subjecting every expence in every department to the Treasury. 4. The appropriation of the money saved. Surely none of these, except the suppression of some few places (and that only as a temporary arrangement) can be done but by Parliament.' *The Correspondence of Edmund Burke* (Cambridge, 1963), iv, 424.

[62] *The Speeches of Edmund Burke* (London, 1816), ii, 42.

[63] See below, pp. 85–6, for the Treasury reorganization of 1782 undertaken by Shelburne, and J. Norris, *Shelburne and Reform* (London, 1963), 199–215.

[64] 21 Geo. III, c. 48, 22 Geo. III, c. 81 and c. 82.

[65] 25 Geo. III, c. 52, *Statutes at Large, 1780–85*, pp. 675–9.

administration and the creation of the Consolidated Fund – which contributed healthily towards a more rational and economical financial system.[66]

But although the administrative reforms of the 1780s were noteworthy, they were by no means adequate, even to the circumstances of peace. The stress of war very soon revealed the frailty of safeguards against the large-scale waste of public money. Parliamentary supply procedures still proved incapable of enforcing strict conformity to the letter of appropriation, and the reformed machinery of audit was still grossly unsuited to the scale of its burdens. By 1806 the Chancellor of the Exchequer could report that £455 million of public expenditure was unaccounted for in any formal sense.[67]

Other embarrassments soon followed. The faction politics which followed Pitt's death were peculiarly favourable to a renewed attack on administrative malpractices, and scandals were not far to seek. A Select Committee appointed in February 1807 to examine the control of public expenditure[68] was able to reveal substantial misappropriations by Thomas Steele, a Joint Paymaster-General, in circumstances which reflected badly upon the Treasury, the Exchequer and the machinery of audit.[69] Initially the episode was exploited for party-political ends, but in 1810 the fifth Report of the Select Committee had the great good sense to review the problems of audit objectively and historically (Doc. 15(a)). As a result, they re-discovered the significance of the 1667 Commission of Accounts, and the remarkable lapse of parliamentary scrutiny between 1714 and 1780 was noted, if not fully understood. Set in this historical context, Pitt's Audit Office (reinforced as recently as 1806) was seen for what it was – an over-cautious piece of tinkering which had simply preserved the worst evils of the old system. For it had made no real provision for Exchequer reform and it had not assisted parliamentary scrutiny. The officials of the Audit Office were still yoked to the redundant formalities of the ancient course, waiting for the King's Remembrancer to issue his cumbersome writs and the Clerk of the Pipe to produce his expensive *Quietus* – simply and solely, the Committee believed, 'as having no other object than the profit of fees arising therefrom'.[70]

The findings of this Committee usefully promoted the closing stages

[66] J. Ehrman, *The Younger Pitt: the Years of Acclaim* (London, 1969), pp. 239–81; Binney, *Public Finance*, pp. 109–16, 272–82.

[67] 21 May 1806, Cobbett, *Parliamentary Debates*, vii, 299–300.

[68] D. Gray, *Spencer Perceval, the Evangelical Prime Minister* (Manchester 1963), p. 148. The Committee was strong in financial experts and included Lord Henry Petty, Francis Horner, W. Sturges Bourne, Henry Thornton, Thomas Baring, Samuel Whitbread and Henry Grattan.

[69] *PP* 1807, ii, 315, 325, 345.

[70] *PP* 1810, ii, 403.

of Exchequer reform which were to culminate in the abolition of 1834.[71] But its central claim to attention is that it demonstrated what no one since Burke had grasped, the fallibility of Treasury control. The deficiencies of the Audit Office were only partly linked to the anachronisms of the Exchequer: they arose in some measure because the Office was dependent upon an arbitrary and preoccupied Treasury, which appeared to have no consistent standards of accountability. Its discretionary power to allow or disallow items in accounts declared before it was being exercised with an increasing, and dangerous, freedom: the Audit Office, in contrast, was deprived of all initiative and compared badly with those great departments, such as the Navy, which had their own, independent machinery of audit. Thus, in their report, the Select Committee urged the reassertion of historic powers of parliamentary scrutiny and the creation of a new Audit Office, independent of the Treasury. It was to take responsibility for the whole range of public expenditure accounts, deal with them on a uniform basis and report its findings directly to the House of Commons (Doc. 15(a)).

This was an important contribution to the line of thought which was to lead to the Exchequer and Audit Departments Act of 1866, but in the circumstances of a major war this report was too easily eclipsed by the more immediate problems of war expenditure. Provision was made for the separate audit problems of the peninsular campaign and colonial expenditure,[72] but the ideal of a uniform, unitary system of account was further off than ever. The Select Committee's report on sinecures and emoluments likewise risked eclipse by considerations of expediency or partisan politics.[73] Fortunately, at this point in the economical reform campaign the tide was beginning to turn in favour of a more constructive attitude to the problems of officeholding. It was no longer a matter of sweeping away the menacing 'influence of the Crown' in the form of sinecures and pensions: it was time for politicians to think more carefully about providing for those public servants who were efficient – to ensure decent conditions of service and adequate provision for retirement. Thus, in response to the Select Committee's Third Report, on emoluments, the House of Commons registered a series of resolutions, recommending the general application of a superannuation

[71] Legislation of 1817 (57 Geo. III, c. 60 and c. 84) regulated sinecures in the Upper and Lower Exchequer; the abolition of the main structure of the Upper Exchequer was secured in 1833 (3 & 4 Will. IV, c. 99) and of the Lower Exchequer in 1834 (4 & 5 Will. IV, 15); see Sainty, *EHR* (1965), pp. 472–3.

[72] 53 Geo. III, c. 100 and 53 Geo. III, c. 150 were designed to facilitate the audit of army accounts in Spain and Portugal; 54 Geo. III, c. 184 set up a Colonial Audit Office.

[73] Gray, *Spencer Perceval*, pp. 150–9. George III felt compelled to remark on 'the incalculable mischief which attends the existence of a Committee of Finance originally instituted for bad purposes', ibid., p. 155.

formula which the Treasury had applied in the Customs service in 1803. Graduated according to length of service, these pensions were to be paid either from departmental funds or from the Civil List or from parliamentary votes, but in every case, the House resolved,

> 'It is also expedient, that no such Pension or Allowance should either be granted in any Office, or presented by way of Estimate to this House, until it shall have been submitted to the Commissioners of His Majesty's Treasury, and approved by them, whose duty it will be to take into their consideration the circumstances and fortune of each individual applying to be placed upon the Superannuation Fund; that the Public Money may in no case be paid for duty not performed. . . .'[74]

These resolutions of 31 May 1810, and the legislation which embodied them,[75] have a good claim to be regarded as the beginning of the process which was to produce a unitary civil service under the Treasury's financial control.

Thus the proceedings of the 1807 Select Committee on Public Expenditure had bred two, apparently divergent, lines of parliamentary policy – for independence of the Treasury in matters of financial control, and for dependence on the Treasury in matters of administrative control. These contradictions were to be reconciled in the course of the next fifty years, and of the two policies the second had surprisingly strong attractions. In the wake of the Napoleonic wars, with a National Debt amounting to nearly £850 million and public expenditure at more than three times its pre-war levels, there were powerful incentives for retrenchments which should be as comprehensive as they were severe. The inhibitions which had opposed the extension of Treasury sovereignty in the 1780s were now overwhelmed. The 'system of Departments', which had characterized English central government for so long was discredited. Again and again, Members of Parliament demanded that the Treasury resume what they vaguely felt to have always been its traditional role – central supervision of expenditure and the conditions of employment in all civil departments.

The case for Treasury control of establishments was made with repetitive emphasis in the reports of the 1817 Select Committee on Finance (Doc. 15(b)), and the larger case, for Treasury sovereignty over a comprehensive and uniform system of public expenditure, was

[74] *PP* 1810, ii, 366–7.
[75] 50 Geo. III, c. 117 defined the terms of civil service superannuation and required accounts of public salaries, pensions and allowances to be laid annually before parliament. See E. W. Cohen, *The Growth of the British Civil Service, 1780–1939* (London, 1941), pp. 56–8.

made with even greater cogency, in 1828 (Doc. 15(c)). The eleven-year interval deserves comment, perhaps, as do other long intervals in this narrative of protracted reforms. It is a symptom of unstable political circumstances which had made 'economical reform' one of the few uniting issues of a demoralized Whig party[76] upon which it could sometimes force a debate. But the lion's share of the credit for its impact on Lord Liverpool's administration must go to the small group of radicals – Joseph Hume in particular – who had made the issue of public expenditure their own. Their persistent sniping at the government's estimates, their crushing indictments of anomalous accounting, stiffened the Tory resistance but it also brought its rewards. The government's response to one such series of onslaughts provides a landmark in the history of Treasury control.

The Treasury Minute of 10 August 1821 (Doc. 16) is, however, a rather ambiguous landmark. Its own preamble admits that it is a response to formidable external pressures mounted by the two Houses of Parliament. And the first victim that it sacrifices is the Treasury's own establishment, pared down in numbers and in emoluments by as much as 60 per cent.[77] But the Minute then goes on to urge the same scale of economies upon all other departments, and it is this comprehensiveness which is the significant symptom of things to come, when the Treasury would be strong enough to direct uniform standards for a unitary civil service. But the Treasury Minute of 1821 was hardly a directive: it was an appeal, backed up by example, and the very mixed response betrays just how far Treasury influence fell short of 'control'. It was one thing for the Treasury to enforce regulations upon the establishments of its subordinate departments, the revenue boards; it was quite another to call the traditionally independent departments of the Secretaries of State into line. At the Foreign Office, Palmerston greatly relished his use of 'a vigorous and unsparing Pruning Knife'[78] but at the Colonial Office the recommended economies were circumvented and the Treasury was defied.[79] Whatever the Houses of Parliament might require, there was still no adequate sanction which the Treasury could enforce against departmental autonomy: Parliament would have to produce its own.

[76] A. Mitchell, *The Whigs in Opposition, 1815–1830* (Oxford, 1967), pp. 12, 15, 104, 113, 125, 142, 181–3; A. Foord, *His Majesty's Opposition, 1714–1830,* pp. 457–61.

[77] See below, pp. 92–4, for the impact of these retrenchments, and Roseveare, *The Treasury: the Evolution of a British Institution* (London, 1969), pp. 160–1.

[78] D. M. Young, *The Colonial Office in the Early Nineteenth Century* (London, 1961), p. 41.

[79] Ibid., p. 62. The Under-Secretary of State refused to acknowledge the coercive authority of anything less than an Order in Council.

The process by which this sanction was evolved had at least five aspects which eventually converged in the 1860s to form Gladstone's completed 'circle of control'. The control was essentially financial in its objectives and parliamentary in its basis, but it brought the Treasury into a close working relationship with the House of Commons and laid foundations upon which the Treasury could, for nearly 50 years, exercise administrative control of the Home Civil Service. In the meantime, it resolved the long-standing contradictions which baffled parliamentary inquiries had been contemplating for over 150 years – the malversation of public funds, the laxity of official audits, the inconsistencies of published accounts and, at their heart, the institutional deficiencies of the Exchequer and the Treasury.

To take these concurrent aspects of development in their logical sequence, one must first note the process by which the estimates placed annually before Parliament were successively extended to include *all* the costs of government, civil as well as military. This resolved the anomaly, rooted in the post-1688 financial system, by which only the military estimates, for Navy, Army and Ordnance, had been presented for perfunctory but regular inspection. The costs of civil government, as we have seen, had been met partly from the Crown's discretionary funds, the Civil List, and in larger part from the fees and profits of the departments themselves, both areas beyond the scope of parliamentary scrutiny. But the 'Economical Reform' campaign of the 1780s, which had attacked the maladministration of the Civil List, had also called in question the whole system of fee-taking. The philosophy of the Eleventh Report of Lord North's Commissioners (Doc. 14(a)) exemplifies the kind of pressure which, through a long succession of inquiries, resolutions and legislation, gradually edged public servants into carefully graded (and by no means ungenerous) salary-scales. The salaries were still met, where possible, from departmental fee-funds, but an increasing burden of expenditure was now thrown upon parliamentary supplies and therefore brought within the annual scrutiny of the House of Commons. This category of 'miscellaneous estimates' was to grow more rapidly still as the Civil List was whittled down until, by the accession of Queen Victoria, it provided for little more than the personal expenditure of the sovereign.[80]

It was now possible for the House of Commons to exert an informed pressure upon the expenditure of government departments. Joseph Hume's crude but effective yardstick of the expenditure levels of 1792 was superseded as, in 1824, 1831, 1837 and 1843, the estimates of civil expenditure were reclassified to yield meaningful comparisons. But the principal beneficiary was the Treasury which, nudged forward by

[80] B. Chubb, *The Control of Public Expenditure* (Oxford, 1952), ch. 1; P. Einzig, *The Control of the Purse* (London, 1959), chapter 18.

Parliament, was now obliged to submit all departmental estimates to a preliminary scrutiny. It had the responsibility of presenting and defending these figures to the House of Commons: it was entitled to demand that the figures should be defensible. Thus, every year now saw the Treasury calling for the draft estimates of government departments, submitting them to inspection and, where necessary, demanding revision (Doc. 17(a)). In this way, 'Treasury control' acquired a much more methodical, consistent and, above all, responsible character. It still suffered from limitations: as the evidence given before the 1847–8 Select Committee on Miscellaneous Expenditure was to reveal, the Treasury could not exert quite the same disciplines against the Foreign Office, Home Office or War Office that were applied to the smaller departments[81] and this was a problem which long survived the limits of this study. But the evidence of 1847–8 displays a system in being which was soon to approach a point of maturity.

Meanwhile, a second line of development was making progress in close harmony with the first. This was the elaboration of financial accounts to provide a clear, comprehensive, annual picture of government income and expenditure. It proved more arduous than one might expect; but the anomalies which Burke had derided proved remarkably tenacious, rooted in the historic peculiarities of the Exchequer and the ancient revenues of the Crown.[82] The creation of the Consolidated Fund in 1787 had not eliminated the accounting oddities of the unreformed system and the investigators of the early nineteenth century were confronted with some bewildering medieval survivals. The essential problems were that the accounting years of the various revenue departments did not coincide, and that their returns for accounting purposes tended to be net rather than gross. (Indeed, the practice by which the revenue departments remunerated themselves from their cash receipts without submission of parliamentary estimates was the principal loophole in the system reviewed in 1847–8.) The obligation to inform Parliament with annual statements of account had been imposed upon the Treasury in 1802, but absurd inconsistencies survived, and it was the exposure of these by Joseph Hume in 1822 which shamed the Treasury into some kind of reform. It mounted inquiries into departmental accounting at home and abroad and a report of experts in February 1829 helped to set standards which were gradually conformed to by other departments.[83] The Treasury could only

---

[81] Evidence of Charles Trevelyan, Q.1190, *PP* 1847–8, xviii (i); cf. M. Wright, *Treasury Control of the Civil Service, 1854–74* (Oxford, 1969), pp. 196–7.

[82] R. C. Jarvis, 'Official Trade and Revenue Statistics', *Economic History Review* (2nd series 1964), xvii, pp. 43–62.

[83] Report from the Select Committee on Public Accounts, *PP* 1822, iv, 293; Report on the Mode of Keeping the Official Accounts, *PP* 1829, vi; Papers

recommend – it could not compel – the adoption of double-entry book-keeping in all government offices, and it was not until 1840, for example, that the War Office conformed. It had to wait until Gladstone's 'Public Revenue and Consolidated Fund Charges Act' of 1854 before gross revenue and expenditure accounts were made available to the House of Commons on the basis of a financial year which agreed in ending on 31 March.

Accompanying this consolidation of accounts was the consolidation of administration. The Irish and Scottish Treasuries were united in the United Kingdom Treasury in 1816 and 1833 respectively. The emergence of civil estimates as a distinct entity in parliamentary supply was matched by the creation of a Paymaster of Civil Services in 1834. In 1848 his office was consolidated with that of the Paymaster-General who had controlled Army, Navy and Ordnance payments since 1835. Thus, funds were now channelled thriftily through a single pair of hands. But, as a symbol of efficiency and propriety even the new Paymaster-General took second place to the 'Comptroller General of the Exchequer' – residuary legatee of the ancient Exchequer which, with all its quaint, cumbersome and maddening anomalies, had been effectively abolished by Acts of 1833 and 1834. This was the fourth and most dramatic aspect of reform – it led, as everyone knows, to the burning down of the Palace of Westminster – but it was also the least satisfactory. It involved a transfer of functions without sufficient reappraisal of roles. The new Comptroller of the Exchequer took over the duties once performed by the Auditor of the Receipt and the Clerk of the Pells. He recorded the receipts of revenue and his signature was essential to the issue of funds – the cash, in both instances, being handled at the Bank of England. It might seem a book-keeper's job. But Lord Monteagle, appointed Comptroller in 1839, took his duties literally, as ones of control. A former Whig Chancellor of the Exchequer, with a grudge against some of his colleagues, he exercised control pedantically, rejecting Treasury warrants to issue money in every instance where he thought the instructions were defective or improper, and quibbling too about the wording of remittances paid into him.[84]

Relating to Public Accounts, *PP* 1831, xiv; A Statement of the changes which have been introduced into Public Departments in the system of book-keeping since 1832, *PP* 1844, xxxii.

[84] See his hostile 'Observations' upon the Treasury's memorandum on financial control, 1857, which includes this consummately silly statement: 'In these observations I do not presume to remark upon the regulations or accounts which the Treasury may judge it necessary to require and enforce with a view to ultimate accountability and to the audit of the accounts. That does not enter into the question of Exchequer check.' (Appendix III, Report of the Select Committee on Public Monies, *PP* 1857 (sess. 2), ix, 556.) The whole point of the Treasury's challenge to the Exchequer was the search for 'ultimate accountability'.

After fifteen years he could boast of a hundred conflicts with the Treasury – and the Treasury hungered for his extinction.

Yet it was logic, not rancour, which argued that the Comptroller-General's functions were virtually meaningless unless they were linked to a process of retrospective audit which could check that the details of expenditure accounts properly matched the purposes for which they had been appropriated by Parliament. It was for this that the Treasury argued when it presented its case before the 1856 Select Committee on Public Monies, and its evidence is remarkable on several counts. Presented by a permanent official, it is impressive testimony to the calibre of the Treasury's senior staff. It is striking too for its confident vision of the Treasury's administrative supremacy as the department of control (Doc. 17(b)). It is also a very cogent argument for a creative species of control founded upon the collaboration of the Treasury and Parliament. Monteagle believed that the basis of financial control must be mistrust: but William Anderson, head of the Treasury's finance division, argued more imaginatively for confidence. As the steward of the public purse, the Treasury could be trusted to superintend the departments' expenditure of public money far more closely and flexibly than the Exchequer, which could see no further than its Bank of England accounts. The Treasury would account for that stewardship, and it would be the task of an independent audit office to report on the propriety of its accounts.

This principle of a restrospective appropriation audit – the fifth and concluding line of development – was not novel in 1856. Sir James Graham, First Lord of the Admiralty in the reforming Whig administration of 1830, had discovered some alarming misappropriations in his department and in 1832 had voluntarily submitted to Parliament an account which would demonstrate that the Admiralty, now chastened, had strictly adhered to the letter of parliamentary appropriations.[85] However, this annual gesture of rectitude remained an isolated one and it was not until 1846 that the Ordnance and War Office began to follow the example. Even then, the significance of this voluntary submission was not fully appreciated by the House of Commons, although in 1831 a Royal Commission on Public Accounts had argued that the House should appoint an investigating committee to review such annual accounts.[86]

[85] A. B. Erickson, *The Public Career of Sir James Graham* (Oxford, 1952), pp. 95–105, 109; J. T. Ward, *Sir James Graham* (London, 1967), p. 126; Chubb, *Public Expenditure*, pp. 11, 21. See also *English Historical Documents, 1833–1874*, ed. G. M. Young and W. D. Handcock (London, 1956), pp. 563–4 for Sir William Anderson's memorandum on Graham's naval reforms.

[86] See the First Report of the Commissioners of Public Accounts, 8 October 1831, in Appendix I of the Report of the Select Committee on Public Monies, *PP* 1856, xv, 480.

The 1856 Select Committee broke through this inhibition. It was not prepared to accept the Treasury's case in its entirety, but in the various recommendations of its report it drew together our five themes of development and urged their consolidation. Civil estimates, for example, were to be presented more speedily and accurately; income and expenditure accounts were to be based on *actual* receipts and payments; the Paymaster-General was to be a non-political official, and double-entry book-keeping was to be extended to all departments and maintained under Treasury control. Its key proposal was to extend the appropriation accounts to all departments, submit them to audit by a greatly enlarged Audit Board which would report, independently of the Treasury, to a select committee of the House of Commons.[87]

There is a deceptive appearance of inevitability about the implementation of these proposals. In fact, ten years were to elapse before the programme was completed. Even in 1856 the Committee had to reject the draft proposal which most precisely foreshadowed the ultimate solution, i.e. that the Exchequer and the Audit Office should be consolidated in one department, 'responsible to Parliament and reporting directly to Parliament, [which] should henceforth control the original issue, and both by concurrent and final audit, superintend the application of the public monies to the services voted and sanctioned by Parliament'.[88] This went too far, too fast. While Lord Monteagle lived, an eloquent dissentient, he held to his quasi-judicial life tenure in the Comptrollership. Not until his death would it be possible to undertake a reconstruction of his department. But in 1861, with Gladstone's encouragement, the House of Commons set up its Public Accounts Committee, and in 1862 Gladstone moved the resolution which made this Committee a permanent part of the machinery of the House.[89]

The time was now ripe for consolidation. With Monteagle's death the way was clear for the final reconstruction of the Exchequer and the Audit Office as one great department, under the provisions of the Exchequer and Audit Departments Act of 1866.[90] Like Monteagle, the new head of the department, the 'Comptroller and Auditor General', was to enjoy quasi-judicial status answerable only to Parliament, but to his routine responsibility for the issue of parliamentary grants from Bank of England accounts was added a more demanding function – the

[87] Report of the Select Committee on Public Monies, *PP* 1857 (sess. 2), ix, 495–501.
[88] Report of the Select Committee on Public Monies, *PP* 1857 (sess. 2) ix, 503.
[89] See Reid, *Financial Control*, pp. 75–6, 95; Chubb, *Public Expenditure*, p. 32.
[90] 29 & 30 Vict. c. 39.

audit and critical inspection of their expenditure, and the submission of his findings to the Public Accounts Committee of the House of Commons.

This completed the 'circle'. It was now that parliamentary and Treasury interests converged to become something that can be meaningfully called 'control' – a responsible, constructive relationship which enabled positive principles of financial management to emerge, quite literally, by trial and error. The errors, of course, would be those of the spending departments, detected in some breach of financial propriety by the Comptroller and Auditor-General; the trial would be the subsequent inquisition by the House of Commons committee. The Treasury, which might conceivably find itself in the dock as a party to some maladministration, soon established its role as an assistant prosecuting counsel, working in close harmony with the Comptroller and Auditor-General and the Public Accounts Committee to expose evasions of Treasury, as well as Parliamentary, control. Indeed, this collaboration, by which the sanction of parliamentary exposure could be backed up by the administrative remedies of the Treasury, was specifically provided for by sections 27 and 33 of the Exchequer and Audit Departments Act (Doc. 18). At long last, Treasury control had the kind of comprehensive, sovereign authority which it had always lacked.

The landmark of 1866 therefore marks the beginning of a new phase in the history of the Treasury. Presented annually, the reports of the Comptroller and Auditor-General were to enable the Treasury, as well as Parliament, to refine its conceptions of public accountability, advancing from the merely negative ideal of propriety to seek out standards which would guarantee both the wisdom and the efficiency of public expenditure. With his large staff and a roving brief from the Treasury, the Comptroller and Auditor-General was also well equipped to do what had hitherto lain beyond the strength of the Treasury alone – penetrate the internal workings of the departments of government and bring to light some of the less obvious problems of cost-accountancy.

The Treasury Minute of April 1868 (Doc. 19) was designed to put this relationship upon a firm footing, and in this it succeeded. Its definition of the scope of Treasury control was to prove an historic one which is still appealed to today.[91] It must therefore take its place with the Order in Council of January 1668 as a fundamental registration of Treasury authority, adapted to the novel context of parliamentary control. Its main criterion of propriety lies in the estimates approved

---

[91] See §§18, 19 of the Treasury's memorandum on the control of expenditure, submitted to the Select Committee on Estimates, 1958, Sixth Report from the Select Committee on Estimates: Treasury Control of Expenditure, 1957–8, p. 3.

by the House of Commons, but in its last paragraph it looks beyond the mere letter of parliamentary appropriations to the whole field of public expenditure. In inviting the Comptroller and Auditor-General to report upon any item of expenditure which, in his opinion, should be the subject of special Treasury authority, the Treasury was opening up for itself a very considerable area of responsibility, which it has been exploring ever since.

With the measures of 1866 and 1868 we therefore come to the brink of a new era beyond which it is not now possible to explore. Though supplemented in 1912 (with the creation of the Estimates Committee), amended in 1921 (a slightly revised Exchequer and Audit Departments Act) and submitted to searching reappraisal in the late 1950s and early-1960s by the Plowden Committee and other inquiries,[92] the principles and machinery of modern accountability were now essentially complete. Turning away from this, however, it is now time to look at an essential counterpart of these developments of formal power – the internal development of the Treasury which by 1870 could provide men qualified and competent to make the system work. Who were the professional civil servants of the Treasury administering this apparatus of control – and in what sense were they professional? It is not to be taken for granted that by 1868 the Treasury was properly equipped to exercise its powers, as the next chapter will demonstrate.

[92] For the subsequent evolution of accountability see Chubb, *Public Expenditure*; Reid, *Financial Control*; Roseveare, *Treasury*, pp. 287–312.

3

The Treasury Establishment: the Problem of Professionalism

REMINISCING in 1890 about his earliest Budget, Gladstone was to recall the incapacity of the Treasury's officials to provide him with any technical assistance.

'There was literally nobody, he said, to whom he could turn in 1853, when he had the most difficult measure on hand that he ever had to do with (the Succession Duty Bill). He proceeded to contrast the Treasury of those days with the Treasury he knew in more recent times, and the contrast was very complimentary.'[1]

There are grounds for feeling that Gladstone was a little unfair to the Treasury of 1853 and rather indulgent towards its officials in 1890. But, unquestionably, the internal reforms which Gladstone fostered did much to 'professionalize' the Treasury and give it a structure and character which survived virtually unchanged until the First World War. The small, self-confident organization of first-class men, the exclusive élite of the Victorian civil service, was the deliberate creation of reforms which reached completion between 1850 and 1870.

A major objective of this chapter is to document and reappraise these measures because the problem that was being solved was a much larger one than the provision of budgetary expertise. It was a fundamental task affecting the organization and methods of the department as a whole and the clerical establishment in particular – a question of its recruitment and training, its management and morale, all of which had implications for the civil service at large.

But the problem was not of recent origin. Long before the mid-nineteenth century the Treasury had been obliged to recognize, if not fully comprehend, the administrative shortcomings of its permanent staff, and the piecemeal responses of the department make up a lengthy process which begins, as do others already discussed, in the Treasury of the 1660s. Like those other themes it is not a simple story of unbroken

[1] The Diary of Sir Edward Hamilton, 15 July 1890 (BM Add. MSS. 48, 653, f. 78).

progress. Intervals of inertia were succeeded by spasms of reform but the reforms were not always wise ones and there was regression. There were even intervals when the requirements of the Treasury seemed modest enough to be matched by the abilities, and exceeded by the numbers, of its permanent staff. Consequently, the line of development is a rather patchy one, sometimes difficult to document, and underlying its hesitance in the same kind of shortcoming which hampered the development of effective accountability – the Treasury's failure to perceive precisely what the problem was.

The point can be illustrated by referring at once to a document upon which much of my argument hinges.[2] Here, in 1828, is a comparatively junior Treasury clerk addressing himself to a careful analysis of the Treasury's organizational problems and offering detailed, logical solutions. He was able to do this largely because he, rather than the Lords of the Treasury, was best placed to appreciate what the problems required and what they had so signally failed to get. Indeed, his perceptive diagnosis, rooted in a sound understanding of the establishment's recent history, is the unique exception among Treasury memoranda which proves the general rule – that the transient political heads of the Treasury were generally incapable of discerning what measures were most likely to induce their officials to give of their best. It was to be some years before the Treasury Board's solemn injunctions to arrive punctually, work harder and merit promotion gave way to enlightened efforts at the management of Treasury careers.

These efforts, unwarrantably dominated by the reputation of Sir Charles Trevelyan, produced an interesting literature of inquiries, reports and reorganization minutes which is represented in the documents. For the late seventeenth and eighteenth centuries, however, the material is comparatively meagre, only hinting at the underlying problems of running a major department of state. Indeed, for some time after 1660, it is far from clear that the clerks in whom we are interested were regarded as an intrinsic part of the Treasury as an institution. They had no legal tenure, no settled salaries and no clear allocation of responsibility.[3] They figure rarely, if at all, in the Treasury's official records and tend to be entirely eclipsed by the growing significance of the Secretary to the Treasury. *His* evolution as a major figure in English administration was far more pronounced, although like the clerks he enjoyed only a precarious official tenure. Indeed, he was rather more vulnerable to dismissal, his post being held at the disposal of each incoming Treasurer or Treasury Board.

---

[2] See Doc. 23, discussed at greater length below, pp. 89–92.
[3] For these and associated problems of the Treasury establishment the essential reading is *Treasury Officials, 1660–1870*, ed. J. C. Sainty (London, 1972), pp. 1–15.

The Secretary, however, was the beneficiary of the process by which, in the 1670s, the parliamentary management of an emergent Court party passed from the hands of the Secretaries of State to those of the Treasury. No doubt it was as Danby's brother-in-law as much as his Secretary that Charles Bertie acquired the discretionary control of the secret service funds in 1676;[4] but with Henry Guy's long tenure from 1679 to 1689 and 1691 to 1695 this function had evidently become an inseparable attribute of the secretaryship, with the important difference that Guy was handling the secret service money for the king – indeed, for three kings in succession. The confidential power and public prestige of the Secretary could scarcely grow higher. However, Guy's career also demonstrated the dangers of the post becoming too exclusively a political one, and in 1695 his dismissal and imprisonment for taking bribes was not unwelcome to the parliamentary world. Members of the House of Commons had expressed a pointed regret for the premature death of William Jephson during his secretaryship, 1689–91, and as a 'financial' rather than a 'patronage' secretary Jephson's loss was acknowledged to be 'irreparable' by the First Lord, Godolphin.[5]

With Henry Guy's successor, however, the administrative dimension of the secretaryship was firmly reinstated. William Lowndes was the nearest thing to a professional civil servant which the post had yet produced, and despite his long and influential membership of the House of Commons his role at the Treasury seems to anticipate that of a 'Permanent' rather than a 'Parliamentary' Secretary. Like Downing, Lowndes was to identify himself with the practical, financial and administrative aspects of his role, and although he also handled the secret service funds of the Crown he escaped any damaging associations with party politics. He served without interruption from 1695 until his death in 1724, having reached this eminence after a twenty-years' apprenticeship as a Treasury clerk.

The evolution of the clerical establishment to the point where it could produce a Lowndes therefore makes more insistent the questions one wishes to ask about these early Treasury officials. One wonders not only who they were and what they did, but to what kind of background did they belong and to what sort of career did they aspire? Was the advancement of Lowndes from clerical obscurity a freak of administrative evolution, a special case which proves nothing about

[4] A. Browning, *Thomas Osborne, Earl of Danby, Duke of Leeds, 1632–1712* (3 vols., Glasgow, 1944–51), i, 110, 196; S. B. Baxter, *The Development of the Treasury 1660–1702* (London, 1957), pp. 187–90.

[5] Baxter, *Treasury*, pp. 195–7; W. Cobbett, *Parliamentary History of England*, v, 666. (The distinction between a 'financial' and a 'patronage' secretary is, of course, anachronistic at this time and for many years to come: see Sainty, *Treasury Officials*, pp. 29–31.)

the class from which he came? Or should one, as I suspect, press the more difficult question – why did the Treasury establishment fail to produce more of its own rulers before 1885, when it first began to find Permanent Secretaries within its own ranks.[6]

To the last question the answers can only be tentative, and to the others they will not be readily forthcoming. The clerks of the late seventeenth-century Treasury remain a shadowy generation which has left no clear image of its character in the Treasury's papers. It is only after 1714 that their identity as part of the departmental establishment becomes the subject of regular entries in the Minute Books. Before that date one can only make deductions from the kind of entries in Downing's Minute Books and memoranda[7] which make it clear that he was assisted by two or three men – Roger Charnock, Philip Lloyd and Lawrence Abbott – who were regularly deputed to perform responsible tasks, preparing accounts, drafting reports and interviewing departmental officials. Even the scrappier Minute Book of Sir Robert Howard betrays, in its interesting marginalia, the Secretary's dependence on the clerks at his elbow: 'Lloyd remember it', 'Aram take charge of this', 'Mr Wolseley remember me of this'.[8] The actual entry of minutes in several clerical hands testify to a delegation of responsibilities by the Secretary in a way which clearly gave the clerks a good opportunity to master routine official business. They evidently attended the proceedings of the Board, noting and executing the instructions of the Lords in collaboration with the Secretary.

It should therefore be no surprise to discover that by 1673 a well-informed observer quite naturally listed the four clerks *with* the Secretary as the official embodiment of 'the Treasury'.[9] Indeed, more than twenty years before Lowndes was promoted, one of these clerks could have serious pretensions to succeed Howard as Secretary.[10] He

[6] The precedent set by Lowndes was followed when John Taylor, a Treasury clerk since 1690, became Joint Parliamentary Secretary, Nov. 1714–Oct. 1715. The only other examples are of Charles Lowndes, Joint Secretary 1765-7 after forty-one years service as a Treasury official, and Edward Chamberlayne, who committed suicide on his selection in 1782 after twenty years in the Treasury. Thomas Bradshaw, the former War Office clerk who became Joint Secretary after five years in the Treasury, is not such a significant example, but there are enough instances to show that the Lowndes precedent was not irrelevant in the eighteenth century. It is the interval 1782-1885 which requires explanation.

[7] See below, Doc. 8; cf. Baxter, *Treasury*, pp. 219-19.

[8] PRO T 29/4. Regrettably, Shaw's printed calendar of Treasury Minutes does not retain the marginalia. Other editorial omissions and contractions make it always desirable to consult the original document.

[9] *Letters to Sir Joseph Williamson, 1673-4*, ed. W. D. Christie (Camden Society Second Series, 1874), i, 67.

[10] Ibid., pp. 81, 127, 146. For the career of Philip Lloyd see Baxter, *Treasury*, pp. 220-5.

failed to do so, but a subsequent career, which led him to a knighthood
and a clerkship of the Privy Council, is a useful clue to the social and
administrative status of his colleagues. John Evelyn might regard their
work as 'servile enough'[11] but he was not sorry to see his son and a
nephew hold clerkships in the Treasury. By the 1690s, with the
political dimension of the Treasury's role now highly developed, the
incidental attractions of the office must have been considerable.
Sinecures came their way, and the probable yield of fees and gratuities
may well have been £700 per annum.[12] Some of them could seek, and
one or two obtained, membership of the House of Commons.[13] They
were, in the main, well-connected gentlemen with gentlemanly expectations.

To suggest that these characteristics were incompatible with real
professionalism would be unjustified. Individual Treasury clerkships
sometimes approached, but they never wholly attained, the status of
sinecures. The generation of the 1680s and 1690s may have been as
hard-working as its predecessors, and when we reach a clear definition
of their duties in 1714 (Doc. 21(a)) they will appear to be demanding
enough. The suspicion must remain that, in this field of government
as in others, the effects of competitive political patronage may have
been damaging. By 1689, and probably for some years before,[14] a
distinction had emerged between the group of five, then four, 'chief
clerks', and an inferior grade of 'under-clerks' whose duties were
without doubt 'servile enough'. There was clearly some danger of the
chief clerks becoming drawn into the political spoils system, too grand
to sit upon a Treasury stool. But the scanty evidence suggests that by
the end of the seventeenth century the Treasury establishment was an
embryo hierarchy of capable public servants, advancing by merit as
well as seniority towards responsible and rewarding duties.

From this context, therefore, there was nothing incongruous about
William Lowndes becoming a leading public figure as Secretary to the
Treasury. He was exceptional only in the breadth of his experience and
the degree of his competence. Unfortunately, this point is rather
obscured by the special circumstances of his appointment. Lowndes
was the party to a deal which allowed the imprisoned Henry Guy to

[11] John Evelyn to Mrs Boscawen, 29 June 1691 (Evelyn MSS., Christ Church,
Oxford). I am indebted to John Sainty for this reference.
[12] Baxter, *Treasury*, p. 231.
[13] William Shaw, a Treasury clerk 1680–97, did so in 1685, and Christopher
Tilson (1684–1742) and Henry Kelsall (1714–62) held seats in early Hanoverian
parliaments. Baxter mistakenly asserts (p. 232) that Shaw's position would have
been impossible after 1688, but it not until the Place Act of 1741/2 (15 Geo. II,
c. 22) that departmental clerkships became incompatible with membership of
the House of Commons.
[14] Sainty, *Treasury Officials*, pp. 33, 34, 36.

retain a financial interest in his secretaryship, for, as Lowndes was to confess to the Parliamentary Accounts Commission in 1703, as long as Guy lived he was under an obligation to hand over to him one half of his earnings.[15] This may not have been the condition of his appointment, which the king had approved, but it clearly undermined Lowndes's status as Secretary in his own right.

Yet, if Lowndes began his secretarial career as the curate of his predecessor, he very soon vindicated himself as the embodiment of Treasury professionalism. He has already been noted as the architect of the important Exchequer Regulation Act of 1696, and the same year saw him deeply involved in the planning and execution of the great recoinage of 1696-7.[16] Entering on his new parliamentary duties as member for Seaford, he was immediately plunged into the most arduous period of fiscal improvisation in English history. Although the exact extent of his personal initiative in shaping the 'financial revolution' of these years is less easily charted than Downing's, it is clear enough that he had a large hand in constructing the annual array of tax proposals which were Budgets in all but name.[17] He drew, as any expert must, upon the special knowledge of other experts. The growing empire of revenue boards dependent upon the Treasury made its own contribution to the efforts which helped pay for the War of the Spanish Succession, but, as the Treasury's spokesman in the House of Commons and its representative on the Committee of Ways and Means, it was Lowndes as Secretary who consolidated the Treasury's mastery of parliamentary finance.

An interesting reflection of the demands now made upon the Treasury and its Secretary in this new world of banks and stockjobbers, tontines and Exchequer Bills, is a memorandum submitted to Robert Harley in August 1710, within a week of his appointment as Chancellor of the Exchequer (Doc. 20). It is typical in one respect of the kind of 'projects' which poured in on all Chancellors – it barely conceals the interest of the promoter in profiting from his own scheme. The author, Slyford, was an indefatigable projector with a finger in several financial pies.[18] Nonetheless, his is a remarkably precocious recommendation

[15] PRO T 64/126, p. 248.

[16] For the role of Lowndes in this controversial enterprise see Sir John Craig, *The Mint* (Cambridge, 1953), pp. 185-7; J. K. Horsefield, *British Monetary Experiments, 1650-1710* (London, 1960), pp. 49-50; Ming-Hsun Li, *The Great Recoinage of 1696 to 1699* (London, 1963), pp. 45-6, 95-9.

[17] P. G. M. Dickson, *The Financial Revolution in England, 1688-1756*, pp. 58-9; D. M. Gill, 'The Treasury, 1660-1714', *English Historical Review* (1931), xlvi, pp. 610-22.

[18] For some light on Slyford's other enterprises see E. Hughes, *Studies in Administration and Finance, 1558-1825* (Manchester, 1934), pp. 229, 233, 236, 255-60, 395, 405, 428.

which anticipates by several generations the provision of expert financial knowledge and specialist functions at a senior level in the Treasury, and it effectively demonstrates the kind of pressures which were now bearing upon the department.

Yet Lowndes was exceptionally competent to provide himself the kind of fiscal inventiveness and organizational powers which were needed to see the Treasury through this very difficult period, and it is no coincidence that these years of his secretaryship also witness a distinct clarification of the department's clerical structure. During Queen Anne's reign the Treasury 'establishment' visibly emerges with formed characteristics which will remain recognizable well into the nineteenth century. Lists of June 1711 and October 1715 appear to represent the earliest efforts to define the full extent of what 'the Treasury' had now become, showing us that, in addition to the joint secretaryship created on Guy's death in 1711,[19] the staff consisted of four Chief Clerks, nine Under Clerks, three Under Clerks for keeping accounts, an Office Keeper, a Doorkeeper, a sweeper, a bag-carrier, a letter-carrier, four Messengers of the Receipt with three deputies and one Messenger of the Chamber.[20] No clear idea of the functions performed by the clerks (with whom we are primarily concerned) is revealed by these lists or by the records of their remuneration, but an important Treasury Minute of 18 November 1714 (Doc. 21(a)) sets out clearly the division of responsibility among the Chief Clerks. The underlying principle appears to be the purely utilitarian one of the division of labour along commonsense lines, although it may also reflect the specialized aptitudes and past experience of the individual Chief Clerks. There is no reason to suppose that this kind of distribution reflects a novel departure, but what is new and interesting is the decision to set it out in detail in the Treasury Minute Book. It seems to mark the beginning of a practice by which the Treasury Board henceforth put on record its decisions on the organization and methods of the Establishment's tasks, and it thus becomes possible after 1714 to discern, or deduce, a growing code of professional conventions (Doc. 21).

One of the most important and least explicit of these is a convention of permanence which guaranteed the Treasury clerk's security of tenure regardless of his political affiliations. That Treasury clerks had such political affiliations need not be doubted although they have yet to be

---

[19] Thomas Harley's appointment as Joint Secretary with Lowndes must be regarded as a piece of jobbery by Edward Harley rather than a response to Slyford's memorandum. The differentiation of functions between the Secretaries evolved later – see D. M. Clark, 'The Office of Secretary to the Treasury in the Eighteenth Century', *American Historical Review* (1936–7), xlii, 22–45.

[20] Harley MSS., BM Loan 29/45B, 12/259, 265; *CTB 1714–15*, ii, 297–8.

demonstrated in detail. Indeed, Godolphin, Walpole, Newcastle and other First Lords could scarcely hope to rival the fertility of Lowndes in staffing the Treasury,[21] but Treasury clerks were usually their clients, if not their nephews, and this constituted a state of dependence which sometimes had to be acknowledged, as in December 1761 (Doc. 21(m)). Fortunately for the professional development of the Treasury the price of patronage did not extend to serious risk of dismissal on the arrival of a new and possibly hostile Board. The ousting of Charles King in April 1721 is really the exception which proves the rule, for Walpole was simply rectifying the unjust dismissal of his relative, Thomas Mann, some years before, and he did not fail to offer compensation (Doc. 21(f)). There was no question, therefore, of Walpole or any other First Lord sweeping the Treasury clean on entering office. Certainly they seized every opportunity to fill vacancies, a process in which they were sometimes assisted by freaks of mortality,[22] but the existing tenures and seniority were generally respected with results which become apparent in clerical careers of undisturbed tranquillity. Thus, while twenty-two of the sixty men who served on the main clerical establishment between 1714 and 1760 disappeared within ten years of appointment (ten of them within five years), another twenty-seven remained for over twenty-five years (eleven of them for over forty).[23] The notorious extreme is Thomas Pratt with seventy-four years on the active establishment (1724–98) and another six in pensioned retirement, but clerks like Edward Burnaby, with thirty-four years as an Under Clerk and two as a Chief Clerk, or George Herbert and Henry Fowler who spent forty-one years in the Revenue Room, are more typical of the Hanoverian Treasury. Edward Webster, who survived for sixty years as an Under Clerk, was lucky enough to be given the opportunity of secondment from the office in 1717 (Doc. 21(d)) and he was rarely seen there again, but for the majority there was no question of promotion to positions outside the Treasury, and promotions within the department waited upon seniority – which could mean a very long wait indeed.

[21] Sainty, *Treasury Officials*, pp. 137–8, reveals that nine members of the Lowndes family served in the late seventeenth- and eighteenth-century Treasury, although it is difficult to establish which of them are the offspring of William Lowndes's four marriages.

[22] Harley was able to appoint five clerks in 1711–12. Walpole made a series of thirteen appointments in the first five years of his ascendancy, but it is noteworthy that of sixteen men appointed between 1712 and 1722 nine had died between 1718 and 1725. Walpole made no appointments between May 1726 and September 1732 and only four occurred before 1742 when a batch of five appointments occurred, mainly in the Revenue Room.

[23] These figures, and those in the note above, are based on the Under Clerks, Chief Clerks, Revenue Clerks and supernumerary clerks, as listed in Sainty, *Treasury Officials*, pp. 37, 40, 64, 101–2.

One may reasonably infer that these circumstances did something to induce apathy and inefficiency among the clerks who remained, and in such a context the decision to appoint two outsiders to Chief Clerkships in 1759 (Doc. 21(k)) is highly significant. Both men, James Postlethwaite and Robert Yeates, were well equipped to make specialized contributions to the Treasury's work, the first with his extensive knowledge of the fiscal system of which his *History of the Public Revenue* is the surviving testament,[24] the second with his experience of parliamentary drafting as a clerk of the House of Commons.[25] When Postlethwaite died in 1761 he was immediately replaced by another experienced outsider, Thomas Bradshaw of the War Office, whose talents and connections were to make him a Secretary to the Treasury and a Lord of the Admiralty.[26] In his case one may discern an element of political patronage but in all three appointments the interests of professionalism may well have been uppermost in the Treasury's mind. Anxiety on this score is already evident in the Minute of 27 July 1757, providing for the training of junior Under Clerks by service in the 'Accomptant's Office' (Doc. 21(i)). This branch of the Treasury, otherwise known as the Revenue Room, had evolved as a small and distinct hierarchy of clerks specializing in the recording of financial accounts,[27] and the exacting, technical nature of the work probably ensured that this was the most professional element in the whole department. Successive Chief Clerks of the Revenue Room could fairly boast of the skilled and unremitting nature of their duties (Docs. 22(d), 24), to which an early introduction might well be salutary for novices on the main establishment. If that was the intention of the Minute of 1757 it can claim to be the first to show concern for the technical training of Treasury clerks.

Unfortunately, the department responded badly to these promising innovations. The interchange between the clerks of the Revenue Room

---

[24] James Postlethwaite, F.R.S., *The History of the Public Revenue, from the Revolution in 1688, to Christmas 1753; with an Appendix completing the same to Christmas 1758. Containing a minute and comprehensive View of all our Public Transactions relative to Money and Trade within the said Period ... concluding with a practicable Plan for reducing all the Public Funds into One ...* (London, 1759), republished in facsimile, Gregg International Publishers Ltd, Farnborough, 1971.

[25] For the career of Robert Yeates, see O. C. Williams, *The Clerical Organization of the House of Commons, 1661–1850* (Oxford, 1954), pp. 165–9; and Sheila Lambert, *Bills and Acts: Legislative Procedure in Eighteenth Century England* (Cambridge, 1971), pp. 45–7, 67–8.

[26] See *The House of Commons, 1754–1790*, ed. Sir Lewis Namier and John Brooke (London, 1964), ii, 110–11.

[27] Sainty, *Treasury Officials*, pp. 8–9, 63, 64. William Kent's new Treasury building, 1733–6, embodied a large room for the Revenue branch equipped with specially-fitted filing cupboards: *The Survey of London – Parish of St Margaret's Westminster*, xiv, part iii (1931).

and the main establishment was brought to an end in 1776 and was not resumed until 1834. It had not proved possible to combine training with mobility between the two departments and once clerks entered the Revenue Room they invariably remained there. Meanwhile, the intrusion of outsiders at the top of the hierarchy had provoked resentment and something like demoralization. That, at least, one may conjecture from the Minutes of 4 September 1759 and 22 December 1761 (Doc. 21(l) and (m)). The refusal of three clerks and the reluctance of a fourth to accept promotion to a Chief Clerkship in 1761 looks suspiciously like a collective boycott of the intruders, self-wounding gestures of resentment against the patronage of the Treasury Board. But when the refusals recur in 1776 (Doc. 21(n)) one is led to suppose a genuine, if deplorable, reluctance among senior Under Clerks to assume the more demanding duties of a Chief Clerk. It is not inconceivable that the older Under Clerks were sufficiently well-provided with by-employments, sinecures or other sources of income to find the higher fee-scale of the Chief Clerkships a poor compensation for heavier attendance.[28] Absenteeism was possible among the Under Clerks whose numbers had been swelled from twelve to sixteen during the reign of George II; it was unthinkable among the four Chief Clerks. One thing is clear: by the accession of George III the Lords of the Treasury were facing a serious problem of morale.

The problem was to occupy their attention for more than a century, and the Treasury Minutes of 1776 and 1782 (Docs. 21(n) and (o)) are early landmarks in the search for a solution. Of the two, Lord Shelburne's minute embodies the more complex and radical reconstruction of the department, but it leans heavily on Lord North's which is, perhaps, the more remarkable for the commonsense way in which it establishes three fundamental principles. These were (a) the personal responsibility of each Treasury official for the business allocated to him – a responsibility quite incompatible with absenteeism or worksharing with obliging colleagues; (b) the concept of *training* for responsibility by transition through all branches of the Treasury's business; and (c) the criterion of merit, not seniority, as the basis of promotion to the higher rewards of the department. In their simplicity

---

[28] The scale of pluralism among late eighteenth-century Treasury clerks is partially revealed by the inquiries of the 1785–6 Commission on Fees, cited below, p. 86 and Doc. 22, and by the 1797 Select Committee on Finance, Fifteenth Report, Appendix C, pp. 291–5. Evidently, most senior Treasury officials held minor revenue posts and colonial agencies. William Brummell, who retired as an Under Clerk in 1782, was estimated (*Gentleman's Magazine* (1794), lxiv, 285) to have been earning £2500 p.a. from official appointments acquired as private secretary to Lord North. His brother Benjamin, while Senior Clerk in 1797, at £380 p.a., was also Sluice Master at Purfleet, at £77 p.a., and a Lottery Commissioner at £148 5s. p.a.

and obviousness they are a striking comment on what had gone before and mark a very deliberate break with the unregenerate past. Explicitly, or implicitly, these principles were to govern all future regulations of the Treasury establishment.

But it was necessary to place these ideals within a practical, organizational framework, and in the climate created by the 'Economical Reform' campaign it was desirable that the Treasury should make some further sacrifices to the demands of the public interest. Shelburne cleverly resolved these requirements by his elaborately planned reorganization of November 1782[29] which added one more fundamental principle to those laid down by Lord North – that the renumeration of Treasury officials should be dissociated from the work they did. Lord North, despite his careful reallocation of duties, had not broken with the practice by which clerks took their earnings at source, from fees and gratuities levied directly upon the warrants, orders, debentures, contracts and other papers which passed through their hands. This had tended to mean that the areas of business in which a clerk specialized would be determined by their estimated yield of fees rather than their logical compatibility. It worked against the interests of professional specialization as well as creating the danger of collusion between the Treasury clerk and the clients he served.[30]

Shelburne went a long way to resolving these shortcomings by setting up a Treasury fee-fund from which salaries, upon a settled scale, would be distributed to the Secretaries, the Chief Clerks and the Under Clerks. The latter now had their status redefined to distinguish between 'Senior Clerks' and 'Junior Clerks' as distinct grades within the Treasury hierarchy, performing distinct duties. These were related to Shelburne's distribution of business, not between individual Treasury clerks as had always been the practice, but between six 'divisions', in each of which a Senior Clerk would conduct, with a Junior Clerk's assistance, a fixed allocation of duties. This gave practical effect to Lord North's ideal of training at the base of the career-ladder and at the same time ensured that there could be continuity in the handling of Treasury business. The principle that a 'Division' was an official entity which transcended the individuals who worked within it was henceforth a basic feature of the Treasury's organization.

Shelburne's measures were deftly adjusted to the prevailing demands for economy, efficiency and probity in the public service and they

[29] For the background to Shelburne's measure, see J. Norris, *Shelburne and Reform* (London, 1963), pp. 99, 203.

[30] It is worth noting that there is no real evidence of such collusion or corruption among Treasury clerks in handling government contracts: see N. Baker, *Government and Contractors: the Treasury and Army Supplies, 1775–83* (London, 1971), and the same author's 'The Treasury and Open Contracting, 1778–1782,' *Historical Journal* (1972), XV, 433–54.

ensured that the Treasury could hold up its head when it was eventually submitted to parliamentary inquiry. The Commission for Inquiring into Fees in the Public Offices appointed in 1785[31] owed something of its conception to Shelburne's influence, and when it examined the Treasury's structure of renumeration found, not surprisingly, much to admire and nothing to condemn. 'Wise, judicious and effectual' was their verdict on the reorganization of 1782; 'how little is wanted for its completion and perfection.'[32] Yet, as Pitt may have discovered before he pigeon-holed the report, there were substantial discrepancies between the theory and practice of the Treasury's affairs. The point is exemplified by an anonymous booklet, *The Business done in the Treasury*, evidently drawn up for Pitt's instruction some time before June 1783.[33] The specious attractions of this convenient little guide may not have deceived Pitt for long, but they have frequently misled modern historians with results which I shall shortly discuss. Despite its merits as a précis of Treasury functions it should be recognized for what it is, a formalistic account of the way the department was supposed to perform rather than a portrait of the way it actually worked, and I have decided to omit it from this collection.

In contrast, the verbatim testimony of forty-six Treasury officials, given under oath, is an infinitely better (if repetitive) account of the department's character in 1786.[34] It reveals that, notwithstanding the complacency of the Commissioners' report, there were still well-rooted anomalies in the Treasury's organization. Fee-taking had been curbed but not abolished. Many Treasury officials were pluralists, with stipends and sinecures elsewhere in financial administration, and there are clear hints of absenteeism (Doc. 22). It would be fifty years before these anomalies ceased to obstruct the professionalism of Treasury careers, for in this respect as in others, Pitt's preoccupation with the conduct of a great war served to retard a clear line of administrative reform.

It is not until 1805 that the Treasury experienced any major adjustment to the demands being made upon it. It had experienced an inflation of numbers and of salaries in the course of the 1790s, but no organizational change was attempted until 19 August 1805 when three alterations were made to the structure of 1782. The first of these was in the spirit of Shelburne's Minute: it revised the distribution of business among the divisions to give each one a more homogeneous

---

[31] For its inception and operations see J. E. D. Binney, *British Public Finance and Administration, 1774–92*, pp. 16–17, 280; Norris, *Shelburne and Reform*, pp. 203, 204, 210.

[32] Second Report of the Commission appointed to Inquire into Fees (1786), *PP* 1806, vii, 60.

[33] PRO Chatham MSS., PRO 30/8/231.

[34] Appendix to Second Report of the Commission appointed to Inquire into Fees (1786), *PP* 1806, vii, 49–91.

character; but the second went completely against the whole tradition of Treasury organization. It directed each of the four Chief Clerks to take up responsibility for one or more of the six divisions. The significance of this may not immediately appear, but one may see from the distributions of November 1714 and particularly, July 1759 (Doc. 21(a) and (k)), that the Chief Clerks had always combined their special responsibilities for certain areas of Treasury business with a general responsibility for matters coming before the Board. William Mitford, in his evidence to the Commissioners of Inquiry into Fees (Doc. 22(b)) had stressed the breadth of a Chief Clerk's jurisdiction over 'every part of the business that may be required by the Board or the Secretaries, or that arises in the Office.' This was now ended. The Chief Clerks were to become specialists of a narrow and unrewarding kind, superintending a mere fragment of routine business and displaced from their attendance upon the Treasury Board.[35]

They were to be displaced by the third and most significant innovation of 1805, the Assistant Secretary or Law Clerk, whose duties

'will be to attend the Board at every sitting, to take the minutes, to see that the same are regularly transcribed and carried into effect without delay by the Chief Clerk, or in his absence the Senior Clerk in each branch, to revise the minutes and drafts of letters and special warrants prepared in conformity thereto for the signature of the Board or the chief Secretaries; to sign all references and directions for carrying Orders in Council into execution, to accept bills of exchange drawn upon their Lordships, to examine and report upon all such matters as may be specially referred to him by order of the Board ... and generally to take care that all regulations for the conduct of business are punctually attended to.'[36]

These comprehensive, professional duties were recognized to be incompatible with membership of the House of Commons. The incumbent was to be a permanent official and, quite clearly, head of the permanent establishment.

This 'palace revolution' at the expense of the Chief Clerks has been recognized as a major landmark, not merely in the history of the

---

[35] On 2 March 1831, William Cotton (Chief Clerk 1820–32) wrote to Assistant Secretary Stewart: 'It always appeared to me that the Minute in 1805 which established the place of the Assistant Secretary entirely changed the character of the Chief Clerks, their principal duties having been transferred by that Minute to the Assistant Secretary they no longer continued Board Room officers but were thrown back into their respective Departments to take a share in the general business attached thereto' (PRO T 1/4306). There is no justification, in Cotton's diagnosis, for the assertion of D. Gray, *Spencer Perceval, the Evangelical Prime Minister, 1762–1812* (Manchester, 1962), p. 313, that this represented a welcome liberation or gain in specialization.

[36] PRO T 29/85, pp. 346–51.

Treasury but of the Civil Service at large. It is seen as an early and most significant stage in the development of bureaucratic neutrality, a vital contribution to responsible government.[37] The 'Assistant Secretary' of 1805 is understood to be the precursor of the 'Permanent Secretary' of 1867 who, in due course, was to be acknowledged Head of the Civil Service, and it has been demonstrated that the first incumbent, George Harrison, was a man exceptionally well-equipped to promote this role.[38] A professional lawyer, with experience of fiscal problems, he was an able and ambitious administrator who soon acquired a remarkable degree of confidential influence upon successive First Lords. He amply filled the vacuum left by the Joint Secretaries who were now retreating into predominantly political roles,[39] and as spokesman for the 'official' Treasury he vigorously promoted his conception of the department as the 'superintending and directing' heart of central government. He championed the interests of Treasury control in general and in detail, and his career is inseparable from the process of Treasury self-assertion which has been noted in the preceding section.

However, there are dangers in an interpretation so strongly coloured by hindsight. It would be a mistake, for example, to seize upon the minute of August 1805 as a purposeful anticipation of the Permanent Secretaryship of 1867, let alone the 'Headship' confirmed in 1919. It will be shown, shortly, that the changes of the 1860s involved so much more than a revision of nomenclature that they can be seen, in some degree, as a reversal of the arrangement of 1805. Furthermore, it would be unwise to relate the appointment of 1805 uncritically to the recommendation of the 1786 report on Fees for the creation of a non-parliamentary Secretary.[40] This recommendation was clearly part of the general campaign for the 'reduction of the influence of the Crown' which, in the wake of the electioneering of 1784, wished to see one of the Joint Secretaries taken out of politics. The creation of the Assistant Secretaryship in 1805, on the contrary, enhanced the influence of the executive by liberating the two Secretaries for their parliamentary work, and the appointment of Harrison was to provide a valuable recruit for the Tory establishment.[41] It would be more realistic to recognize the arrangements of 1805 as a belated *ad hoc* adjustment to William Pitt's unconventional style of doing Treasury business – a style which

---

[37] Gray, *Spencer Perceval*, p. 312; Henry Parris, *Constitutional Bureaucracy* (London, 1969), pp. 45–7.

[38] J. R. Torrance, 'Sir George Harrison and the growth of bureaucracy in the early nineteenth century', *English Historical Review* (1968), lxxxiii.

[39] The chronology of the process is elusive, but see J. C. Sainty in *Treasury Officials*, p. 29.

[40] *PP* 1806, vii, 56; cf. Torrance, 'Sir George Harrison', p. 53.

[41] Torrance, 'Sir George Harrison', p. 57.

kept Pitt physically remote from the Treasury, its Board and its clerks. Harrison's appointment was therefore a fitting reward for his personal services and a shrewd way of getting Treasury business done in a way that suited Pitt – simply, directly and confidentially, without the cumbersome ritual of delegation to four Chief Clerks of questionable competence.

This would seem to make for efficiency, but it would be most dangerous to assume that the 1805 reorganization was wholly beneficial for the clerical establishment – that it 'professionalized the Treasury',[42] improved clerical influence on decision-making and made it more attractive to aristocratic young aspirants.[43] These are misconceptions which appear to derive, quite directly, from the document of 1783, *The Business done in the Treasury*. From this is it not at all apparent how large a share the Chief Clerks of the late eighteenth century had actually had upon the decision-making procedures of the Treasury Board, and it is possible to imagine that for them the arrangements of 1805 represented a gain rather than a regression.[44] But, as the evidence abundantly shows, the arrangements of 1805 mark the beginning of a process which destroyed the Chief Clerks, stunted the Under Clerks and, in due course, demoralized the department as a whole. Unless this process is understood, much of the significance of Trevelyan's reforms and the reorganizations of 1856 and 1870 will be missed.

The most appropriate way of approaching this phase of Treasury evolution is through the analysis of S. R. Martin Leake, in his 10,000-word 'Observations' of 1828 (Doc. 23).[45] He was an Assistant Clerk at the time, but he had already served twenty-five years in the department and was the son of a former Chief Clerk. It was his accurate sense of Treasury history which gave weight to an analysis of what had gone wrong with the morale and efficiency of the department over the last fifty years. He was writing at a time when it was possible to discern no less than six concurrent processes of deterioration, which stood out all the clearer against his sense of what had been, and might again be, an harmonious organization. He traced most of the evils to the principles

---

[42] Gray, *Spencer Perceval*, p. 313.

[43] Torrance, 'Sir George Harrison', p. 78.

[44] Torrance ('Sir George Harrison', pp. 59–60) appears to follow Gray (*Spencer Perceval*, p. 313) in making this deduction from a reading of *The Business done in the Treasury*. The same document misleads them into believing that the Revenue Branch was first set up in 1776 (Gray, p. 307; Torrance, p. 59, n. 1) when it is simply noting the rearrangements of 22 February 1776 – Doc. 21(n.) below.

[45] The copy among the loose bundles of documents relating to the early nineteenth-century establishment – T 1/4306 – runs to 107 small pages, from which it has been possible to print only a few essential passages, discussed above, pp. 89–92, and presented in Doc. 23, but the complete text is worth consulting for its analysis of the handling of Treasury business.

introduced with the best of intentions in August 1805, when Harrison's appointment launched the first of these processes – the practice of creating positions at the top of the Treasury hierarchy and filling them without regard to experience of Treasury business or the claims of departmental seniority. Harrison, as we have noted, was an outsider and so were his successors of 1826 and 1828. (They would continue to be until 1885.) Meanwhile, in 1815, 1816 and 1824 several more senior posts were created and filled in a controversial manner. The Principal Clerk Assistant to the Secretaries joined the Assistant Secretary in 1815 as a senior official, superior to the Chief Clerks and privileged with general access to the decision-making activities of the Board.[46] In 1816 the post of Auditor of the Civil List was set up under statutory authority[47] and although not formally incorporated in the Treasury hierarchy until 1831 it was immediately filled by Treasury appointment and became another valued promotion prospect outside the old establishment. Likewise the post of Principal Clerk of the Commissariat, created in 1816, became an influential position outside, but intruding upon, the traditional hierarchy. Lower down the scale, the post of Superintendent of Parliamentary Returns, set up in 1812, became the Clerkship of Parliamentary Accounts in 1824 and in both guises this valuable and responsible position was held by newcomers to the Treasury.[48]

Thus the former heads of the Treasury Establishment, the Chief Clerks, found themselves doubly superseded – by new posts and new men – and to make things worse the Minute of August 1805 had thrown them back upon completely stultifying duties which were quite unworthy of their experience. Martin Leake's description of their dilemma cannot be bettered (Doc. 23). Wedged between idleness and interference there was little which the Chief Clerks could usefully do to promote the business of the department, and a thoroughly unhealthy state of resentment and frustration was generated at a crucial point in the Treasury's career structure.

This, the second process of deterioration, was closely linked to a third, in which the arrangements of 1805 had led to a marked inefficiency in the handling of business. According to Martin Leake – and the evidence supports him – the pressure of war and the new style of decision-making inaugurated in 1805 had led to a vast and burdensome multiplication of paperwork, much of it superfluous and some of it harmful.[49] Even at the best of times, the work of junior officials on the

[46] PRO T 29/133, pp. 745–6; Sainty, *Treasury Officials*, p. 59.
[47] 56 Geo. III, c. 46, s. 8; Sainty, *Treasury Officials*, p. 60.
[48] Sainty, *Treasury Officials*, p. 58.
[49] Estimates of the volume of Treasury business, based on the number of documents registered in the Treasury's indexing system, were made in 1805,

Establishment had consisted largely of penmanship – the copying of formal documents according to prescribed forms – but by the 1820s it is clear that the unremitting drudgery of this work had become so great as to preclude any intelligent interest in the subject. Martin Leake, with twenty-five years of this behind him, could speak with feeling of the stunting consequences: the morale and training of the younger and abler men were being gravely impaired.

This made it all the more exasperating to contemplate a fourth process, a paradoxical one which could hardly be foreseen in 1805. But it followed that, while the main Establishment was immersed in the mounting flood of paperwork, the class of 'Extra Clerks' – a temporary and inferior grade of copyists appointed to help wherever they were needed[50] – had tended to become the free-wheeling confidential secretaries to the new senior officials, underpaid perhaps but privileged with access to responsible duties. They were now outflanking the Under Clerks in the same way that the Principal Clerks had superseded the Chief Clerks, gaining opportunities for advancement which were denied to the established body. Martin Leake may have had one conspicuous case in mind – the career of William Hill who, although never an Extra Clerk in name, was appointed in that kind of role in 1808, a mature intruder in the main Establishment.[51] It was Hill for whom several of the new senior posts had been created: Superintendent of Parliamentary Returns in 1812, Principal Clerk Assistant in 1815, Principal Clerk of the Commissariat in 1816. Finally, the Headship of the department in 1826, as Assistant Secretary, was Hill's reward for remarkable abilities and (Martin Leake evidently thought) exceptional opportunities. It was his death in June 1828 which must have liberated Martin Leake's 'Observations'.

1815 and at later dates. Their accuracy, and the components of this business, cannot be readily confirmed: Martin Leake attributes the sharp increase after 1805 to changes in the handling of business rather than to a commensurate increase in responsibilities.

1767	906 papers	1805	7,220 papers
1783	2,892 papers	1810	14,805 papers
1795	4,764 papers	1815	19,761 papers
1800	4,812 papers	1820	24,373 papers

By 1847 the volume of business was given as 29,914 papers.

[50] For the problem of defining their status and numbers see Sainty, *Treasury Officials*, pp. 42–3.

[51] At a time when entrants to the Treasury had an average age of 20, Hill was 30 when Harrison brought him into the Establishment as a Junior Clerk. The careers of the three Crafers, Charles, Thomas and Edwin, likewise exhibit the phenomenon to which Martin Leake was referring. Beginning as Extra Clerks, all three attained high and confidential positions in the Treasury which would appear to have been well-deserved. See Sainty, *Treasury Officials*, p. 121.

Clearly, this kind of career only aggravated, by contrast, the fifth general factor in decline – the deteriorating career-prospects of the junior Establishment. The war years had inflated the ranks of the Under Clerks – five were added in 1797, three in 1805, four in 1808, one in 1811 and four more in 1813 – and although five were pruned away in 1821 there remained a generation whose ordinary prospects of advancement were greatly inferior to those of the eighteenth century. Martin Leake himself, although destined to become a Principal Clerk, had only moved one grade forward in his twenty-five years: the ordinary apprenticeship of a young Treasury clerk might last thirty.[52]

To all these must be added the sixth and concluding factor – the salary retrenchments of 1821–2 and the unpopular superannuation deductions which accompanied them. Justified in themselves as an overdue curtailment of war-time inflation, the cuts were more grievous for the younger than for the older men. The expectations of a Junior Clerk at the top of his scale were no longer £520 but £200. It was the last straw, tending, in Martin Leake's words, 'permanently to paralyse the little zeal still remaining in the department' (Doc. 23).

This elaborate diagnosis of a misconceived system is tinged with some bitterness but it remains a fair one which can be substantiated by the ascertainable facts. More interestingly, however, it was a constructive diagnosis which intelligently anticipated the kind of measures which in thirty years' time were to assist in healing the department. In particular, Martin Leake seized upon the principle which Trevelyan was later to make his own – a proper regard for the division of labour between intellectual and mechanical work (Docs. 23, 25). The physical drudgery of copying and entering superfluous papers was to be pruned by a rational codification of Treasury business and the remainder handed over to that class of Extra Clerks which had been created to deal with it. The Established Clerks would meanwhile return to those worthwhile executive responsibliities which would fit them for higher office. Martin Leake yields nothing to Trevelyan in his confidence that the Treasury man, properly trained, was peculiarly equipped to serve anywhere in the administrative system, and in his own case that faith would seem to be justified. In the clarity and logic of his detailed recommendations Martin Leake shows himself to be a frustrated professional with considerable potential which, happily, was to find its fulfilment in time.

[52] The ten Chief Clerks appointed between 1782 and 1820 had served between twenty and twenty-five years as Under Clerks. No further promotions were made until 1829, and thereafter the previous service of Chief Clerks (with the exception of Edward Drummond's eighteen and a half years) was between thirty and forty years.

But, beyond some scribbled and petty criticisms by the new Assistant Secretary, it is not clear what reception was given to the 'Observations'. The fact that they have survived among a few bundles of unclassifiable Treasury papers may suggest that they remained in circulation to influence a later generation, but the initial response was negative. Indeed the Whig administration which took office in 1830 soon took steps to consolidate just those features of Treasury organization which had proved so controversial. Their elaborate reconstruction Minute of 17 October 1834[53] (too lengthy and verbose to present among the Documents) is significant for its explicit approval of the division of the Treasury's work between the new decision-making hierarchy, created since 1805 and recently enlarged,[54] and the executive hierarchy of the old Establishment headed by the Chief Clerks. In both structures, promotion was to be determined by merit, not seniority, and in the appointment of the highest officials candidates would still be sought outside the Treasury.

Its main object, however, was to reorganize the department in a more economical way, cutting down numbers and curtailing salaries. This was achieved by contracting the six Divisions into four, incorporating the Revenue Branch as a fifth Division and reducing the body of Under Clerks by four.[55] Death and retirements allowed a clean sweep among the demoralized Chief Clerks and other retirements lower down the scale allowed a general upward movement in the Establishment. At the end of the day the Treasury Board could congratulate itself for a notional saving of £8,479 p.a. which had been the real object of the exercise. It had done nothing for morale.

On the contrary, the Whig leadership, for so long pledged to cleanse the Augean stables of Tory maladministration, was intent on some unpalatable reforms. Their unsympathetic probing among the Divisions had uncovered habits of laxity and indiscipline in the performance of the younger clerks, and absenteeism among the older ones. The requirements of the superannuation system set up in 1824[56] were a

---

[53] PRO T 29/358, pp. 317–33; printed in Appendix 4 to the Report from the Select Committee on Miscellaneous Expenditure, *PP* 1847–8, xviii(i), 78–85.

[54] The senior post of Clerk for Colonial Business was created in 1832 with general Treasury responsibilities in addition to his colonial audit duties. In 1834 his status was established as that of Principal Clerk, ranking fourth in the official hierarchy. See Sainty, *Treasury Officials*, p. 62, and D. M. Young, *The Colonial Office in the Early Nineteenth Century* (London, 1961), p. 195.

[55] Three Senior Clerkships and three Assistant Clerkships were abolished, while the Junior Clerks were increased by two, thus aggravating the promotion problem.

[56] In 1824 the government was obliged to undertake the full cost of civil service pensions, after a stormy experiment with the contributory scheme of 1821. The contributory principle was reintroduced in 1834. For the early history of civil service superannuation see M. Raphael, *Pensions and Public Servants* (Paris, 1964).

convenient excuse to inaugurate attendance registers. By the Treasury Minute of 24 June 1831 all Treasury clerks were to be signed in daily with a record of their time of arrival. Hours were still the traditional ones – from 10.30 or 11.00 at the latest, until the work of the day had been discharged – but it was necessary to break with the old habit of closing down the department for its eight-week vacation in the summer. A Minute of 20 January 1835 noted that in recent years 'the business of the Treasury has become incessant, in consequence of the protracted sessions of Parliament and the increase of public business', and holidays – still a generous seven weeks – would have to be staggered.

These trivial innovations provoked disproportionate resentment among the irritable and despondent Under Clerks, and some of them petitioned angrily. But the Treasury Board was undoubtedly justified in its concern for departmental discipline: the prolonged deterioration in morale had been revealing itself in individual acts of resentment and in a general decline in the quality of recruits. Moral and physical unfitness for the demands of Treasury work revealed itself in a disturbing number of cases during the 1820s and 1830s and there was an unprecedented rate of dismissals and 'retirements'. Ill-health figures largely among the ostensible grounds for withdrawal, but there are several hints of financial embarrassments and certain acts of indiscipline go a long way to confirm Martin Leake's picture of departmental friction and frustration.[57] The following senior officials (with age in brackets) were retired during the reorganization of 1834: W. Speer (69); J. Vernon (64); J. Grange (58); G. West (54); T. Hoblyn (53); C. Woodford (? – after 35 years service); but the wastage of younger men between 1823 and 1834 is indicated in the table opposite. The significance of these figures is heightened if one notes that the only other departures in these years were: 1829, E. C. Bullock, Chief Clerk (64), and 1832, W. Cotton, Chief Clerk (52).

An inquiry into recruitment and training was therefore urgently required when the Treasury Board undertook it in January 1831. They appealed, interestingly enough, to the disgruntled Chief Clerks and asked for their views on the qualities required for service in the Treasury – a challenge which the Chief Clerks failed to meet with much originality. But the least vague, though least concise, reply came from the head of the Revenue Branch, T. C. Brooksbank, whose views combine platitude with some penetration of the requirements of

[57] Among his other offences – absenteeism, carelessness – C. W. St John, dismissed in 1833, had torn up a Sign Manual Warrant and in extenuation argued that he was carrying an unfair share of the duties of his Senior Clerk. William Duke had likewise torn up his attendance record, resenting the fact that his movements should be spied upon by an Extra Clerk. His pleas for reinstatement reveal that he too had 'pecuniary difficulties' (T 1/4310).

Treasury work (Doc. 24). Founded upon an uncompromising belief in the Treasury's sovereign status among departments of government, Brooksbank's requirements are of course élitist, but the emphasis is upon the social, rather than the intellectual, criterion of an élite – the education of a gentleman to a certain minimum standard. His attitude to mere academic attainment is amusingly revealed by the story of the distinguished mathematicians floundering among the intricacies of the National Debt; and against this kind of narrow specialism Brooksbank opposes his conception of *training* in the comprehensive requirements of Treasury work. In the modern jargon, he combines a 'generalist' philosophy of intellectual background with an emphasis on 'relevant' studies for those who wished to serve in the Revenue Branch. Indeed, all Brooksbank's thinking on this subject is coloured by his sense of the special nature of his department which we have already noted for its self-conscious professionalism, but in his concluding rhapsody on the self-sufficient continuity of the *permanent* Establishment (from which he excludes the Assistant Secretary) he may be taken to express views common to all his colleagues at this stage in the Treasury's evolution. It is a valuable testimony.

			Age	
1823	J. R. Hislop	Assistant Clerk	41	resigned, mentally ill.
1824	A. F. Pococke	Junior Clerk	26	resigned.
1825	H. Cotterell	Junior Clerk	24	died.
1826	P. A. Compton	Assistant Clerk	38	resigned, ill; died 1827.
1827	Hon. W. Rodney	Junior Clerk	33	resigned.
1830	E. A. Vesey	Junior Clerk	23	died.
1831	P. H. Earle	Assistant Clerk	47	resigned, ill.
1832	W. Duke	Assistant Clerk	32	dismissed.
	A. Salwey	Assistant Clerk	35	resigned, ill; died 1833.
1833	C. W. St John	Junior Clerk	24	dismissed.
	T. Bulteel	Junior Clerk	25	resigned, 'pecuniary difficulties'.
	E. Baker	Junior Clerk	25	resigned, ill.
1834	F. G. Vandiest	Assistant Clerk	34	resigned, ill.

The Treasury Board's immediate response was unadventurous. The concept of probationary service for Junior Clerks dates from 1808, when it was fixed at three months. The decision of 12 April 1831 to defer permanent appointments for one 'or two' years probation of the 'talents, conduct and assiduity' of recruits reflects the more serious nature of the problem but was hardly imaginative. However, in September 1834 Lord Melbourne expressed his desire for a more discriminating test of fitness and potential, to be assessed by a competitive examination between three nominated candidates. The nature of the examination was not elaborated, but one of the earliest appears to have required the candidates to précis a correspondence of nineteen items exchanged between the Foreign and Colonial Secretaries, H.M. Commissioner at Havannah and the Treasury. . . .[58] By January 1840 the frivolity of these exercises may have prompted the department to require something more relevant to its needs. On 14 January a Minute called for post-probationary tests in double-entry book-keeping – a topical subject at this time of reform in government accountancy. Indeed, the particular interest of the decision lies in its recommendation by the Treasury to all other departments of government. Like the 'economy' circular of 10 August 1821[59] it is a symptom of the Treasury's limited, yet growing, concern to influence standards in the civil service as a whole.

For the Treasury, however, these were but half-hearted gestures which left the central problems of recruitment and morale virtually untouched. Neither Trevelyan's appointment as Assistant Secretary in January 1840, nor Sir Robert Peel's administration, appear to have made any immediate improvement, and when the Treasury was submitted to one of its most searching parliamentary inquiries in 1848 its shortcomings were still essentially those of the 1820s and 1830s deriving – as I have been at pains to argue – from the reconstruction of 1805.

This point was not overlooked by the Select Committee on Miscellaneous Expenditure. When Trevelyan gave his evidence he was prepared to admit it:[60] but he declined to make the obvious deductions (Doc. 25). On the contrary, Trevelyan aligned himself with the principles of the Treasury Minutes of 1805 and 1834 and only sought their logical completion. The decision-making élite of the Secretaries and the Principal Clerks was to be reinforced, preferably by experienced outsiders. The old clerical establishment, headed by the Chief Clerks, should be encouraged to wither away so that it might be replaced by a modestly-paid body of copyists. Liquidation, not reform, was Trevelyan's answer to the deeply-rooted problems of the old Establishment.

There is a hard-headed logic about this solution which one supposes to be characteristic of the man, and, given his position in the hierarchy, it was natural that he should subscribe to it. Unlike Martin Leake, he had no sentimental attachments to the traditional character of the department, no roots in its evolution and – one infers – no friendships among its members. The abrasiveness of his recommendations owes something to the self-conscious isolation of a man prepared to be thoroughly unpopular with his colleagues. Indeed, Trevelyan's views about the Treasury and its role jarred awkwardly with the received ideas of those outside, as well as inside, the department. While his

---

[58] PRO T 1/4310, Assistant Secretary's report to the Board, 31 October 1834.
[59] See above, p. 67 and Doc. 16.
[60] See his answer to Q 1391 (Doc. 25).

recommendations for economies were well-calculated to appeal to a parliamentary Select Committee, particularly in 1848, his conception of Treasury suzerainty within the public service went rather further than anything which was then acceptable.[61] Likewise, while Treasury men might share his opinion of the status and requirements of a Treasury élite, they recoiled from his divisive vision of Treasury business separated between exclusively 'superior' and 'inferior' roles. Two other witnesses, with long experience of the Treasury, rejected Trevelyan's diagnosis and affirmed their belief in the homogeneity and continuity of Treasury business. Both believed that a useful Treasury career at the highest level of responsibility could be founded only upon a painstaking apprenticeship in routine copying.[62] It was pointed out, quite justly, that Trevelyan's examples of the successful recruitment of outsiders to the Treasury at the highest level were misleading.[63] On the contrary, it could be shown that many long-serving Treasury men had successfully carried their expertise elsewhere to other departments of Government, in vindication of the traditional Establishment's excellence as a nursery of public servants.[64]

The conflict of views appears extensive and in the evidence given to the Committee one can sometimes discern the antagonism which Trevelyan provoked. But, in fact, the disagreement was of an irritatingly narrow kind. Trevelyan and the 'orthodox' or 'old-school'[65] Treasury men were agreed on the nature of the malaise – the wasteful, frustrating discrepancy between the 'superior' and 'inferior' duties of

[61] The report of the Select Committee flatly rejected Trevelyan's proposals, and even Gladstone warned Northcote in 1853 against 'any unnecessary lodgement of power in the hands of the Treasury' (BM Add. MSS. 50,014, ff. 76–81), cited by J. Hart, 'The Genesis of the Northcote-Trevelyan Report' in *Studies in the Growth of Nineteenth-Century Government*, ed. G. Sutherland (London, 1972), p. 76.

[62] See the evidence of Sir Alexander Spearman (formerly Treasury Clerk of Parliamentary Accounts and Assistant Secretary) and George Boyd, Chief Clerk, particularly questions 1879, 1960–67, 1980, *PP* 1847–8, xviii(i).

[63] Spearman made the point that the men cited by Trevelyan, i.e. G. W. Brande, Clerk for Colonial Business, and R. Hankins, Law Clerk, had simply transferred their previous duties to specially created posts in the Treasury – Q 1959, *PP* 1847–8, xviii(i).

[64] Spearman cited the cases of Matthew Winter (1777–98), appointed Secretary to the Board of Taxes; Edward Bates (1800–23), who succeeded Winter; Robert Mitford (1796–1823), appointed Chairman of the Board of Taxes, and J. C. Freeling (1813–26), Secretary to the Board of Excise. He could have added G. T. Goodenough (1766–82), Secretary to the Board of Taxes, J. Martin Leake (1763–85), Commissioner of the Audit Office, C. A. Gore (1834–9), Commissioner of Woods and Forests, and perhaps G. E. Anson (1834–40), private secretary to Prince Albert.

[65] Trevelyan's own phrase, writing to Gladstone 9 February 1854 (BM Add. MSS. 44,333, ff. 158–62).

Treasury men – and they were broadly agreed in their vision of a solution – a select, tightly-knit establishment of highly-trained professionals. The conflict was rather over the means to this end. Did it have to involve the extinction, however gradual, of the traditional hierarchy of Chief Clerks and their juniors ? Did it have to require the incursion of favoured outsiders upon the career-prospects of established Treasury men ? And, at its heart, this was not a dispute about abstract measures but about particular men. Trevelyan had not concealed his disdain for the incapacity of some of the senior men, nor his despair at the unfitness of some of the younger, and he was repaid with personal hostility. He could be accused of heartless ingratitude to those permanent colleagues who had unselfishly coached him, a novice outsider, in the intricacies of Treasury affairs.[66]

Yet, Trevelyan was no ruthless doctrinaire. The objectivity of his judgments on individual Treasury men cannot be confirmed, of course, but one must respect his sense of a discrepancy between the resources of the Treasury's personnel and the administrative needs of the hour. As the previous chapter has shown, the developing demands of parliamentary control upon Treasury control were reaching their peak in mid century. Trevelyan was keenly aware of this pressure and it underlies the urgency of his complaint to the 1848 Select Committee that the Treasury was simply not strong enough to exercise its potential powers.[67] Trevelyan was joined by two other senior Treasury officials in elaborating this theme in some important memoranda of 1850. Here it was admitted that the Treasury was failing to administer its general superintendence over the country's financial affairs. On crucial fiscal problems the First Lord and Chancellor of the Exchequer had to turn for help elsewhere – to the Board of Trade, to the heads of the Revenue Boards, or to their own private secretaries.[68] It is precisely the situation which Gladstone was to discover three years later and recall in 1890.

This agreement adds up to a convincing indictment, yet it requires closer scrutiny. A department which contained George Arbuthnot, W. H. Stephenson and C. L. Crafer[69] could not really complain of a lack of competent financial advisers. Arbuthnot was a distinguished

---

[66] See G. Arbuthnot's strictures on the Northcote-Trevelyan Report, 6 March 1854, *Reports and Papers relating to the Reorganization of the Civil Service*, PP 1854-5, xx, 405-6, printed in *English Historical Documents, 1833-1874*, pp. 575-6.

[67] See Q 1646, PP 1847-8, xviii(1), cited Roseveare, *The Treasury: the Evolution of a British Institution* (London, 1969), p. 166.

[68] See G. W. Brande's and S. Martin Leake's contribution to 'Memoranda on some Branches of the Business of the Treasury', March, April 1850, in *PP* 1854-5, xx, 432-8.

[69] For full details of their Treasury careers see the alphabetical index of Sainty, *Treasury Officials*, pp. 110, 121, 153.

currency expert who became Auditor of the Civil List in 1850. Stephenson was rising through the Treasury to the Chairmanship of the Board of Inland Revenue in 1862, and Crafer, who began his career as an Extra Clerk, had exceptionally wide experience of parliamentary finance. All were accustomed to working closely with Treasury ministers. Yet, it would appear that the death of T. C. Brooksbank in March 1850, aged 71, severed a long and irreplaceable tradition of professional experience, which Trevelyan had tried vainly to preserve.[70] Arbuthnot, Stephenson and Crafer were committed to other responsibilities, and the dissatisfaction of Trevelyan and Gladstone must be seen to reflect narrowly upon a single official, Charles Litchfield, to whose infirm shoulders the Chief Clerkship of the Finance Division descended in February 1851. The inadequacy of Litchfield must have been a vexatious burden to endure for three crucial years which saw the inauguration of Gladstone's budgetary career. Yet to those capable of taking a broad and dispassionate view of the situation it would have seemed unjust to found upon Litchfield pessimistic conclusions about the Treasury as a whole. Even Gladstone did not share Trevelyan's confidence that the only remedy was to import experienced outsiders,[71] and it was Trevelyan who had to bear (unfairly, as it happens) the considerable odium which attended W. G. Anderson's transfer from the office of Assistant Paymaster-General to be Principal Clerk for Financial Business in 1854.[72]

In the event, Trevelyan's views on reform in the Treasury, as elsewhere, were tempered by the caution of his colleagues. Only grudging adjustments were made to the half-implemented principles of the Northcote-Trevelyan Report.[73] After February 1856, recruitment to the Treasury was determined ostensibly by the Civil Service Commission's modest examination of three candidates for each vacancy, but considerable latitude was retained by Treasury ministers in the selection and encouragement of nominees. Youths of between 18 and 25 continued to provide the raw material of Treasury recruitment and there was no question of surrendering the Establishment to Trevelyan's ideal of veteran administrators. Indeed, the major reorganization of

[70] Trevelyan claimed to have made several attempts to persuade Brooksbank to record his extensive knowledge of public finance (PP 1854–5, xx, 437) and he was apparently instrumental in securing Brooksbank's papers for the Treasury library – Trevelyan to Gladstone, 31 March 1853 (BM Add. MSS. 44,333, f. 30).
[71] Gladstone to Russell, 20 January 1854 (BM Add. MSS. 44,291, ff. 93–104), cited by Hart, 'Northcote-Trevelyan Report', p. 79.
[72] Trevelyan to Gladstone, 18 June 1855 (Trevelyan Letter Book 35, p. 252, formerly Bodleian Dep. d. 125).
[73] M. Wright, Treasury Control of the Civil Service, 1854–1874 (Oxford, 1969), pp. 14–15; Roseveare, Treasury, pp. 171–3.

the Establishment promulgated on 4 July 1856 represented a firm rejection of Trevelyan's principles and – more significantly for my argument – a reversal of the principles which had been governing the Treasury's organization since 1805. The Treasury Minute of 4 July (Doc. 26) deliberately *reintegrated* the department, ending the exclusive division between the decision-making and executive hierarchies. The Assistant Secretary, the Auditor of the Civil List and four other Principal Clerks were brought back into direct working relations with the rest of the clerks who now had before them a clear line of advancement leading to the highest permanent appointments. Much of the routine drudgery of copying documents was shifted to the separate Registry Department staffed by 'supplementary' clerks, and to that extent Trevelyan's insistence on a proper division of labour was satisfied.[74] But for the main Establishment, united in the preparation and implementation of Treasury Minutes, the homogeneity of Treasury business had been restored. Behind changed nomenclature,[75] the divisional organization of the department was essentially what it had been before 1805.

The effectiveness of this reconstruction cannot be illustrated with much vividness. The litany of complaints since the 1820s was not succeeded by any audible murmur of content. There were simply no more complaints. In any case, the purely organizational merits of the 1856 Treasury Minute tended to get overshadowed by the more controversial significance of the Civil Service Commission's examinations. Deliberate assessments of the Treasury's character usually asked whether the products of limited competition represented a better type of recruit than their predecessors. In 1860, George Arbuthnot, who had always opposed Trevelyan on civil service reform, thought perhaps not,[76] and Charles Rivers Wilson, who entered the Treasury through one of the earliest competitions, was ready to agree that, while the average level of intelligence had been raised and there were fewer 'QHB's' (Queen's Hard Bargains!), there were none of this generation to eclipse the best products of the old school – and he named Arbuthnot, Stephenson and Anderson.[77]

Yet, in any broad survey of the Treasury's nineteenth-century

[74] Wright, *Treasury Control*, p. 10.

[75] The grades Chief Clerk, Senior Clerk, Assistant Clerk and Junior Clerk were replaced by Principal Clerk, First Class Clerk, Second Class Clerk and Third Class Clerk; see Sainty, *Treasury Officials*, pp. 71–3. The reorganization of 1870, involving the early retirement of five officials, allowed the grade of Third Class Clerks to be abolished; below, p. 105.

[76] Evidence given by Arbuthnot (Q 767) to the Select Committee on Civil Service Appointments (*PP* 1860, ix).

[77] Sir Charles Rivers Wilson, *Chapters from My Official Life*, ed. E. MacAlister (London, 1916), pp. 27–8.

recruits, the generation appointed between 1856 and 1870 does stand out with certain significant characteristics. Predominantly well-connected, public-school men (eight of them Etonians), they appear socially and educationally better-equipped than any preceding generation to make their mark in public life, and in due course several of them attained to high honours. Francis Nowatt and Reginald Welby, the earliest of this generation, and Edward Hamilton, one of the last, were to become Permanent Secretaries of the Treasury. George Ryder, appointed in 1857, became Chairman of the Board of Customs, as did Henry Primrose, appointed in 1869. J. A. Kempe and Horace Seymour, both joining in 1867, passed through the Treasury and the Customs Board to responsible posts in the Mint and the office of Comptroller and Auditor-General. C. R. Wilson likewise passed from the Treasury to a distinguished career as a financial adviser to the Egyptian and British Governments. All obtained knighthoods (Welby a peerage) for their public services.[78]

A closer analysis would detract from this superficial evidence of success: some of these men were kicked upstairs, and all could be accused of benefiting from the Treasury's favoured position in the late-Victorian Civil Service.[79] But the fact remains that this comparatively small generation of twenty-two men produced a high proportion of officials who, for good or ill, exercised leadership in British government, and it is an achevement worth examining. Did it owe everything to selection by limited competition? Evidently not. The same generation exhibits some conspicuous failures, men endowed with education and connections but without ability, who failed to respond to the Treasury's opportunities and drifted away into idleness or resignation. One became an amateur comedian, another wrote operettas and a third took up water-colours. One resigned within nine years of appointment.[80] All the evidence indicates that the Civil Service Commission examination was no real test of ability and only a flimsy obstacle to favouritism.[81]

It might be more reasonable to believe of this generation, what has

[78] H. A. D. Seymour is an exception, but it is claimed that he was due to be knighted when he died, June 1902; *Alumni Cantabrigienses*, compiled by J. A. Venn, Part II, vol. v (1953), p. 469.

[79] For the stormy controversy over the 'Treasury ring' of privilege and patronage see *The Times*, 24, 25, 27, 28, 29, 30, 31 January 1890.

[80] These were, respectively, Q. W. F. Twiss (1856–92); F. E. Clay (1857–74); C. R. Baillie-Hamilton (1868–89); and B. C. Stephenson (1857–65).

[81] The incomplete records of examinations for Treasury clerkships show that it was possible for candidates to compete more than once for a vacancy, and eventually win admission against weaker rivals. This does not confirm the story of the 'Treasury idiots' (Roseveare, *Treasury*, p. 172) but it indicates the possibility of manipulation of favoured candidatures. See PRO CSC. 2/35, and T 1/6760A/20269/1867.

been proposed for an earlier one,[82] that its best elements had been positively attracted by the reformed character and opportunities of the Treasury. Certainly any cursory survey of a First Lord's correspondence will reveal the considerable pressure for nominations to the Treasury's Junior Clerkships[83] but the pressure is invariably parental. As far as the aspirations of Treasury recruits are concerned, the little evidence there is tends to be negative. For example, Welby, the embodiment of the late-Victorian 'Treasury mind', had had no clear ideas about a career when he took his ordinary pass degree at Cambridge. Prompted by a friend, the son of a Treasury minister, he accepted his nomination to the Treasury 'on the impulse of the moment'.[84] Likewise Edward Hamilton, faced with the choice of becoming tutor to the children of the Prince of Wales or remaining at the Treasury, which he had only just joined, found it difficult to decide. 'Somewhat gloomy prospects of future in Treasury' was a factor weighing against remaining; the dangers of 'giving up profession' argued against leaving.[85] Other Treasury clerks of this era, who have left impressions of their early lives in the department, give no evidence of positive ambitions to serve there. They came because they had been secured nominations by their parents or friends, and they stayed in spite of the discovery that the work 'did not then seem . . . of a very attractive or important nature. There was too much useless duplication in the shape of copying out, and making précis in books of decisions and matters which were merely formal.'[86]

This is fair comment on the amount of routine drudgery which had survived the reorganization of 1856. Nevertheless, the prospects for younger men were now distinctly brighter, as the memoir writers soon discovered. Those broad and profound changes in the scale and character of British government which might be discerned by mid-century had produced in the Treasury, as elsewhere, a closer working relationship between minsters and civil servants,[87] and a specific symptom of this was an increased ministerial reliance on official private secretaries. Such appointments were certainly not novel: eighteenth-century Treasury officials had been selected to serve the First Lord

[82] Torrance, 'Sir George Harrison', p. 78.

[83] For published examples, see Parris, *Constitutional Bureaucracy*, pp. 53–6 (cf. *Some Records of the Life of Stevenson Arthur Blackwood, K.C.B.*, compiled by a friend (1896), p. 30); Sir J. A. Kempe, *Reminiscences of an Old Civil Servant, 1846–1927* (London, 1920), p. 28; *Sir Robert Peel from his Private Papers*, ed. C. S. Parker (London, 1891), iii, ch. xv.

[84] See his obituary, *The Times*, 1 November 1915, p. 12.

[85] *The Diary of Sir Edward Hamilton*, ed. D. W. R. Bahlman (Oxford, 1972), i, pp. xv–xvi.

[86] Kempe, *Reminiscences*, p. 34.

[87] For an excellent treatment of this large and important theme see Parris, *Constitutional Bureaucracy*, chs. iii and iv, pp. 80–133.

and Chancellor of the Exchequer and by 1812 all three Secretaries, permanent and political, were laying claim to official assistance.[88] But the 1850s saw a distinct accentuation of these demands. The Chancellor (Disraeli) insisted on a second Private Secretary in 1852 and the senior Parliamentary Secretary acquired additional official assistance in 1857. During its brief existence (1868–9) the office of 'Third Lord' likewise claimed a Treasury clerk.[89] Thus, at any one time there might be between five and seven of the younger members of the Treasury Establishment serving in close contact with the decision-makers. Of the 1856–70 generation, at least twelve had done so by 1870 and another five were soon to have the opportunity.

There were material benefits in the form of supplementary salaries, but the incalculable benefits were the ones that mattered. Merit necessarily played its part in the rapid advancement of former private secretaries, but it was merit developed and exposed under the most favourable conditions, directly under ministerial eyes. Welby's ten years as private secretary to successive Financial Secretaries put him almost ten years ahead of his contemporary, Francis Mowatt,[90] and Edward Hamilton likewise reaped exceptional rewards from his five years of personal service under Gladstone.[91] And, whatever the gains in material terms, the sheer interest and variety of the work was its own reward.

Work in the Treasury divisions was never to have comparable attractions, but the closer relationship between ministers and civil servants was telling, even there, and interest and variety of a more professional kind than in private office were increasingly accessible. In a small way, but with growing frequency, it was becoming possible for the junior Treasury official to identify himself with a particular administrative or legislative enterprise. J. H. Cole (1843–84) for example, earned special commendation in 1851 for his work on the Commission for the New Palace of Westminster. William Law (1838–81), as a Principal Clerk, had devoted years to the reforms which culminated in the Courts of Justice Act of 1874 and the Judicature Act of 1878. By 1877, C. C.

[88] Sainty, *Treasury Officials*, pp. 74–81. Mr Sainty's success in establishing the identity of private secretaries is a particularly notable achievement in view of the comparative informality of the early appointments.

[89] Sainty, *Treasury Officials*, p. 78.

[90] Mowatt was Welby's senior by a few months but never held a private secretaryship. Welby was promoted First Class Clerk *and* Principal Clerk in 1871, Assistant Secretary in 1879 and Permanent Secretary in 1885; Mowatt, First Class Clerk in 1870, became Principal Clerk in 1880, Assistant Secretary in 1888 and Permanent Secretary in 1894.

[91] He was made a Companion of the Order of the Bath and promoted, in one year, from Second Class Clerk to Principal Clerk of the Finance Division in succession to Welby; see Bahlman, *Diary of Sir Edward Hamilton*, i, pp. xxxiv–xxxvi.

Puller (1865–97) had become the Treasury's expert on superannuation, and Welby, most successfully, had identified himself with statistical and financial problems by 1871. His appointment as Principal Clerk of the Finance Division in that year marked the end of twenty years of weakness in which the Treasury had had to look outside the department for its financial advisers.

The increasingly professional and self-sufficient character of the department was reflected, at the highest level, in some significant adjustments of the 1856 structure. In December 1859, within a year of George Hamilton's appointment as successor to Trevelyan,[92] he had secured his release from the specialized management of a Treasury division. Instead, the Assistant Secretary was to be more usefully employed, in general supervision of the department, preparing material for parliamentary discussion and advising the Chancellor and Financial Secretary on general questions of finance.[93] This ensured his position at the centre as well as the head of the permanent Establishment, and by 1867 Hamilton's vigorous omnipresence made it seem fitting that he should be given a more ample recognition. The Treasury Minute of 10 May 1867, conferring the title of 'Permanent Secretary', emphasized his special responsibility for the control of civil service establishments and salaries, but made no enlargement of his powers.[94] That was not necessary. It simply gave recognition to an established fact which, among other things, subtly distinguishes the 'Assistant Secretary' conceived in 1805 from what the post had become by the 1860s. Then, the Assistant Secretary had been the agent of the Board, put in by the politicians virtually as a bailiff, if not official receiver, to manage a nearly bankrupt concern. By 1867 it would be too much to claim that he had become the agent of the Establishment, but he was, in some unacknowledged sense, its representative, and his weight and effectiveness depended heavily on the professionalism around him.[95]

In this respect, as in others, the significance of the changes taking place in the 1850s and 1860s was to become more clearly apparent

[92] For an important account of G. A. Hamilton and his achievement see Wright, *Treasury Control*, pp. 21–8, 34–43.

[93] Wright, *Treasury Control*, pp. 23–4.

[94] This controversial Treasury Minute has strong claims to be represented among the accompanying Documents of this chapter, but I have taken advantage of the fact that it is conveniently published and commented upon in Wright, *Treasury Control*, Appendix I, pp. 363–6.

[95] Junior Treasury clerks took a disrespectful view of this: 'Do you remember', said one Permanent Secretary to another, *ca.* 1911, 'that in those days [the 1880s] the Permanent Secretary was some old dodderer and we did most of the work without consulting him, so that he never knew much of what was happening in the office?' – Sir Frederick Leith-Ross, *Money Talks* (London, 1968), p. 21.

after 1870, but it has been worth stressing now lest the novelty of the 1870 reforms should appear to be exaggerated. Yet, 1870 was a year of immense importance, a true turning-point in the development of the permanent department. Two circumstances contributed to this. Perhaps the least important, although most celebrated, was the Order in Council of 4 June 1870 inaugurating Open Competition as the dominant mode of entry into the civil service.[96] Unquestionably, this was to affect, if not transform, the academic quality of the men entering the Treasury. In social and educational background the 'competition-wallahs' were almost indistinguishable from the generation which preceded them, but in intellectual calibre and academic honours they were sometimes embarrassingly over-endowed and included some of the most brilliant products of the reformed universities.[97] But what had attracted them? What had made a nomination to the Treasury a prize worth weighing against a university fellowship or an assured career at the Bar? Why, if unsuccessful, should highly-placed candidates turn down alternative offers from the great departments of state?[98] Undoubtedly, one factor which attracted aspirants was the Victorian Treasury's special, if contested, status as the premier department and the department of the premier. Furthermore, the select generation of 1856–70 had successfully established their status as a completely professional, though gentlemanly, élite in the eyes of those social and educational circles where it mattered. Not even Jowett could doubt that a Treasury clerkship now represented a desirable kind of distinction for double-firsts from Balliol.

Yet all this would have been meaningless if the Treasury had not been able to offer work commensurate with these abilities, and to offer it not merely at the senior levels but at the outset. That it could do so was the outcome of the last major reorganization in the sequence which commenced in 1776. The Treasury Minute of 25 May 1870, as amended on 31 December that year, did three simple things (Doc. 27). 1. It freed the Establishment from the remaining elements of mechanical labour required by its over-elaborate system of duplicating letters and minutes. 2. It was thus enabled to make a significant reduction in its numbers and abolish a whole junior grade in the hierarchy. 3. It specifically encouraged the younger men to take the responsibility of recommending and drafting decisions. The last of these points was the one that mattered most. Although the amended Treasury Minute of 31

[96] For an account of its inception and administration see Wright, *Treasury Control*, pp. 74–109.

[97] I have given some impression and analysis of this generation in Roseveare, *Treasury*, pp. 177–81.

[98] For reactions of this kind (*ca.* 1882) see Sir Charles Oman, *Memories of Victorian Oxford* (London, 1941), pp. 100–1.

December still provided for some period of apprenticeship in mechanically learning the formulae of Treasury documents, it did not impair the opportunities of junior clerks to exercise their judgments. They 'got first bite at the papers: they could put minutes or drafts on them before passing them up to their superiors, thus getting a chance of showing their quality.'[99] This was the opportunity which rewarded successful aspirants and particularly impressed men coming to the Treasury from other departments. For some it was like stepping into a new world.[100]

Indeed, for the Treasury it was a comparatively new world, or at least the beginning of a new era, which lies beyond the scope of this study. The reforms narrated in Section 2 had launched the department upon a distinctive phase in the history of Treasury control. Sometimes feeble and incompetent, and invariably less formidable than has usually been supposed,[101] late-nineteenth-century Treasury control was nonetheless founded upon certain elements of institutional strength. Streamlined and economical, stimulating responsibility among its youngest members, the Treasury was now internally harmonious (to the point of cosiness) and externally self-confident (to the point of arrogance). These were indeed mixed blessings, which were eyed without enthusiasm by those outside the charmed circle, but at least they indicate how far the department had developed since the days of 1828 and 1848 (Docs. 23 and 25) and they allow one to suggest, perhaps, that after a prolonged adolescence the Treasury as we know it had come of age.

[99] Sir Laurence Guillemard, *Trivial Fond Records* (London, 1937), pp. 20–1; cf. Leith-Ross, *Money Talks*, p. 22; Sir James Grigg, *Prejudice and Judgment* (London, 1948), pp. 35–6.

[100] Guillemard, *Fond Records*, p. 19. For the distribution of responsibility in the Colonial Office, *ca.* 1870, see R. C. Snelling and T. J. Barron, 'The Colonial Office: its permanent officials, 1801–1914,' in *Studies in the Growth of Nineteenth-Century Government*, ed. G. Sutherland (London, 1969), pp. 155–7.

[101] Wright, *Treasury Control*, pp. 340–51; Roseveare, *Treasury*, pp. 203–7.

SUGGESTED FURTHER READING

S. B. Baxter, *The Development of the Treasury, 1660–1702* (London, 1957).

J. E. D. Binney, *British Public Finance and Administration, 1774–92* (Oxford, 1958).

Basil Chubb, *The Control of Public Expenditure* (Oxford, 1952).

G. Reid, *The Politics of Financial Control* (London, 1966).

H. Roseveare, *The Treasury: The Evolution of a British Institution* (London, 1969). This contains a 25-page bibliography of Treasury history.

J. C. Sainty (ed.), *Officeholders in Modern Britain: Treasury Officials, 1660–1870* (London, 1972).

Gillian Sutherland (ed.), *Studies in the Growth of Nineteenth Century Government* (London, 1972).

M. Wright, *Treasury Control of the Civil Service, 1854–1874* (Oxford, 1969).

DOCUMENTS

1. Treasury control asserted: Treasury Minutes, 1667–8

A series of Treasury Minutes reveals the determination of the 1667 Treasury Commission to secure acknowledgement of its authority from the King, the Privy Council and the Secretaries of State.

FROM: *Calendar of Treasury Books, 1667–1668*, edited by W. A. Shaw (London, 1905), pp. 2–3, 35, 46, 61, 66, 67, 85, 91, 111, 114, 129, 135, 226, 257, 277.

[1667]

May 30. Application to be made to His Majesty that before any warrant be signed by His Majesty for issuing money or charging the revenue or making any grant of any part thereof my Lords be acquainted with the address made to His Majesty concerning it, and make their report of their opinion to him as to the matter of fact and as to the condition and present state of the revenue. (Granted, and order given to the Secretaries to observe it.)

July 12. Ordered that the King be moved not to pass any more Privy Seals for discharge of [the fee of £1,095 from] Baronets: but that the money be actually answered into the Receipt of the Exchequer.

July 26. The King to be moved that he sign nothing for secret service but what really is so.

August 14. The King to be moved in Council against granting more places for life.

August 19. On Dr Creighton's business the King to be again moved against reversions, that my Lords may have opportunity to prefer such as merit . . .

August 21. On the order from the King about Holman's grant of the Receivership of Oxford and Berks the King is to be moved to declare that he will give no more of these places for life.

September 17. *Resolved:* that the King be moved that no warrant be tendered to His Majesty by either of the Secretaries for anything relating to the revenue.

September 24. *Memorandum.* The King to be moved about his verbal order to Sir John Denham without any further examination . . .; that such things pass not but by regular way of examination, so that his Majesty be not taken by surprise.

October 28. Ordered that all docquets for the Great Seal and Privy Seal be for the future signed by my Lords themselves.

October 31. The King to be moved in Council that the Secretaries sign nothing relating to the Customs or aught else of the revenue; but that all such matters begin in the Treasury, and so go hence to His Majesty for signature.

November 27. Sir Robert Long reports that the Privy Council did not use the words 'direct' or 'order' in any order to the Lord Treasurer for money unless when the Treasurer applied to them; as when he would have a bargain confirmed, &c., by the Council: otherwise the Council only used the words 'pray' or 'desire'. Sir John Nicholas to be acquainted herewith by Sir George Downing.

December 3. Complaint to be made to the King in Council of the warrant for Sir Dan. Hervy for hay for New Park, countersigned by Secretary Morice: as having been begun without the privity of my Lords, and not having been presented to them.

[1668]

January 13. Write the Lord Keeper to give notice to my Lords of any reversions of places come to him relating to the revenue.

February 18. The Order of Council for regulating the question of the King's signature as between the Treasury Lords and the Secretaries of State is to be written fair on a board and hung up in the Treasury Chamber.

March 13. Ordered that in all leases and acts of bounty there be inserted a clause of resumption at pleasure. The lease to be void when otherwise penned. This to be moved in Council.

2. Treasury control confirmed: Orders in Council, 1667–89

The Order in Council of 31 January 1668 (written out on a board and hung up in the Treasury) is the fundamental statement of Treasury authority, appealed to and re-asserted in the face of all challenges.

FROM Privy Council Register, 2 October 1667 to 28 August 1668, Public Record Office, P.C. 2/60 pp. 46, 157–8, 176–7.

[a] 1 November 1667

It was this day ordered by his Majesty in Council that neither of his principal Secretaries of State nor any other person whatsoever do at any time hereafter prepare or offer to his Majesty for his royal signature any grant, order or warrant relating to his Majesty's Customs, or any other branch of his revenue unless the business first take rise and begin with the Lords Commissioners of the Treasury or the Lord Treasurer for the time being, and that they be acquainted with and consenting to the same.

[b] 31 January 1668

It was this day ordered by his Majesty in Council that the ensuing rules and orders relating unto the procuring his Majesty's royal signature to any warrants for payment of money out of his Majesty's Treasury, and all grants of bounty or grace, and other gifts and grants, should be procured and pass henceforward according to the form and method hereafter prescribed, and not otherwise.

(1) That all offices belonging to his Majesty's revenue and all other offices formerly disposed of by the Lord Treasurer, or by his recommendation, pass by the Commissioners of his Majesty's Treasury as they have anciently done, and they to countersign what his Majesty signs therein.

That other offices passing by the Secretaries of State or by any other officers, pass with this caution, that they include not in the warrants any other fee, or salary, than the ancient fee in King James's time.

(2) That all warrants for privy seals for money to be imprested to the Treasurers of any of his Majesty's offices, as the Navy, Household, Guards, etc, whether for ordinary or extraordinary service, pass by the Commissioners of his Majesty's Treasury, and they to countersign.

(3) That all orders and warrants for regulation of any matter either in the Exchequer or any branch of his Majesty's revenue, or any regulation of any office for managing his Majesty's expense, pass by the Commissioners of his Majesty's Treasury.

(4) That all warrants and privy seals for pensions of grace and free gifts or other beneficial grants pass by the Secretaries of State, but with this regulation, that they present none to his Majesty's signature until a petition have first been signed by the petitioner in which he shall set forth the value of the thing sued for, which petition shall be transmitted to the Commissioners of the Treasury for them to report in writing to his Majesty their knowledge or opinion of that matter, and if need be, to inform his Majesty of the State of his treasure or revenue with other circumstances of his profit or disadvantage in that matter before his Majesty be engaged by his signature to consent to any such favour to the party petitioning, and that if a warrant shall after such report be granted, the said report and the date thereof be mentioned in the preamble of the warrant.

(5) That warrants for secret service pass by the Secretaries of State but that they be restrained to such things as indeed are so, and that other payments go not under that name which, after having been paid under the notion of secret service and perhaps in another man's name, may rise again afterwards and obtain a second payment under its proper name or a new fiction.

(6) That the Secretaries of State draw no warrants for release of any forfeiture relating to Excise, Customs or any other way touching his Majesty's treasure or revenue, until a report of the state of it have been presented to his Majesty from the Commissioners of his Majesty's Treasury.

(7) That the Secretaries of State forbear drawing any warrants directed to any of his Majesty's offices, [such] as the Navy, Household, paymaster of Guards or other offices for provision of which distinct Treasurers are appointed for the issuing any sums of money by the said Treasurers or offices, upon any extraordinary occasions, or for pensions, or free gifts, whereby his Majesty's treasure is issued without any privy seal, and without the privity of the Commissioners of his Majesty's Treasury, and by it the officers may become indebted, the money which should defray the necessary charge of the said offices being diverted to other uses by such warrants; the like caution to be used as to warrants for delivery of plate in the Jewel House, unless to Ambassadors or other [of] the King's officers on account, to be returned, and not as free gift.

(8) That the passing patents by immediate warrant may be restrained to such services as necessarily require it and that no grants for the benefit of particular persons may be so passed, and in case any such shall come to the Great Seal by immediate warrant that the Lord Keeper be enjoined to return them.

That all letters, orders, warrants, etc., into Ireland for disposing any of his Majesty's treasure or revenue in that kingdom, not comprised in the civil and military lists there established, may be first communicated to his Majesty's Commissioners of the Treasury in England, that his Majesty may receive their opinion in writing before he be engaged by his signature.

[c] 12 February 1668

All things relating to the Treasury in England or Ireland to be immediately referred to the Lords Commissioners of the Treasury, from whence it may come again to the Council Board, in case the matter be of such a nature as they cannot or would not willingly give their determination therein.

[d] FROM Privy Council Register, Public Record Office, P.C. 2/65 p. III.

28 January 1676

His Majesty having been pleased to declare in Council that by reason of the great anticipations upon his revenue and for preservation of the due payment thereof he finds himself necessitated to make a suspension upon some part of his yearly expense, and having communicated to this board a scheme for regulating the same accordingly, to commence from the first day of this instant January and to continue until the 31st day of March, 1677, it was this day ordered by his Majesty in Council that the said scheme of expense which is hereto annexed shall be the rule for the payments of money to all the uses therein set down during the time aforesaid, and that the Lord High Treasurer of England do govern himself by the same scheme and make payment of no greater sums than are therein expressed to any of the uses therein named, wherein the public payments are to be preferable to the rest, and that each proper officer do receive his Majesty's direction in writing under his royal sign manual for the particular payments to each of the said uses.

This limitation nevertheless to be understood and intended, that such persons from whom any part of their salaries, board wages, or other just perquisites shall in the said time be suspended shall have a good right to and may claim the same as formerly immediately from and after the expiration of this order.

And in case it shall happen that his Majesty's occasions within the said time should necessarily require greater or other payments to any of the uses in the scheme annexed or to some other use or uses not therein mentioned, it is provided that the Lord High Treasurer shall make such payments from time to time (over and besides the particular sums limited in the scheme annexed) by warrant from his Majesty under his royal sign manual and not otherwise.

[e]   FROM Privy Council Register, Public Record Office, P.C. 2/68 p. 385.

11 February 1680

It was this day ordered by his Majesty in Council that for the future no grant whatsoever wherein his Majesty's treasure or revenue may be any way concerned be permitted to pass the Privy Seal until the Lords Commissioners of the Treasury or Lord Treasurer of England for the time being shall have signified to the Lord Privy Seal, by attesting a docquet, that they have been made acquainted therewith and do approve thereof, and of this his Majesty's pleasure the Lord Privy Seal is to take notice.

[f]   FROM Treasury Outletters, General, Public Record Office, T 27/6 pp. 181–2.

14 February 1681

Lords Commissioners of the Treasury to Lord Conway, Secretary of State

Our very good Lord, We find by an Order made by His Majesty in Council the 31st of January 1677 [sic for 1667/8] it is required that all letters, orders, warrants, etc., unto Ireland for disposing any [of] His Majesty's treasure or revenue in that kingdom, not comprised in the Civil and Military Lists there established, should be first communicated to the Commissioners of His Majesty's Treasury in England that His Majesty might receive their opinion in writing before he be engaged by his signature, and we being informed that some letters and directions in such cases as aforesaid had nevertheless been formerly obtained and sent into Ireland without our knowledge and contrary to that Order we have taken this occasion to acquaint your Lordship with the said Order of Council and do desire that your Lordship will be pleased in your station to see it complied with. We do also desire that what returns shall be made upon such letters, orders, warrants, etc. from the Lord Lieutenant may also be communicated to us before any further progress be made therein to the end we may have it in our power from time to time to represent to His Majesty matters of convenience or inconvenience to his service when such directions are desired relating to His Majesty's revenue or treasure in that kingdom. And so we remain, our very good Lord, your Lordship's most humble servants.

[g] FROM Treasury Outletters, General, Public Record Office, T 27/9 p. 242.

9 January 1686

Henry Guy, Secretary to the Treasury, to the Commissioners of the Privy Seal:

My Lord and Gent.

My Lord Treasurer desires you to take care that no grant pass under the Privy Seal of any lands or money or any other thing relating to his Majesty's revenue, nor that pardons of fines, forfeitures, etc. do pass the Seal until his Lordship have first signed the docquets of such grants or pardons according to Orders of Council heretofore made in that behalf. I am, my Lord and Gent., your most faithful humble servant.

[h] FROM Treasury Minute Book, Public Record Office, T 29/7 p. 47.

18 June 1689

Present: Lord Godolphin, Sir H. Capell, Mr Hampden

His Majesty came in. His Majesty being moved upon the docquets for the Commissioners of Prizes, that the warrant ought to have begun at this Board, was pleased to declare his pleasure, that it should do so but in regard that that business required a present despatch His Majesty did direct the Commission should proceed at present but that the right of this Board should be saved and that for the future such warrants should begin here.

3. The rule of 'Specific Sanction': the Order in Council of 17 June 1667.

Although issued in the emergency of the Dutch attack on the Medway, this Order defines a fundamental principle of Treasury control: that the Treasury may regulate expenditure in detail, even though that expenditure may have received a general sanction from the Crown.

FROM Privy Council Register, May 1666 to September 1667, PRO. PC 2/59 f. 233.

17 June 1667

Whereas the present posture of his Majesty's affairs requires that his treasure should with all imaginable care be reserved for his Majesty's most necessary and pressing occasions, and not be paid according to the ordinary rules of the several offices and treasuries from which his Majesty's treasure is issued until some greater plenty of money may give way to the satisfying the creditors of the several offices, the safety of his Majesty's government being first provided for; it is therefore ordered that the several treasurers and other persons who receive money by way of imprest . . . do forbear making any payments without directions from the Commissioners of his Majesty's Treasury, who are hereby authorised and required to give and prescribe such rules to them as they shall judge for his Majesty's service, except only in relation to such payments as are, or shall be charged and registered upon the Acts of Additional Aid, Poll Bill, and Eleven Months' Tax. And to that end the said treasurers and other persons are hereby ordered and required that they do weekly send to the Commissioners of his Majesty's Treasury a certificate of the several sums of money by them received and paid the instant week, and what is in remain; and likewise that they bring to the said Commissioners a list of such payments as they propose to themselves to pay the week succeeding and judge to be of necessity, to the end that the said Commissioners of the Treasury may direct what shall be paid that succeeding week, and what shall be deferred: to which the said treasurers are to conform . . . [with the exception of the Navy Treasurer's payments on seamen's 'tickets', wages, pilotage charges and ordnance.]

4. Treasury control of departmental estimates: the Navy, 1676

Extensive in theory, the Treasury's power to control departmental expenditure was often limited in practice, and the Navy was the biggest of the spending departments. Danby (a former Treasurer of the Navy) was determined to bring it under control.

FROM *A Descriptive Catalogue of the Naval Manuscripts in the Pepysian Library at Magdalene College, Cambridge*, IV, edited by J. R. Tanner. Navy Records Society, 1922–3; pp. 265–6.

Admiralty Journal, 15 January 1676

My Lord Treasurer was pleased to take notice to his Majesty of the necessity of bringing again into practice the ancient method of the navy, by which no works upon which any part of his Majesty's treasure is to be issued are to be entered upon without an estimate of the charge thereof first prepared, and signed by the Officers of the Navy, then by the Lord High Admiral, and afterwards presented and approved of by his Majesty in Council, and a privy seal granted thereupon warranting the Lord Treasurer to issue money for the same. The non-observance of which, and consequently the entering upon works without particular estimates and sums especially appointed thereto has (as his Lordship was pleased to shew) occasioned (among other ill effects) that the charge of the navy has never had any certain measures taken of it, to the leading his Majesty insensibly to a much greater expense, and contracting upon himself a much greater debt than probably would ever otherwise have been; And therefore moved, that for the time to come the said ancient method of proceeding by estimate be taken up and strictly conformed to, upon every occasion of expense not already provided for by some privy seal. Which his Majesty was pleased with the advice of my Lords, fully to agree to and direct both their Lordships and the Officers of the Navy to see duly observed.

5. The Treasury on revenue and expenditure: the report of 20 October 1668.

In this careful analysis of the King's revenue and liabilities, the Treasury Commissioners' attempt to bring home to Charles II the gravity of his situation. The clarity of their exposition owes much to their success in marshalling the king's liabilities 'in course' for payment in strict sequence.

FROM BM Add. MSS. 28,078 ff. 11–15, 'Scheme for settling his Majesty's expense upon the several Branches of his Majesty's Revenue, presented to his Majesty by the Lords Commissioners of his Treasury,' 20 October 1668.

May it please your Majesty, in pursuance of your Majesty's commands signified by your Orders in Council of the 22nd of July and 26th of September last requiring us to cause the particulars of the report of the Committee for Retrenchments to be put in execution, we have taken into consideration the present state of your Majesty's revenue thereby the better to assign supplies from the particular branches of your Majesty's revenue to the several issues especially committed to our care by your Majesty's aforesaid Orders and have with submission to your Majesty's pleasure proposed the assignations hereunto annexed which we humbly present to your Majesty as the best we could do considering the straitness and difficulties of your Majesty's revenue at the present, for the success of which we dare not be answerable to your Majesty foreseeing that many of your Majesty's officers and servants may complain of the remoteness of divers of the assignments, and therefore for the right information of your Majesty and for preventing such complaints we humbly take leave to annexe likewise a list of the several branches of your Majesty's revenue, and under each head have put the payments assigned on them for one year's expense whereby it will evidently appear to your Majesty that we have gone as far as the several branches of your Majesty's revenue would bear, and that the overplus of the several branches above the assignations with which they are charged will fall short of supplying those payments which are charged upon the Exchequer in general.

§ Customs. The rent of the Customs is paid by £32,000 *per mensem*, eight thousand pounds whereof is applied to the paying of tallies struck upon the late Farm of which there remain unpaid to the value of £214,213 4s 10d, which at £8,000 *per mensem* will not be paid in two years time.

So that, that present part of the Customs can be of no use to your Majesty's expense either by receipt or credit, none being willing to lend money upon assignments so remote, especially upon a revenue depending upon your Majesty's life (which God preserve.)

One other part consisting of £8,000 *per mensem* is assigned for repaying the £200,000 advanced by the present Farmers of which the sum of £112,000 being already paid, and the remainder at the rate of £8,000 *per mensem* extinguishing the debt by the month of September next, we hope that it may be rendered useful to your Majesty for borrowing money thereon monthly (vizt.) when the debt of one month shall be paid off, we hope the money may be borrowed again, and for this hope we have some encouragement by discourse we have had by the Farmers, though we dare not deliver it to your Majesty as a certainty, because it depends on the minds and affairs of others.

Out of the remaining £16,000 *per mensem* we reserve £3,000 *per mensem*, making £36,000 *per annum* wherewith to pay the constant payments hereunder mentioned (vizt.):

[26 items, mainly pensions and salaries, including £12,000 p.a. for the Judges and £11,000 p.a. for the Masters of Chancery.]

So the total charged upon the £3,000 *per mensem* of the £16,000 of the Customs being £33,252 0s 6d, there will remain thereof to be paid into the Exchequer for your Majesty's other occasions £2,747 19s 6d. So there will remain of your Majesty's Customs applicable to your Majesty's other present occasions as a fund of credit, notwithstanding the anticipations at present upon that part, about £264,000 – upon which is intended to be charged according to the paper annexed for the year beginning the first of January next – for the Navy, £200,000; for the Ordnance, £25,000; for Tangier, £55,000; for the Treasury of the Chamber, £20,000; for the Great Wardrobe, £16,000; for Ambassadors, both English and foreign, £27,000 – so that the total charged on the Customs being £343,500, exceeds the sum of £264,000 before mentioned applicable to your Majesty's use £79,500. So that from this branch of your Majesty's Customs nothing can be expected to come into your Majesty's Exchequer for paying any of those sums charged upon the Exchequer in general, though a considerable part of your Majesty's debt upon the old tallies will likewise be paid off in that time.

§ Excise. The rent of your Majesty's Excise being £340,000 *per annum* is at present anticipated at the least to the value of £455,547 8s 9d in so much that Sir Stephen Fox sometime since declared as well to your Majesty as to us, that unless the assignments formerly charged on that branch might be lessened, it would be impossible for him to provide money for the pay of your Majesty's soldiers, which is the reason why we have transferred Tangier to be paid on the Customs, and intend to charge on the Excise, for your Majesty's Household, £90,000;

for your Majesty's Forces, £182,673, which we understand from Sir Stephen Fox to be the just sum of the establishment. [Further items, for the Duke of York, Monmouth, the Excise office, etc.] So the total charge upon that office being £294,413, there will remain overplus £45,587, which nevertheless cannot come to pay any payments in your Majesty's Exchequer but must according to the rule be applied to the paying of the anticipations in courses.

§ Chimney money. The Chimney money stands charged at the present with an anticipation of at least £446,677 which is to be paid in course, so nothing can be expected thence for the supply of any present occasions.

§ Lands, fee-farm rents, &c. Your Majesty's lands, fee-farm rents, etc., are about £96,000 *per annum* including the jointures of the Queen Consort and Queen Mother, upon which we have resolved to charge [the Queen's and Queen Mother's households, Ambassadors, intelligence, Robes, the Jewel House, gifts, the Master of Horse, etc.] So that from this branch of your Majesty's revenue may be expected towards the supply of your other occasions, £11,600, out of which somewhat will fall short for Schools, Hospitals, Churches, etc., paid in the counties by ancient grants.

§ [Other petty revenues – coinage of tin, First Fruits and Tenths of Clergy, profits of the law courts, petty customs farms, the Post Office – are all over-charged with expenses.] So nothing can be expected thence.

So the total of moneys which may be depended upon for defraying such sums as are by former orders yet unpaid, or by the design of the annexed proposal intended to be charged on the Exchequer will amount unto £17,567 19s 6d. And if your Majesty shall resolve to stop the whole of those pensions, etc., before mentioned, concerning which your Majesty's pleasure is herein desired, then the whole will amount unto £21,527 19s 6d.

§ Exchequer in general. The sums chargeable upon the Exchequer may be according to the best computation we can make as follows – [24 items for official fees, courtiers' pensions, gamekeepers, tents, etc., totalling £59,894 19s 10¾d]. Besides interest of money borrowed, defalcations on several branches of your Majesty's revenue, and expenses not foreseen, estimated by your Majesty's Order of the 22nd of July at £250,000 and by that of the 26th of September at £200,000, for which we are not able to assign any particular funds.

[The report concludes:]

Now in regard that this present state of your Majesty's revenue may appear to differ from that supposition, upon which your Majesty's Order of the 22nd of July may seem to be grounded, we humbly take leave to offer to your Majesty some reasons upon which we conceive the appearing difference may arise – vizt. that all the branches of your Majesty's income being there cast into one total of £1,030,000 appear to have been reckoned useful to your Majesty's present support. Whereas upon examination it is found that the Chimney money, which in that computation is reckoned at £170,000 is wholly useless to your Majesty's present occasions, though in the mean time it payeth off a debt lying upon your Majesty. Likewise the Customs were therein reckoned as if the whole £400,000 were useful to your Majesty's present support, whereas we cannot hope for this year to use more than £300,000 thereof, though the other £100,000 be in the meanwhile employed for paying off a debt which lies upon your Majesty.

A great part of the profits arising from alienations, all the profits of the seals of both the Benches, sixpenny writs in Chancery, all moneys paid into the Hanaper, the greater part of the post fines and Green wax, issues of jurors, and sheriffs proffers and payments, though part of your Majesty's revenue, as is mentioned in your Order of the 22nd of July, yet are they by constant practice applied to defraying the charges of several Courts of Justice, etc., by the direction and allowance either of the Lord Keeper or the Pipe respectively, and therefore not applicable to the particular branches of the expenses enjoined in the said Order to be provided for. The profits reserved out of the Post Office are since disposed by your Majesty's Order.

In your Majesty's Order of the 22nd of July no provision was made for the payment of wages or salaries to any such officers or servants as ought to be paid in the Exchequer, Customs, or any other branch of your Majesty's revenue, nor for payment of Coldstreamers, and such as were instrumental in your Majesty's escape, nor for the establishment of Jamaica, nor President of Wales, besides pensions to several persons and sums of ready money directed by your Majesty's Order of the 26th of September to be paid.

These we humbly conceive to be some of the reasons why we are doubtful that your Majesty's revenue will not be found capable to perform all what is expected from it by your Majesty's said Orders of the 22nd of July and 26th of September.

But the principal reason is the great anticipation under a devouring interest lying upon the Excise and Customs, which as it is by the interest a very great expense to your Majesty, so by the anticipation it subjects your Majesty's occasions to the will of others, whilst your Majesty is forced to depend upon loans.

If any other means could be found by which those branches might be freed from anticipations, they would be well near sufficient to perform what is enjoined by your Majesty's Order of the 22nd of July, and for other parts of your Majesty's expense we should hope by the other smaller branches to struggle with them, until the anticipations on the Chimney money might likewise be extinguished, which being once accomplished, we should not doubt but your Majesty's revenue would perform with ease and satisfaction what your Majesty's ordinary affairs might require.

In the mean time as we shall according to our duty use our utmost endeavours to prevent all inconveniences which may arise from your Majesty's wants, so we hold it not less our duty to lay before your Majesty the true state of your revenue, that so your Majesty may be pleased to give such directions as in your wisdom shall seem fit.

Having heretofore frequently given your Majesty an account of the particulars of the great debt in which your Majesty is engaged as well in the several offices of your expense as by loans on your Majesty's revenue, we do not at present trouble your Majesty with a repetition thereof, this representation being intended only to shew your Majesty how the state of your revenue will stand in order to one year's future expense, grounded on the late Orders of Council.

All which is humbly submitted to your Majesty.

Albemarle   Ashley   T. Clifford   W. Coventry   J. Duncombe

6. Public credit: the Treasury advertises 'payment in course'.

FROM *The London Gazette*, Nos. 135, 245, and 411.[1]

[a] 28 February–4 March 1667

I am desired to publish this Advice, That such persons as have lent Moneys for His Majesties Service in the present War, upon the credit of the late Act for 1250000 L. whose Orders are of the Numbers 99,100 and so forwards, to the number of 126. are to take notice, That there remains Money in Bank for them, at the Receit of his Majesties Exchequer, ready to pay both their Principal and Interest; And are therefore desired to cause their respective Orders and Tallies to be brought into the Exchequer, and to give their Acquittances that they may receive their Loanes and Interest according to the said Act: And that all persons whose Orders do in course succeed the aforesaid Numbers, shall be paid as fast as the Tax comes in upon the same Act, as they stand Registred in their course.

[b] 19 March–23 March 1668

Whereas the Tallies struck heretofore upon the Farmers of His Majesties Customs, have used to be paid promiscuously, without any certain Order, the Lords Commissioners of his Majesties Treasury have lately caused so many of the Tallies on the Customs unpaid, as have come to their knowledge, to be registred in a certain course in which they are to be paid; which Register is to be seen, either in Sir Robert Long's Office, or at the Customs House; where all persons concerned may see the Course in which they are to be paid: and if any persons have Tallies unpaid, which are not in the said List, they are desired within 14 dayes from the date hereof, to shew their said Tallies to Sir George Downing, that he may take notice thereof, to the end they may be put in a Course of payment after those already registred, least otherwise any new Charge upon the said Revenue exclude them.

[c] 21 October–25 October 1669

The Officers of the Receipt of His Majesties Exchequer having paid the 1153 Order in number registred on the Act for 1250000 l. shall proceed to the payment of the subsequent Orders as the remains of that Act and the remains of the first Moneth of the Eleven Moneths Tax shall be brought in.

---

[1] Spelling, capitalization and punctuation unaltered.

Also the said Officers are come to the payment of the 1344 Order Registred on the Eleven Moneths Tax, and shall goe on to the payment of the following Orders as the Money shall come in.

Moreover they hereby give notice, That they are come to the payment of the 167th Order Registred on the Countrey-Excise; and that there are yet divers Orders preceding that number, which the parties concerned are desired to bring into the Exchequer that they may receive their Money due upon them which is reserved in Bank.

The said Officers have also paid Forty thousand pounds in part of the first Order Registred on the Hearth-Money, and will proceed in their payments of that and the ensueing Orders on that Register as the Money shall be brought in.

7. The Treasury Board at work: a day's business, 22 July 1667.

FROM *Calendar of Treasury Books, 1667–1668*, edited by W. A. Shaw (London, 1905), pp. 42–3, corrected from the original Minute Book, PRO T 29/1 pp. 78–90 – numbered for cross-reference.

July 22nd 1667

Monday afternoon Present: Duke of Albemarle, Lord Ashley, Mr Controller, Sir W. Coventry, Sir John Duncombe.

[1][1] A warrant for Sir Edm. Pooley to substitute a Deputy for his Receivership of Norfolk.

[2] The farmers of the Customs appeared about their new patent for the Customs, and their striking tallies for their £200,000. That the Lords will first read their patent.

They complain of great quantities of Tobacco planted this year in England. The Lords desire them first to put what they say in writing, and that the business be represented to the Council.

[3] Referred to Sir Robert Long, Sir Philip Warwick, and Sir George Downing to draw up a state of the revenue as charged when the Lords entered upon the Treasury.

[4] Sir John Shaw moves that process stop against him and the rest of the Dunkirk paymasters. Ordered that process be stopped.

[5] Farmers of the Customs, their patent delivered to them to be written in paper and margined; and that they present it against this day sennight; and that the day after they shall have an answer as to their tallies.

[6] Every Monday to be laid before the Lords what money ordered out of the Exchequer for the week ending Saturday before inclusive.

[7] The King to be moved about Mr Warren – Docquet for a prize ship.

[8] Mr Fenn to be spoke with about a privy seal for Sir George Carteret for the new companies of the maritime regiments for Mr Willes, &c.

[9] Earl of Bath's docquet for £1,000 for the King's laces to pass.

[10] That £2,000 p. week be issued to the Lord Anglesey to pay tickets and the officers of the Navy are desired to appoint some person to be present to distinguish seamen's and their relation's tickets from bought tickets, and to see the former first paid.

[11] The petition of Mrs Estcourt (relict of Mr Estcourt, late Receiver of the Hearth money of Wiltshire) read: that she must pay in the £261 10s by the 10th of August and process stopped till then.

---

[1] My numbering.

[12] Major Reeves book for arrears on Chimneys looked into. That he be here tomorrow at 3 afternoon.

[13] Mrs Moon called in about the quarter of a year of her allowance of £500 per annum in dispute during the Tin farmers patent. Mr Napier and the rest of the officers to be here when this settled, this day sennight.

[14] Mr Brown about nutmegs seized referred to the farmers of the Customs upon the Order of Council.

[15] Mr Copinger called in. That Mr Rawleigh pay up to the great Roll, and then he shall be discharged to make up his account by Michaelmas next.

[16] Sir George Downing reports the age of Mr Eccleston, present Receiver of the revenue for Suffolk, to be about 40 years. Mr Deering to be here Wednesday morning.

[17] Warrant for Mr Packer for £200 odd money upon Sir Robert Long his certificate due to him.

[18] Mr Mellish to be here with Sir Daniel Harvey or Sir Eliab Hervey when the arrears paid of Mr Hervey's receipt.

[19] Sir Paul Neil's petition read for several copyhold fines in the Duchy of Cornwall. Sir Charles Harbord to certify all fines on any of the King's lands and revenue of the Duchy of Cornwall since the King's coming in.

[20] That the Cofferer's certificate be monthly and to be brought in the first Monday after every month.

[21] The petition of the London farmers read praying the Lords' assistance to obtain an Act of Parliament for avoiding frauds in Excise. That they draw the heads for such an Act.

[22] Letter to Sir John Norton's Deputy that if he take not care of paying the arrears on the aids, he will be taken into custody.

[23] Sir John Wintour called in. That so soon as the Order of Council comes the Lords will settle this business.

[24] Letters to be written to all the Lords and noblemen's Ladies that have not paid their Chimney money to pay it by —. This written to avoid further trouble. These letters to be given to Major Reeves, and he to be spoken to about them.

[25] Letter to Sir Robert Long to certify what allowance given to public ministers of all ranks in Queen Elizabeth's, King James's, King Charles I's and II's time.

[26] Letter to Sir Edward Griffith to know whether he hath taken up any money at interest, and what interest he hath paid.

[27] Mr Lawrence to take the person of Cadwallader Jones by a special bailiff. To consider first with him about it; he to be sent for.

8. The inauguration of Treasury records: Treasury Minutes, 1667–9.

These Minutes reflect the proliferation of Treasury memoranda books which were essential to control of the Treasury Order system of 'payment in course'.

FROM *Calendar of Treasury Books, 1667–1668*, edited by W. A. Shaw (London, 1905), pp. 1, 5, 37, 268, 285, 317, 376, 378, 380, 381, 442, 450; *Calendar of Treasury Books, 1669–1672* (i) pp. 143–4.

[1667]

May 27. Ordered that Sir George Downing, the Secretary attending this Commission, should keep a book singly for registering the brief notes he should take for framing any orders upon or pursuing other their Lordships' directions; which notes at their next meeting, and before they entered upon any new business, he should acquaint them with and what was done thereupon, and so from time to time what progress was made upon any directions then unperfected: that he should enter the names of the Commissioners present at every meeting and constantly observe this method.

June 1. Sir George Downing to write to Sir Philip Warwick to send to the Treasury Chamber such books and papers as he hath which may be for the use and service of my Lords.

June 3. A register book to be kept in the Treasury Office of all tallies struck on any branch of the revenue that they may be paid orderly.

July 16. Ordered that whatever directions the King gives upon any application of my Lords to him they be entered in a book apart.

[1668]

March 3. Sir George Downing to keep a distinct registry of all such as are on each branch of the revenue. Distinct books hereof to be prepared, and one for the rest of the revenue.

March 27. Every Monday certificates to be made out of the books in the Treasury of what warrants are granted on the Exchequer and elsewhere to the preceding Friday of each week.

May 13. A book of establishments for the new retrenchments [is ordered to be kept]: establishments to be made and a letter sent to each office to know if they have received the King's order for the retrenchments. Charnock to make a book of all the establishments.

July 8. Charnock to keep a book of all petitions [to state] when read and what is done on them.

Charnock to make a great book of orders wherein are to be particularly set down heads for each branch of the revenue.

July 9.   Charnock to get a book for all accounts that are declared and enter their passing in it.

July 10.   A register book to be kept for orders of the Privy Council. Charnock is to number every book of each sort, whereby it may be seen which is first and which second of a sort.

September 22.   A register book [is to be kept in the Treasury] for the Customs, in which there is to be a leaf for each month on which each warrant for that month is to be charged. Charnock to prepare it under the direction of Sir G. Downing.

October 5.   Charnock to keep a particular book in which an entry is to be made of all accounts that are declared; expressing the day on which and for what time.

[1669]

October 8.   Ordered that there be a list made of such offices as are required to return certificates with the respective times when [such returns are to be made]. Ordered that this be posted on a board and hung up in the office and Charnock is from time to time to inform my Lords who are defective in returns.

A book to be kept in which is to be entered the total [issues or assignments] charged each year on each branch of the revenue and on the Exchequer in general, as also what part of what is so charged remains unpaid.

9. The 'ancient course' of the Exchequer: the duties of the King's Remembrancer.

The King's Remembrancer carried a heavy responsibility for expediting the audit of accounts in the Upper Exchequer. The emphasis, in this treatise, on what he *ought* to do, is a clear hint of the laxity revealed in Doc. 11 below.

FROM BM Add. MSS. 24,689, supplemented and corrected from Egerton MSS. 2436.

A Book of all the Several Offices of the Court of Exchequer, Together with the names of the present officers, in whose gift, and how admitted, with a brief collection of the chief heads of what every officer usually doth by virtue of his office, according to the state of the Exchequer at this day [*ca.* 1702].

The King's Remembrancer

Richard Fanshaw, Esq., is the present officer and holdeth his place, by Letters Patent under the Great Seal of England, is in the King's gift, and admitted by taking oath in open court before the Barons of the Exchequer; and he hath yearly a fee out of the Receipt of the Exchequer of £55 17s 4d.

He hath eight clerks or attorneys within his office in his own gift, which are admitted by himself, and an oath administered before him, by virtue whereof they enjoy their places during their lives.

All English Bills within the Exchequer are in this office, and the proceedings thereof much agreeing to that of the Chancery, as by Bill, Answer, Replication, and Rejoinder. The cause being at issue, witnesses are examined in court before the Barons, or by commission in the country. And being ready for hearing, if set down, to be heard by the Lord Treasurer, Chancellor of the Exchequer, or Barons. The writs are first Subpoena, upon not appearing Affidavit is made of serving of the Subpoena, upon which an Attachment goes out of course, then an Alias and a Pluries, afterwards a writ of Proclamation, and lastly Commission of Rebellion. Brief notes of all orders pronounced either in the Exchequer Chamber upon hearings, or in the outer Chamber upon motions, are taken by the King's Remembrancer himself, or such of his office as he shall appoint to do it . . .

At certain days prefixed to the Term, he ought to call to accompt, in open court, all the great accomptants, as the Treasurer of the Chamber, Cofferer, Paymaster of the Works, Master of the Robes, Master of the Great Wardrobe, Clerk of the Hanaper, Treasurer of the Navy and [Treasurer of] the Ordnance, Victualler of the Navy,

Paymaster General of the Army and Garrisons, and such like; and all Collectors of Customs and Subsidies, and all searchers for the moiety of all forfeitures.

He receiveth the duplicates or rolls of assignment or Subsidy rolls of all the counties of England and calleth to an accompt all the Receivers, Collectors of Subsidies and Fifteenths as they are appointed and certified into his office by the respective Commissioners everywhere for the assessing and levying of the same according to their days of payment appointed them by the statute whereby they are charged and payable.

He receiveth certificates half-yearly from the writer of the tallies (called the Auditor of the Receipt) of all money imprested out of the Exchequer for which men ought to come to accompt.

He maketh out process of Distringas (or ought so to do) against all accomptants that are slack, to bring them to accompt, and such as come not in upon the first process against them, he is to issue an Alias Distringas, and then a Pluries, and then a Capias to take the bodies to compel them to an accompt, and may also make out process against lands, goods, and tenements where need shall require, which is done by order of court.

He also takes all Bonds and Recognizances to the King's use, of all Sheriffs, Customers, Receivers, Bailiffs, and all other persons whatsoever that are bound in the Exchequer . . .

He receiveth all Sheriffs Foreign Accompts, Accompts of Escheators, and accompts of Customers, Receivers and Collectors of Assignments, Subsidies and Fifteenths and other Aids and impositions granted in Parliament; Post Office, Wine licence and Coinage Duty, &c; and of the Treasurer of the Navy and Ordnance, Victualler of the Navy, Cofferer, &c., and taketh the total of the debts due thereupon and transfers them to the Treasurer's Remembrancer to be there likewise entered to the end that the debts may be put into the view of every year's remembrance that he to whom it appertains may make process upon the same, that no super or debt be suffered to be out of process until it be discharged. This article being performed would be much for Her Majesty's service.

He ought to inform the Lord Treasurer or Lords Commissioners of the Treasury, or Chancellor, or Barons, or the King's Attorney of all debts and arrearages, &c., and all suits and pleas in his office depending thereupon, to drive things to an issue for the recovery of the King's debt.

He sendeth every Hilary and Trinity term several parchment blank books to all the Customers, Comptrollers, Surveyors, Collectors and Searchers of all the ports of England and Wales, for the entry of all the Customs and Subsidies, and afterwards receiveth the same again by the oath of the said officers, in open court, or before one of the Barons, that they have made all true entries of the same as they ought to do, which are returned with all bonds entered into with [the Crown] by any masters of ships in the said ports touching their trade from port to port and performance of the condition therein expressed . . .

10. The Treasury chivies the Exchequer: Treasury Minutes, 1667–8.

The Treasury Commission of 1667 made vigorous efforts to speed and improve the processes of Exchequer audit, and dealt severely with defaulters. They procured an Act levying a 12 per cent penalty on persons detaining public money beyond the date due for its remittance to the Exchequer (19 & 20 Chas. II. c. 7).

FROM *Calendar of Treasury Books, 1667–1668*, edited by W. A. Shaw, pp. 2, 6, 15, 21, 25, 27, 34, 39, 76–7, 97, 150, 154, 224, 295, 331, 415, 417, 472, 480, 486.

[1667]

May 27. Write the Auditors of the Imprests for an account what accomptants have passed their accounts and how far and what moneys remain in their hands unaccounted for. The like to the Auditors of the revenue and of First Fruits and Tenths.

June 3. The officers of the Exchequer called in and told that their ordinary hours of attendance are not sufficient while receipts and payments are so great as at present; and as complaint is made by Alderman Backwell of a refusal to attend longer they are to take care that there be no further occasion of complaint of that kind.

The King's Remembrancer's officers to bring in writing to my Lords their way of proceeding to get in the King's money from accomptants.

June 20. Write the King's Remembrancer to press to accompt all treasurers upon imprest, and to issue process against all who have not passed their accompt to this year.

June 28. Write the Clerk of the Pipe to send an account of the foot of the accounts of all accomptants against whom process is now taken; and to give an accompt after the end of every term what has been done on said process.

July 2. Auditor Persons called in. It is ordered that all accompts when stated and sworn be brought before my Lords to be passed.

Write the Auditors to certify the state of the accompts to this day of all the receivers of the King's revenue.

July 3. Ordered that all deputies to the auditors be sworn before they enter on their office. Write the auditors to send in the names of their deputies.

July 11. The Auditors of the Imprests called in and are desired to be very strict in passing accounts.

July 17. That a day be appointed to heare the Auditors and the Pipe and settle the carryeing all accounts when finished by the Auditors to the Pipe.

Memorandum. That in the beginning of the next term my Lords meet in the Treasury Chamber at Westminster and dine there with the Barons [of the Exchequer] to settle all matters of order among the officers of the Exchequer and what else may be of import to the King's service.

September 5. Sir Robert Long, Sir George Downing and Mr Sherwyn to confer with Sir Robert Crooke about the business of the Pipe. Sir Robert Long informs and complains that the Pipe make allowances by acquittances without tallies, as [for instance] in the Greenwax farm and by this means can never know what the revenue or farm makes. So [in the same way] the Pipe have put the sheriffs' proffers out of charge in the Great Roll. Ordered the Pipe should make no allowance but by the Lord Treasurer's [direction].

October 2. A table of the fees of the officers of the Exchequer to be brought to my Lords.

December 17. All interest accounts to be referred hereafter to Auditors Chislet and Aldworth. Auditor Phelips to deliver all interest papers to Aldworth, and to be suspended from the execution of his place till further order; my Lords not being satisfied with some accounts he has stated to them.

December 20. Write the Lord Keeper not to grant *habeas corpus* to any in prison for debt to the King.

[1668]

January 13. Auditor Aldworth to be made an Auditor of the Imprest for life, and to surrender his place of Auditor of the Revenue to Mr Chislett, who is to hold during pleasure.

Ordered that such of the Auditors as use deputies bring certificates of the proper swearing of such deputies.

April 8. Write the Auditors of the Imprest and the Auditors of the Revenue to certify on Thursday week what accompts are unpassed and not declared that ought to have been passed since 1660.

May 22. Thursday next to be for hearing accompts at 3 in the afternoon and Tuesday and Thursday in every following week to be for accompts, each Auditor to be heard according to his seniority and at least two Auditors to be heard in a day. This to be posted at the [Treasury] door.

August 17. Ordered that each Auditor of the revenue and of Imprests certify next Monday what Receivers have not yet brought in their accounts and who prosecute not the perfecting of same: my Lords noticing how slowly accounts are brought in by said Auditors to be declared.

August 18. Write the King's Remembrancer to certify what Receivers are returned by each Auditor for not bringing in and prosecuting their accounts, and what has been done thereupon towards compelling them. Also write all the Auditors of revenue and of Imprests that in stating all accounts of the Receivers they place 12 per cent upon them for so much of the King's money as they have detained in their hands beyond its time: as by the late Act.

November 4. Write the Auditors of Imprests for a certificate next Tuesday of what accounts have been declared since 1660 of the Treasurer of the Navy, the Victualler of the Navy and the Treasurer of the Ordnance, and what accounts of theirs are now depending before said auditors, what condition they are in, and why they have not been brought before my Lords.

November 11. Write the Barons of the Exchequer to hasten the declaring the accounts of the Royal and Additional Aids.

November 18. Write the officers of the Exchequer for a table to be made of all fees in the Exchequer. Calculation to be made how much is taken [in the shape of Exchequer fees on a money warrant] on each 1,000£: a dispute having arisen yesterday about the said fees.

A computation to be made of the charge the King is at in bringing in each part of his revenue.

11. Exchequer negligence denounced: [A] The Parliamentary Accounts Commission of 1702–3

Despite the Act of 1696 for the observance of the 'ancient course' of the Exchequer, the due processes of audit were still being neglected, but behind the Treasury's denunciation of the Auditors lay a political vendetta against the earl of Halifax, formerly Chancellor of the Exchequer and now Auditor of the Receipt.

FROM Minutes of the Commissioners of Public Accounts, 1702–3, Public Record Office, Treasury Miscellanea-Various, T 64/126, pp. 644, 655, 665, 674–8.

22 January 1703

In the evening a messenger from the House of Commons brought an order signed by the Clerk of the House for the Commissioners further to examine the Auditors and other officers of the Exchequer relating to the passing of the accounts for the public money, and to lay before the House what they shall find to be the cause that the accounts are not annually and duly passed according to the laws in that case, and through whose fault it hath happened.

23 January

Mr Auditor Bridges and Mr Moody attending pursuant to the precept of yesterday afternoon were acquainted that the occasion of sending to them was pursuant to an order of the House of Commons of yesterday . . .

Being sworn they were asked whether they had at all since 5 November 1688 certified to the Queen's Remembrancer the neglects of the annual accomptants who have not brought in their accompts to the Auditors according to the course of the Exchequer. To which Mr Auditor Bridges made answer, that he has as in duty bound, done as his predecessor did, that he has been a great while in the office and knew the method of it before, but that his predecessor never certified in that manner, but he has frequently certified to the Treasury as his predecessors did heretofore. That some of the accomptants being peers or privileged persons, the Treasury took it on themselves to direct what processes should be issued, after having called the Auditors before them to give them a state of the accounts of the several accomptants.

Mr Moody acquainted the Board, that he attended them formerly with copies of orders from the Treasury directing the Auditors to certify the state of the accounts to the Treasury.

Mr Auditor Bridges said that upon the Earl of Rochester's sending to the Auditors to advise with them about this matter of the accounts being so long behind, they were directed to certify the state of the accounts to the King's Remembrancer; that accordingly they did so for some time, viz. for about a year, certify jointly such state of the accounts to Mr Hall, the then King's Remembrancer, who thereupon issued out process against the several accomptants in arrears. But that method being (as he has heard) found inconvenient, the Remembrancer declined issuing out process without direction of the Treasury, and the Treasury directing that the Auditors should certify thither they never after certified to the Remembrancer, looking upon that subsequent direction to supersede the order for certifying to the Remembrancer. That the Treasury seems to have taken this matter on themselves to prevent process issuing out not only against peers or privileged persons, but also against such accountants as were not to blame, though their accounts were not passed, instancing in Sir Edward Seymour and the Lord Falkland as Treasurers of the Navy, it being alleged at the Treasury that the neglect was in the Navy Board not signing their ledgers for want of some few articles to be adjusted.

That there never were any such orders formerly for the Auditors of the Imprests to certify to the Remembrancer besides those in the Earl of Rochester's time, only in Edward VI's time there was an act which required the Auditors of the Land Revenue to make such certificates. That the Auditors can certify no more than what the Remembrancer knows before, the accounts passing through the Remembrancer's hands. He agreed that the Auditors of the Land Revenue were directed how to certify and that the Queen's Remembrancer was thereupon directed to issue a process one term *ad computandum*, the next term a *distringas*, and the third term a *pluries*. But this was in Edward VI's time, whereas the institution of Auditors of the Imprests was but in Queen Elizabeth's time.

That the Treasury generally sends to them twice a year to certify the state of the accounts that process may be issued accordingly; that in those certificates they can only take notice that such and such persons have not brought in their accounts, but not the reasons why. That while they certified to the Remembrancer they did not certify to the Treasury, and that afterwards, when they certified to the Treasury they were not required to certify to the Remembrancer . . .

26 January 1703

Mr Lowndes, Secretary to the Treasury, pursuant to the letter of yesterday attending before the Board sate, gave an account to the Commissioners who were present. That the matter of certifying the neglects of the accountants had been a subject of contention for many years. That the law of the Exchequer is complete and sufficient provision made for obliging the accountants to pass their accounts if it was adhered to. That the year is divided in the Exchequer into two terms, Michaelmas and Easter; that salaries, pensions and the like are not to be accompted for, but for other payments – as to the Army, Navy, Cofferer, etc., the Imprest Rolls should be issued every half year. That in the Exchequer there are two issuable terms, Hilary and Trinity. That as to all accounts determined the Treasurer's Remembrancer should make out the process for the supers, and as to accounts undetermined the Queen's Remembrancer is to do it.

That the first process is a kind of *Distringas ad Computandum*, then next an *Alias*, and then a *Pluries*, and then they proceed to seizure.

That the Auditor of the Receipt is to send the Imprest Roll twice a year to the Remembrancer, and that by the ancient course of the Exchequer the Auditors of the Imprests should certify the Queen's Remembrancer what accounts are not passed. That when the Lord Treasurer Rochester was sworn he attended his Lordship and they went both to the Upper and Lower Exchequer, and his Lordship enquired into the course of it and directed process to issue of course against the accomptants in arrear because it would have been invidious to send particular orders for issuing out process, and this was the law of the Exchequer before, for the Lord Treasurer can make no new law in the Exchequer.

But this was discontinued, because they found process of course was troublesome but the skreening accountants from prosecution was profitable, and the fault is that either the Auditor of the Receipt has not duly delivered out the Imprest Roll or the Auditor of the Imprests has not duly certified, though he knows not whether the Auditors of the Imprests had not some tacit verbal order to discontinue certifying to the Remembrancer. But if the course of the Exchequer be continued for process to issue out of course against those who are in arrear with their accounts it would soon remedy the backwardness of the accounts, and he agrees it to be the duty of the Auditors of the Imprests to certify to the Queen's Remembrancer and refers the Board to Mr Watts and Mr Armiger, two of the clerks in the Exchequer, to give an account whether the Auditors have duly certified to the Remembrancer.

[The Chairman of the Commissioners now arrived. Lowndes was put on oath and testified further:]

That according to the best of his knowledge, experience and understanding, all the monies issued out of the Exchequer in pursuance to the course of the Exchequer and Acts of Parliament ought to be inserted in the Imprest Roll and transmitted from the Lower Exchequer or Receipt of the Exchequer to the officers of the court of the Exchequer. And that the Auditors of the Imprests, or one of them, ought to certify which of the accountants are behind in their accounts, and thereupon process *ad computandum* or other process, as Extent or the like, ought to issue against the accountants in default, which he takes to be the business of the Treasurer's Remembrancer to make out such process for debts determined and of the Queen's Remembrancer for debts depending, and that the said process ought to issue of course against every issuable term. And in case any accountant hath good cause to move for the stay of process, he is to apply to the Lord Treasurer or Chancellor of the Exchequer or to the Court of Exchequer in that behalf. And he believes that the neglect of this method in the officers or some of them is the cause of the accountants are so far in arrears.

As to the reason why the Auditors of the Imprests did not certify yearly to the Remembrancer he says he knows nothing of their corruptions, but apprehends favour may have been unduly shewn to their accountants in not making out process as they ought to have done, and believes they have sometimes made out certificates to the Remembrancer and no process thereon hath issued.

That he was present *anno* 1685 when the Earl of Rochester directed Mr Hall the Secondary to issue process of course upon the certificates of the Auditors of the Imprests and he knows not why it was discontinued unless to show favour to the accountants, and if the Auditors of the Imprests have not made out such certificates to the Remembrancer it is their fault.

The Board enquiring of him how the Auditors came to look upon it not as their duty, he said he has been told that old Hall did not think it safe to issue out process of course, and thereupon the Auditors discontinued certifying to him, but remembers Mr Done was always for doing it; but takes it to be more profitable to the Auditors to screen the accountants than to prosecute them. He believes if the ancient course in this particular was restored it would be of great service to the public.

[Lowndes goes on to explain that the present Treasurer of the Navy cannot pass his accounts until those of his predecessors have been cleared.]

The Solicitor of the Treasury ought also to hunt out what accountants are in arrear.

Being asked if the Treasury did direct the Auditors of the Imprests to certify only to them and not to the Remembrancer he answered, No. He said they would willingly have got such an order but that it is the course of the Exchequer for the Auditors of the Imprests to certify to the Remembrancer.

The Board acquainting him that the Auditors of the Imprests deny it, Mr Lowndes insisted on it to be the course of the Exchequer and that it was allowed at that time when the Earl of Rochester revived it and nobody denied it, the neglect at that time being but a new innovation.

Being asked how the course came to be broke before the Earl of Rochester's time he answered, he could not tell, but is sure when Sir John Duncombe was Chancellor of the Exchequer he held up [i.e. upheld] the ancient course, and while he continued in the office the accounts were not so behind as now.

12. Exchequer negligence denounced: [B] The Parliamentary Accounts Commission of 1713.

This Accounts Commission, like most of the others, was 'politically motivated' in the Tory interest, but its findings were comparatively objective and anticipate some of the points to be made by the 'Economical Reform' reports of the 1780s.

FROM The Reports of the Commissioners of Public Accounts, 16 April 1713: Remarks on the Management and Disposal of the Public Revenue (W. Cobbett's *Parliamentary History of England*, VI. 1176–200).

Your Commissioners, since their last Report, have finished a general State of the Receipts and Issues of her Majesty's Exchequer, from Michaelmas 1709 to Michaelmas 1710, and from Michaelmas 1711 to Michaelmas 1712 . . .; which they humbly offer to your consideration, with their further Remarks on several Misapplications and unwarrantable Practices in persons concerned in the Management and Disposal of the Public Revenue.

We begin with those relating to the oeconomy of the Army, which, in our opinion, have greatly contributed to that exorbitant expence with which the War hath been carried on by this nation . . .

One of the great Mismanagements of the Army is, that of paying regiments without establishments.

The Paymaster-General hath returned on oath to us, That the Regiments of Hogon, d'Assa and Dalzel, were paid by authority of the General's warrant only. Whereas, according to the best information we can receive, no regiment, troop or company, ought to be paid without being first placed on some establishment, signed by the crown, and counter-signed by the Lord High-Treasurer, or Commissioners of the Treasury for the time being . . .

As to the Remittances for the Army in Flanders, sir Henry Furnese was employed by the treasury to make the best bargains he could, and to be accountable to the public for the profit. We have required these accounts, and the auditor of the imprests, who is possessed of them, hath acquainted us, that he hath not yet been able, by reason of their bulk, to go through them. But we have information on oath of an advantage of one per cent. and sometimes more, made by receiving money at Amsterdam and paying it in Flanders.

The next great branch of Expence to the Public is the Navy; and we here present what hath occurred to us on this head. First, we perceive considerable balances have continued in the hands of the treasurers, and of their executors after the time of their dismission or death; which, notwithstanding the great necessities of the government, have lain long unapplied to the services for which they were intended.

The Reasons given for this practice are, That the Treasurers ought by their instructions to detain money in their hands, when they are displaced, for satisfying defalcations, &c, and for defraying the expence of passing their accounts. But we cannot find the first argument favoured by a reasonable interpretation of the instruction, nor is there any just pretence, why the whole balances in the hands of the preceding treasurers, should not be immediately paid over to their successors. On the contrary, there is very good ground for doing it, to avoid the charge of keeping clerks, and other instruments, for displaced or dead officers, and that the money might be employed towards carrying on the current service . . .

We also find large Imprests granted in the time of each Treasurer since the Revolution, whereof there remained uncleared the 31st of October 1712, the sum of £607,851. For which it is alledged, That the accounts have either been brought into the comptroller's office or not sufficiently vouched, or that the accounts, or some of them, are before the comptroller, under the examination, or that the parties are abroad, and have wages due to them, which will not be allowed till their imprests be cleared, or that when the Treasurer brings the imprest to account in his ledger, they are allowed him in part, or the whole; and the parties are set *insuper* in the Exchequer.

But these allegations cannot, we presume, be admitted as sufficient. For the accounts ought to be brought in every year, where the distance of place will permit; and the large sums, which have been imprested to the store-keepers and clerks residing in England from 1704, should have been long since accounted for. Whereas no effectual care hath been taken to compel them to it, and they seem too much left at their own liberty, to the great damage of the public. Though they are to be set *insuper* in the Exchequer, when the imprests are allowed to the Treasurer; yet the Treasurer's accounts are so long generally in passing, that the parties are often dead, or insolvent, before that is done: and of those which have been set *insuper*, there does not appear any considerable sums to have been accounted for. There are some imprests before 1702 which have neither been accounted for, nor set *insuper*, nor mentioned in the Treasurer's ledger; and other sums have been very lately repaid to the Treasurer in money which have been so long imprested that the interest would have equalled, if not exceeded the principal; to the great loss of the public, which paid interest for that money, as well as to the disadvantage of the service.

Your Commissioners further represent, That the exposing to sale offices, relating to the management of the revenue of the kingdom, is a practice against law, and done in defiance of her majesty's repeated declarations. The instances of which have been proved to us by the oaths of the very persons concerned.

The first is this: Henry Meriton, esq. in 1705, treated with Mr Brydges, then Auditor of the Imprests, for the purchase of his office, and agreed to give him £4000 for it. After this agreement, he applied to the Lord Godolphin, then Lord Treasurer, for his approbation. His Lordship proposed to make him Commissioner of Customs or Cashier of the Excise, in consideration of the £4000 he was to pay to Mr Brydges. But he absolutely refused the first, and was with difficulty brought to accept the latter office, on so hard terms as he thought, because it was to be given during pleasure only. However, being persuaded by Sir William Scawen, whom he had consulted and employed in this matter, to rely on the Lord Godolphin's honour, and promised that he should not be displaced, he paid £4000 to Mr Brydges. Whereupon Mr Maynwaring was made Auditor of the Imprests, Mr Hall, Cashier of the Excise, removed from that employment to be Commissioners of the Customs, and Mr Meriton made Cashier of the Excise. By which it is evident, That the Lord Godolphin was not only privy to this bargain and sale, but negociated it.

13. The Treasury and 'corruption': the Committee of Secrecy, 1742, investigates Walpole's secret service expenditure.

There is very little evidence to show how far eighteenth-century Treasury clerks engaged in political work, but the decision to disqualify all government clerks from membership of the House of Commons (15 Geo. II, c. 22) was associated with the facts revealed by this inquiry.

FROM A Report from the Committee of Secrecy appointed to inquire into the Conduct of Robert Earl of Orford during the last Ten Years of his being First Commissioner of the Treasury (W. Cobbett's *Parliamentary History of England*, XII, 628–821).

1742, May 13

[633] Your Committee proceeded, in the next place, to examine into Mr Paxton's behaviour as a public accountant; and find that he entered on his office of solicitor of the treasury on the 22nd of December 1730, from which time till the month of July 1734, being four years and upwards, they find that he passed no account, nor was he in readiness to pass the same; for it appears to your committee, that, on the 2nd of July 1734, he procured a warrant from the Treasury for stopping process till the Hilary term following; but it does not appear to your committee, that, since that time, process has ever been revived against him, or that any other steps were taken towards his passing any account, till about twelve months ago, when his account, ending the 22nd of December 1732, was delivered into the auditor's office . . .

[635] Your Committee finding, that Mr Paxton had actually passed no account, during the whole time of his being solicitor to the treasury, proceeded to enquire, whether any large sums of public money had been entrusted to him, and find, that he stands *in super* £5,382 18s 1d for money paid over to him by Mr Cracherode, when the said Mr Paxton was his assistant; they also find, that he stands charged upon the imprest rolls with a sum of £89,314 19s 2½d upon account . . .

It also appears to your Committee, that besides the said sums, they have already discovered, that Mr Thomas Lowther, one of the messengers of the Treasury, has paid to the said Mr Paxton one sum of £1500 by virtue of a minute of the Treasury; for which sum neither the said Lowther, nor the said Paxton, are public accomptants.

But your Committee are utterly unable to discover, by what arts and methods Mr Paxton could evade passing any account during the time of his being solicitor of the Treasury, which is upwards of eleven years; especially as it appears to your Committee, that it was the duty

of the said Treasury, to oblige him to prosecute all such accomptants, as should appear to be in arrear by the certificates of the auditors of the imprests; for your Committee find, from a report of the said auditors ... that by a warrant of the Treasury, dated the 16th of August 1711, and signed Oxford, the solicitor of the Treasury is directed to take care, that the process be regularly issued against such imprest accountants as shall appear to be in arrear, by the certificates of the auditors of the imprests, to the queen's remembrancer; as also against all persons, standing *in super* upon an imprest, or other account ...

And your Committee are at a loss to determine, what motives could induce the Commissioners of the Treasury, to continue the said Mr Paxton so many years in the office of solicitor of the Treasury, and to direct that such large sums of public money should, from time to time, be lodged in his hands, when they must have been informed, by the half-yearly certificates, delivered in to them by the auditors of the imprests, that he had passed no accounts from the time of his first appointment ...

[788] A Further Report ...

[810] Your Committee now proceed to lay before you the conduct of the Earl of Orford, with relation to the quantity and manner of issuing and receiving that part of the public money, granted for the support of the civil government, which has been employed in what is commonly called Secret Service.

Your Committee, having been informed that this money had been issued under three different denominations, called for an account of all the sums issued for secret service, or for his majesty's immediate or special service (the money issued to his majesty's privy purse excepted) or to reimburse expences during the last ten years in which Robert, Earl of Orford was first commissioner of the Treasury, etc. And the account having been laid before them from the Auditor of the Exchequer's office, there appeared to be issued under these three heads only, including the annual sum of £3000 paid to each of the secretaries of state for secret services, the sum of £1,453,400 6s 3d.

Your Committee now proceed to lay before you the proofs that the money issued under the three heads of secret service, of special service, and to reimburse expences, were understood to mean one and the same thing.

Christopher Tilson, Esq., a clerk in the Treasury, and who came into that office in the year 1684, said on his examination, that he looked on all these monies to be of the same nature; that they were all without account except as to what relates to the solicitor of the Treasury, nor

is there any entry in the Treasury of the application of any of these sums of money.

John Shepherd, a deputy messenger of the Treasury, who has received very large sums under each of these three heads, being examined, said, that the warrants upon which he received money at the Exchequer under any of these three heads, whether in his own name or in the name of other persons, were all without account, and that he made no distinction whether the orders were for special, or secret service, or to reimburse expences.

But your Committee observe, that all the money issued under the head of secret service, is issued in the name of John Scrope, Esq., Secretary of the Treasury, but the orders for the sums which were issued under the heads of special service or to reimburse expences, are payable to Mr Lowther, Mr Richards, and Mr Shepherd, messengers of the Exchequer, and to a great variety of other names, for which sums no receipts appear to have been given; but none of those to whose names these orders are payable, under other of these three heads, appear to have any interest in the sums thus issued.

[817] Mr Tilson being examined said, that he has had secret service money brought to him, but that he never did receive any money at the Exchequer himself; Shepherd always brought it to him; but that he has always delivered all moneys he has received, whether for secret service, special service, or to reimburse expences, to Mr Fane, Mr Scrope, or the Earl of Orford: that he has to be sure, paid very considerable sums of secret service money to the Earl of Orford, but has no way of ascertaining by book what he has paid, the transition was so quick.

Henry Fane, Esq., a clerk of the Treasury, said, that he has received verbal orders from the Earl of Orford to prepare warrants for the King to sign, and to bring to him, the said Earl, the money. That sums of money for secret service have been frequently put into his hands, which were sometimes brought to him by a messenger; and that he delivered this money either to the Earl of Orford himself, or to Mr Scrope, to carry it to the said Earl. That when he gave it to Mr Scrope it was for him to carry it to the Earl of Orford, and he believes all such sums came into the said Earl's hands, excepting some trifling sums of £40 or £50 which he has paid to others. That he has paid many sums to the said Earl, but kept no account; nor could he recollect the particular sums he has thus paid. That what he has received and paid, and what he has acted in these affairs, was by the said Earl of Orford's directions, either from himself or signified to him by Mr Scrope; and that he does not know that any other Lord of the Treasury has ever given him directions for either receiving or paying any secret service money.

[821] Your Committee being further desirous to inform themselves in what manner the vast sums issued for secret service were accounted for to his majesty, sent for Mr Tilson, who being examined, said, that when his majesty signed a sign manual for the paying of any sum of money to Mr Scrope, for secret service, he also signed at the same time a receipt to Mr Scrope for the same sum, but that there was always a blank left for the date, and the dates are at the same time put in at the Treasury to the warrant, the order, the sign manual, and the King's receipt; and this is usually done by the entering clerk, who wrote the sign manual, that it may all appear in the same hand; that the date of the receipt is always made the same as the date of the order.

14. The principles of 'Economical Reform': the Reports of the Commissioners of Accounts, 1781–4.

In working their way through the technical shortcomings of departmental accounting, the Commissioners evolved a broad philosophy of the public interest which demanded sweeping reforms in the basis of office-holding, remuneration and organization in British government.

FROM The Reports of the Commissioners appointed to examine, take and state the Public Accounts of the Kingdom.

[a] Eleventh Report, 5 Dec. 1783; *C.J.* XXXIX, pp. 779–80

We do not mean to violate, in the slightest degree, any right vested in an officer by virtue of his office. The principles which secure the rights of private property are sacred, and to be preserved inviolate; they are landmarks to be considered as immoveable. But the public have their rights also, rights equally sacred, and as freely to be exercised ...

The principle which gives existence to, and governs every public office, is the benefit of the State. Government requires that various branches of business should be transacted, and persons must be found to transact them. The acceptance of a public office implies an engagement to do the business, and a right to compensation. The officer has powers delegated to him necessary for the execution, but he has no other right than to the reward of his labour. He has no right to any specific quantity of business; that quantity must fluctuate according to circumstances, or may be regulated by the convenience of the State. If the good of the community requires a diminution or annihilation of the business of his office, or the transferring it elsewhere, the officer cannot oppose to the regulation, the diminution or annihilation of his profits; because not the emolument of the officer, but the advantage of the public, was the object of the institution. To suppose in him a right to make such an objection would be to suppose the office created for his benefit ... It matters not what the duration or condition of the interest may be, whether for life or years, during good behaviour or pleasure; all are equally subject to that governing principle for the sake of which it was created, the good of the public. Hence, in every proposed official regulation, the advantage or disadvantage of the officer can never be properly a subject of discussion. The only question is, whether the necessity or good of the State actually requires it? This decides the propriety of the regulation; and the determination of it belongs only to the supreme power that watches over the public good, for its improvement as well as its protection.

[b] Fifth Report, 28 Nov. 1781; *C.J.* XXXVIII p. 577

We are well aware of the difficulties that must for ever attend the introducing novelty of form into ancient offices, framed by the wisdom of our ancestors and established by the experience of ages; they are considered as incapable of improvement; the officers educated in, and accustomed to the forms in use, are insensible of their defects, or, if they feel them, have no leisure, often no ability, seldom any inclination, to correct them; alarmed at the idea of innovation, they resist the proposal of a regulation because it is a change, though from a perplexed and intricate, to a more simple and intelligible system.

[c] Sixth Report, 11 February 1782; *C.J.* XXXVIII p. 711

By strict economy we apprehend, is not meant such as either derogates from the honour and dignity of the Crown, or abridges the servant of the public of the due reward of his industry and abilities; we mean an economy that steers between extreme parsimony on the one hand, and profusion on the other; that is consistent with justice as well as prudence; that gives to all their full due, and to none more; that supports every useful and necessary establishment, but cuts off and reduces every superfluous and redundant expence. Some regulations, built upon the principle of economy thus defined, have for their objects, the offices, the officers and their emoluments.

An office of the highest antiquity, that has subsisted for ages under its present form; that has the receipt and custody of the public treasure, upon the due administration of which depends the national credit and safety of the realm; an office of such a description is entitled to the utmost respect and alterations in its establishment should be well weighed, and proposed with caution and diffidence. But as a change in the manners, customs, and above all, in the finances of this nation, since the origin of this office, together with peculiar circumstances of the times, may render regulations necessary, we have judged it part of our duty to examine into the Receipt of the Exchequer, with a view to an economical reform . . .

[d] Twelfth Report, 11 June 1784; *C.J.* XL p. 120

Uniformity in the course and modes of transacting the business of the public ought to be introduced and pursued, as far as is practicable, in similar offices. It causes the intercourse between offices connected to be carried on with greater ease and expedition, and facilitates the means of acquiring official knowledge to those persons who pass through the different departments of the State to the high stations of administration; and thus, when a regulation is clearly of general utility, it should be extended to every office, the constitution and objects of which will admit of the application. The legislature have established important regulations in the office of the Paymaster-General of His Majesty's Forces, regulations suggested by us to be equally applicable to the office of the Treasurer of the Navy, and which, in the judgement we have formed upon the present enquiry, may, with equal propriety, be extended to the office of the Treasurer of the Ordnance.

The Commissioners of the Treasury, whose duty it is to guard the public treasure both against superfluous and improvident issues, should before they direct any issue, have knowledge of the sum remaining in the hands of the officer soliciting the issue, and of the services for which the supply is required. The defects in the annual estimate for the Ordnance service manifestly shew, that the monthly estimate, formed at the beginning of the year, upon a conjecture what services will arise, and what sums will be wanted, in every successive month of that year, can never convey to the Commissioners of the Treasury the accurate knowledge they ought to possess previous to the direction of every issue; and, therefore, we are of opinion, that in every memorial presented to the Commissioners of the Treasury for a supply of money for the service of the Ordnance, the total sum remaining unapplied in the hands, or on the account, of the Treasurer of the Ordnance, ought to be inserted, together with the services that are the ground of the requisition.

[e] Third Report, 7 March 1781; *C.J.* XXXVIII p. 250
As the public money should pass without delay from the pocket of the subject into the Exchequer, so it ought not to issue out of the Exchequer, either before it is wanted, or in larger sums than the service for which it is issued required.

The principal cause of the magnitude of this balance, is, the practice in this office [of the Treasurer of the Navy] of not carrying money issued under one head, towards satisfying a demand upon any other head of service; the consequence of which is, when the money upon the account of any head of service is nearly exhausted, a supply must be procured for that service, how abundant soever the sums upon other heads of account, or the sum total of his cash may be. Were all the sums he receives to constitute and be considered as one common general cash, and be applied indiscriminately to every service, a much less sum than the lowest of the balances in the account last mentioned would, in our opinion suffice to carry on the current services of the Navy, even various and extensive as they now are.

[f] Fifth Report, 28 Nov. 1781; *C.J.* XXXVIII p. 575
The usual course of the receipts and issues in this office [of the Paymaster-General of the Forces] for several years, has constantly put

into the hands of the Paymaster-General a large sum of public money not employed in the public service, expressly contrary to that sound maxim of prudence and economy, that more should not be issued from the Exchequer for any service than that service wants. He asks sums of the Treasury under specific heads of service, and in the form of a computation; the Treasury directs the issue in the terms he asks it, without knowing whether the service is adequate to the requisition, whether the computation be just, and whether he has not already in his hands full as much as he wants. There is no control upon him in the Exchequer; the only attention of that office is, to see that the issue does not exceed his credit, and that his credit does not exceed the supply for the Army services, voted by Parliament that year. Supposing the constitution of this office to continue in its present form, we think the interposition of some check necessary, to reduce and confine this balance within due bounds. The Paymaster-General can receive nothing from the Exchequer but by direction of the Treasury; the Treasury, therefore, should have the means of judging upon the propriety and necessity of the requisition, to which a frequent knowledge of his balance is essential; and therefore we are of opinion, that in the first memorial presented every month by the Paymaster-General of the Forces to the Lords of the Treasury for a supply for the Army services, he should always insert the sum total of the balance of public money, for the service of the Army, at that time in his hands, custody, or power. What those due bounds are, within which this balance ought to be circumscribed, depends upon a variety of circumstances, of which the Treasury may, upon examination, obtain knowledge sufficient to direct their judgement.

[g] Tenth Report, 2 July 1783; *C.J.* XXXIX p. 522

The business of the Auditor of the Imprest, to be selected from his commission, is, to audit the accounts of most of the receivers, and of all the officers and persons entrusted with the expenditure of the public revenue. Possibly this office might formerly have been able to accomplish this duty, but such has been the increase of the revenue within these few years that the accounts are grown to a number, magnitude, and extent, greatly beyond what could have been foreseen. The accounts, which at this day remain for the audit of the Exchequer, are seventy-four millions, the issues of twenty-one years for the Navy service; fifty-eight millions, the issues of eighteen years for the Army service; near thirty-nine millions issued to sub-accountants; together, one hundred seventy-one millions. The receipts and issues of all the provisions for the support of the Land Forces in America and the West Indies during the late war; all these accounts must be passed. The public have a right and good cause to demand it. If, according to the present constitution of the Exchequer, they can be passed no where but in the office of the Auditor, that constitution should be altered. Such of the accounts as may appear the most proper to be removed, should be transferred from his office to such other offices as may, from their peculiar circumstances, and the relation they bear to the subject matter of the accounts, be presumed to be the best qualified for the examination of them.

15. Parliament demands the enforcement of Treasury control: Reports of Select Committees of the House of Commons, 1810, 1817, 1828.

The pressure for economy, during and after the Napoleonic wars, helped to banish earlier misgivings about Treasury sovereignty. Members of Parliament were increasingly prepared to follow the lead given by Burke in demanding comprehensive superintendence by the Treasury over all areas of public expenditure. Sir Henry Parnell, chairman of the 1828 committee, was to enlarge on this theme in his pamphlet, *Financial Reform* (1830).

[a] FROM The Fifth Report (Second Part) from the Committee on the Public Expenditure of the United Kingdom (*PP* (1810) II pp. 381-405).

The Committee ... having been led, in the former part of this Report, into the examination and exposure of more than one instance of default, and delinquency, in the misapplication and embezzlement of public money, and having had occasion to observe considerable irregularity and laxity in the auditing of accounts, by the continuance of which, temptation may be held out to the commission of similar offences; proceed now to lay before the House the result of their inquiry into the general subject of the audit of all accounts of public expenditure and particularly into the provisions of the 46 Geo. III, c. 141 by which the present Board of Commissioners was constituted ...

From the evidence contained in the Appendix the House will perceive that the duty of examining and passing the different public accounts is distributed among a great variety of offices, in some of which, namely in the Customs, Post Office, Stamp Office, Ordnance, Navy and War Offices, the officers themselves will be found to be the auditors of their own expenditure; and that contrary to the received opinion, that the power of examining and auditing the public accounts is vested in the Board of |Commissioners under the Act of 46 Geo. III, c. 141, there is no general power practically lodged in that Board to embrace and comprehend in any degree the whole examination of that important branch of the public concerns.

The Board of Treasury, to whom this duty might be conceived more immediately to belong, has at no time exercised a systematic control over the public accounts; neither would such an employment be compatible with the regular functions, and ordinary occupations of that Board, nor consistent with those urgent executive duties in which it is constantly engaged ...

An examination of public accounts by officers possessed of such very limited powers, encumbered by useless forms, and entirely dependent on the Treasury, could at no time be considered as constituting an efficient check on the irregularities of public expenditure; accordingly it will be found that soon after the House of Commons began to assume those important political functions which it now habitually exercises, the state of the public accounts was brought at different times under the immediate consideration of Parliament.

[The report then reviews the history of Parliamentary Accounts Committees and Commissions since that of 1667–9.]

The facts already stated sufficiently prove what the Committee have it in contemplation to establish, that the House of Commons, upon various occasions, took immediate cognizance of the public accounts, and exercised an effectual control over them by means of Commissioners especially appointed from time to time for that purpose. From the reign of King George the First, until about thirty years ago, either no occasion called for such an interference, or if called for, it was not exerted.

[389] ... The defects in the constitution of the present office [of Audit] are those which result from a 'system of Departments' over which there is practically no general control or superintendence, the heads of the respective Departments being themselves members of the Board which could alone exercise the control ... The present system of audit may therefore with propriety be declared to have failed, in many respects, answering the purpose contemplated by the legislature in the appointment of Commissioners. The principal defects are those which are inherent in the system itself and in the mode of examining and auditing the public accounts according to the course of the Exchequer.

[392] ... It is true that the cash transactions of these great Departments [e.g. the Navy and the Ordnance] are regularly checked and examined; and the public may perhaps derive some security from their being ultimately examined and passed (imperfect as the examination may be) in a distinct office of accounts. But your Committee desire the House to recollect, that there is an essential difference between the examination of a mere cash account, such as has now been described, and that of the actual expenditure; which latter is the real and substantial audit of the account ...

[394] ... Had the public accounts of the Kingdom been under the immediate superintendence of any one department possessing authority (of which the present Board are almost entirely destitute) and immediately responsible to Parliament, it is neither probable, or possible, that the defects or inconveniences of passing accounts according to the

useless forms of the Exchequer could have remained to the present day; neither could the accounts of so many principal and sub-accountants have fallen into arrear, as had been the case in all the great departments of public expenditure, or so palpably defective a system of examining and auditing any account have been allowed to exist . . .

It might fairly be presumed, that an independent and unconnected office for the examination and audit of the public accounts would possess powers and be divested of restrictions, to a degree at least, beyond those offices which examine and audit their own accounts; yet the contrary has been found to be the fact, and the distinction between the Commissioners for auditing the Public Accounts and those Departments is, the increased restriction and dependence to which the former is made subject. The offices of accounts which are not subject to the rules of the Exchequer, possess within themselves much greater powers and means of internal regulation and improvement than the Audit Office; they are not practically subordinated in matters of account to the Treasury, or any other Department; have very ample discretion as to the allowances made to the accountants, and are under no legal restriction as to forms of accounts or modes of examination . . . In all these respects, the situation of the Auditors of Public Accounts appears to be entirely different; for exclusive of their immediate dependence upon the Treasury, without whose previous sanction the power of acting is almost entirely denied to them, they are subject to such a variety of restrictions, imposed on them partly by established official usage and partly by Acts of Parliament, as unavoidably tends to impede all sufficient progress in the discharge of their functions, and renders them wholly subservient to the Board of the Treasury.

[400–1] The question, whether an account ought to be stated to the Treasury previous to declaration, appears to be regulated by no fixed principle, but to depend upon official usage . . . The decision of the Auditors is in no instance final; but the Lords of the Treasury exercise complete authority with regard to all the articles of an account, whether of allowance or surcharge.

The great strictness of the rules by which the Auditors are now bound produces an evident necessity independent of official usage for stating many public accounts to the Treasury . . . Thus, the special jurisdiction of the Treasury is constantly and habitually necessary to the final passing and settlement of the greater part of the public accounts which are examined by the Commissioners of Audit . . . A practice has arisen and been acted upon to a very considerable extent, and much to the prejudice of all regular check and control over the expenditure of the Kingdom, of *issuing money without acccount, other than such as shall be required to be rendered to the Lords of the Treasury.*

The mode of investigating and passing public accounts ought, as nearly as possible, to be uniform in all offices of government.

Your Committee content themselves for the present with suggesting the necessity of allowing to the Commissioners for auditing the Public Accounts the same discretion, respecting all matters of accounts, as that which is now exercised by other auditing Departments, and perfect freedom with regard to all internal arrangements of their office.

[404] ... When your Committee ... consider the great variety and importance of the business transacted by the Treasury, and the inexpediency of allowing the office which regulates and controls the issue of public money, the power also of auditing the expenditure, they have no hesitation in declaring that a regular and independent office of accounts would, in every respect, be a more proper department for the exercise of a vigilant and efficient control; and therefore recommend, that all monies issued by the Treasury for services other than those before stated, should be accounted for to the Auditors of Public Accounts.

[405] Your Committee further propose, that a copy of the annual report of the state of the public accounts made by the Auditors to the Lords of the Treasury on or before the 31st of March in every year, pursuant to the Treasury warrant of 9th October 1806, should be in future annually laid before the House of Commons.

[b] FROM Reports of the Select Committee on Finance, to inquire into and state the Income and Expenditure of the United Kingdom for the year ended 5 January 1817, and state the probable Income and Expenditure for 1818 and 1819, and to consider measures for relief from the said Expenditure (*PP* (1817) IV, 30, 94, 110, 111, 209, 225).

[i] First Report, on sinecures, pensions and salaries:

... Your Committee do not feel themselves competent to recommend any general regulation by which the proper scale of salary ... may be settled ... Your Committee are therefore of opinion that it should be left to the judgment and responsibility of the Lords of the Treasury, for the time being, as vacancies occur, to place the several offices proposed to be regulated upon such an establishment with respect to the numbers and rank of the persons requisite for the discharge of the efficient functions of such offices, and the amount of salary to be assigned to each person, as may appear to them adequate, after a full enquiry into the nature and extent of the duties to be performed, and the degree of official and pecuniary responsibility which necessarily attaches to some of them. If it should be thought proper in any Act to be passed with reference to the subject of this Report, to enact, that whenever any of the said offices shall be reduced and regulated, there should be laid before both Houses of Parliament a comparative statement of the number, duty, and emolument of the respective officers under the old and new establishments, your Committee conceive that the parliamentary check, created by this arrangement, would be sufficient to prevent any abuse of a power which seems properly to belong to the Lords of the Treasury, as the official and responsible advisers of the Crown upon all matters which relate to the superintendence and control over the public expenditure.

[ii] Third Report, on the Ordnance:

Your Committee think it necessary to bring under the notice of the House, the propriety of watching over such augmentations, to whatever department they are first applied; and of requiring that the attention of the Treasury should in the first instance be called to them so as to form the subject of a distinct Minute. The desire of equalizing their emoluments to those of other departments is so natural to all offices, that whenever an advance is made in any of them it will be followed by applications and give rise to pretensions in almost every other, and to dissatisfaction if these representations are not complied with.

Your Committee recommend, that no increase of Civil Establishment, or increase of salary to officers already on the Establishment, nor any superannuation allowance, should be granted without a previous report to the Lords Commissioners of the Treasury, and their formal concurrence obtained, by Minute of the Board, before any report shall be made by the Master General and Board of Ordnance to the King in Council, for the purpose of giving effect to any recommendation for such superannuation or increase of salary or establishment.

... But they earnestly recommend the necessity of subjecting the proceedings of this department to the general control of the Lords Commissioners of the Treasury, from the first preparation of subjects to be proposed on Estimate to Parliament, up to a final audit of accounts.

... and they desire to conclude this part of their report, by expressing again the decided opinion, which has already been applied to various parts of this subject, that no department of large expenditure ought ever to be placed beyond the controlling superintendence of the Lords Commissioners of the Treasury. From them every other office should expect, and from them the House will require, not a judgment as to the best mode of constructing, maintaining or improving the works respectively belonging to each separate branch, but a judicious and economical allotment to every one of them of such limited sums as can be assigned, with a due regard to the necessary expenses of every other service, and of the necessities as well as of the resources of the country.

[iii] Sixth Report, on the Navy:

... What your Committee therefore earnestly recommend is this; that the Lords of the Treasury should call for a return of the present establishments of all the civil offices in the state, the salaries of which have been increased in the last fifteen years, and with a reference to the circumstances now stated, and such other considerations as the altered situation of the country ... that they should make a revision of the same, and direct such prospective reductions therein as may appear to them reasonable without impairing the efficiency of the service.

... They are informed, that in point of practice, no measure that involves an expenditure of public money, is taken by the Board of Admiralty, without previous communication between the First Lord of the Admiralty and the First Lord of the Treasury, and the Chancellor of the Exchequer; and your Committee can easily conceive, that cases will sometimes occur in which such confidential and unreserved communications are likely to be more effectual toward their object, than any official correspondence between the two Boards could be, even supposing that such correspondence could properly take place; but feeling, as your Committee do strongly, the necessity of bringing all financial subjects officially within the view of the Treasury, they suggest, whether, in addition to the confidential intercourse before mentioned, it might not be advisable that it should be made a rule of the Council Office, that every proposition involving an increase of public expense, should, according to the nature of the case, either be submitted to a Committee of Council, consisting of such members as may be connected with the Treasury department, or be made by the Council Office a subject of a direct reference to, and report from the Treasury, to that office, before it is presented to his Majesty for his final approbation. By this arrangement, which will combine the forms which have from the earliest times prevailed in the practice of our government, with that essential control which your Committee judge it necessary to place in the financial ministers alone, they hope that the results which they have so often recommended may be attained.

[c] FROM The Reports of the Select Committee on Income and Expenditure, 1828 (*PP* (1828) V. pp. 7–8 (Second Report, on the Ordnance)).

The Committee particularly desire to draw the attention of the House to the fact, that the ancient and wise control vested by our financial policy in the hands of the Treasury over all the departments connected with the public expenditure, has been in a great degree set aside. Although it is the practice to lay the annual estimates before the Board of Treasury the subsequent course of expenditure is not practically restrained as it ought to be, by one governing and responsible power, but remains too much under the separate management of the Departments.

In pursuing the same objects of reform and retrenchment [as those defined in the last twenty-five years], the Committee feel convinced that it is essentially necessary, in order to give full effect to their efforts, that what they may have to propose shall embrace measures for securing, 1st, A clear and uniform system of accounts in all the offices; 2nd, A principle of simplification and consolidation in the transaction of public business; 3rd, An effectual control in the Treasury over the departments; and lastly, A strict adjustment of the numbers of our military and naval forces, so as not to exceed what is really necessary for the peace and security of the Empire.

With respect to the [third] great object to be secured, namely, the establishment of an effectual control in the hands of the Treasury, this is nothing more than the restoration to the Treasury of its ancient authority. It is necessary that this control should be constantly exercised, in determining the amount of expenditure to be incurred by each department; in securing the application of each sum voted in the annual estimates to the service for which it has been voted; in regulating any extraordinary expenditure which, upon an emergency, may be deemed necessary within the year, although not included in the estimates; and in preventing any increase of salary or extra allowance, or any other emoluments, being granted, without a Minute expressive of the approbation of the Board of Treasury. The Committee have further to observe, that it is expedient, not only to restore this control, but to secure it from being again set aside; which cannot be effected except by the House of Commons constantly enforcing its application by holding the Treasury responsible for every act of expenditure in each Department.

16. The Treasury appeals for departmental economy: the Treasury Minute of 10 August 1821.

Under strong parliamentary pressure for economy in public expenditure, the Treasury sought to procure cuts in government establishments by setting an example with its reduction of Treasury salaries and calling upon other departments to follow its lead. But it is a fundamental feature of nineteenth-century Treasury control that its power to secure cuts was far smaller than its ability to refuse increases. The growth of superannuation allowances in the Civil Service was therefore an important supplementary opportunity for the Treasury to negotiate for economies in return for pay and pension settlements.

FROM Treasury Minute of 10 August 1821 on the reduction and alteration of Departmental Establishments, and control of superannuation (*PP* (1822) XVII pp. 5–10).

My Lords read the Address of the House of Commons of the 28th June last, praying His Majesty to order a minute inquiry into the several departments of the civil government, as well with a view to reducing the number of persons employed in those departments (which, from the great increase of business, were augmented during the late war), as with reference to the increased salaries granted to individuals since the year 1797: Also the Address of the House of Lords of the 2nd of July, in which their Lordships beseech His Majesty, that, for the purpose of affording a further relief to the country, he will be pleased to order a minute inquiry into the several departments of the civil government . . . [After reciting various reports and Treasury minutes relevant to economical reform in establishments, the Treasury Lords proceed to make a sweeping revision of the size and salary scales of the Treasury's own establishment, discussed in Section 3, above p. 92.] My Lords are further pleased to direct letters to be written to the heads of the respective departments under-mentioned, and who will communicate their Lordships directions to the offices immediately under their superintendence, vizt. [over forty departments, including the Foreign Office, Home Office, Colonial Office, War Office, Admiralty, Ordnance Office, all the revenue departments and Exchequer and audit offices in England and Ireland], desiring that they will respectively cause to be made out and communicated to my Lords as soon as practicable, and at any rate before the 10th of October next, such plan for the reduction of their respective establishments as they may think most expedient, with a view of providing for the efficient execution of the duties of their several departments, at the smallest expense to the public.

Let a letter be written to the Chief Secretary for Ireland, directing him to call upon the principals of the different public departments in that country to furnish, for their Lordships consideration, similar plans for the reduction of their respective establishments.

My Lords, in calling upon the heads of the other departments of his Majesty's civil government, to enter upon a revision of their respective establishments, with a view to such economical reductions as may fulfil the intention of his Majesty, expressed in his answers to the Addresses of both Houses of Parliament, think it right to state the principles upon which they have proceeded, and the course they have followed in the revision of the establishment of the Treasury, under their immediate direction.

They have thought that they should best carry into execution the intentions expressed in the Addresses of Parliament, by keeping in view the following General Rules:

1st. That every office was to be restored to the situation, in respect to the number of persons employed and of their respective emoluments, in which it stood in 1797, unless some adequate cause continued to exist which rendered some alteration necessary.

2nd. That where increase of business, or the more correct and efficient execution of the public service, rendered it necessary to preserve establishments either created or enlarged since 1797, the emoluments of the officers composing those establishments should be assimilated, as nearly as the change of circumstances would admit, to those received by persons in similar situations in 1797.

3rd. That if any office, existing in 1797, was found to be no longer necessary to the public service, or that its emoluments might be properly reduced, such office should be abolished, or reduced in value, as the case might admit.

SUPERANNUATION

My Lords are of opinion, that it is essentially necessary that some new regulations should be adopted, with a view of limiting this branch of the public expenditure in future; and they are of opinion that the mode of regulation which seems in all respects most eligible is, to require that the individuals themselves who may hereafter enjoy the benefit of superannuation allowances should be called upon to contribute to a Superannuation Fund, to be administered under the direction of their Lordships ...

[Sixth Regulation] No superannuation to be granted to any such contributor except by the Treasury, and by that Board only at four periods to be fixed in each year (except in cases of immediate urgency)

when a special Board or Boards shall be held for the purpose of considering all applications received in the preceding quarter; notice of
which Board shall be given to the heads of the departments recommending such applications, from each of which some proper officer
shall, if required, attend to answer all such questions as the Board of
Treasury may put, in order to enable them to decide upon the fitness
or relative urgency of each application; and to distribute the disposable
amount of the Fund, or so much of it as may be requisite, in such
manner as, upon all examination of all the cases before them, may
appear most conducive to justice and the public interest.

17. Treasury control of estimates and audit: the Reports of Select Committees in 1847-8 and 1856.

As the ordinary expenses of government were withdrawn from the Crown's Civil List and made the subject of annual parliamentary votes, so the Treasury's opportunity to adjudicate on government expenditure was enhanced. It was entitled to submit departmental estimates (excluding those of the War Office and Admiralty) to careful scrutiny before they were presented to the House of Commons by the Financial Secretary. This kind of discretionary control made the Treasury increasingly impatient with the obstructive, formalistic check operated by the Comptroller of the Exchequer.

[a] FROM The Report of the Select Committee on Miscellaneous Expenditure (*PP* (1847-8), XVIII (I)).

Evidence given by Sir Alexander Spearman (formerly Treasury Clerk of Parliamentary Accounts, Auditor of the Civil List, and Assistant Secretary to the Treasury until 1840) and Charles Long Crafer (Spearman's successor as Treasury Estimates Clerk in 1835).

Question 11. [Chairman to Spearman] Probably you can state to the Committee, during the time you held that office, what was the general course in the preparation of the Estimates for Parliament? – The first step, I think, that was taken, invariably was, that the secretary to the Treasury called upon all the departments to transmit their Estimates for the consideration of the Lords of the Treasury. There were certain other Estimates that were absolutely framed in the Treasury.

12. At what period of the year did that take place? – Generally, at the close of the year, so as to give ample time for the transmission of the Estimates to the Treasury, and then for the Chancellor of the Exchequer and the secretary of the Treasury to consider them.

17. When the Estimate arrived, was it submitted to the Board of the Treasury? – No. The mode that was followed, during the time that I was at the Treasury was this, the Estimates as soon as they were received were placed in the hands of the clerk of Parliamentary accounts, whose business it was to arrange them in classes; by him they were laid before the secretary of the Treasury, and the secretary of the Treasury then communicated with the Chancellor of the Exchequer upon the subject. It was the business of the Chancellor of the Exchequer, and not that of the Board of Treasury.

29. [Mr Henley] What has the clerk of Parliamentary accounts to do with them in the interval between receiving them in the first instance

from the secretary to the Treasury and returning them to him? – In the first place, he should classify them; in the next place he should prepare such memoranda of the expenditure as he is able, from his knowledge of the subject, to prepare for the consideration of his superior; and the whole of the papers are then placed in the hands of the Secretary to the Treasury, who consults with the clerk of Parliamentary accounts as his assistant in such matters.

53. Did the explanation or observation upon the return go beyond noticing any excess or decrease in the expense; did it go to the expense itself? – I should certainly not have considered that I was justified in dealing with the principle of whether such a sum, or such another sum, was necessary for the expenditure of any department. My business was to lay before those who were to decide upon the point the amount of the Estimates, together with such explanation as I was able to give. It was for them, not for me, to decide as to whether the sum was too large or not.

87. [Dr Bowring to C. L. Crafer] When the documents are returned by the Treasury to the departments, are they returned with objections to the specific items, or for general revision? – Both courses have been taken on different occasions. Sometimes the Estimates are returned, if any charge is objected to at the Treasury, by the Chancellor of the Exchequer; they may either be returned by him privately, or with an official letter, pointing out the objection; that is done sometimes. On other occasions he may consider that a general revision of the Estimate should take place, and then it is sent back for the department to reconsider.

88. Is not the case at the present time that the whole of the Estimates have been returned? – The whole of the Estimates have been returned, with a direction to the departments to re-consider them, and to make every reduction that can be made.

91. [Chairman] In point of fact have you yourself known, in ordinary years, any great diminution suggested by the Treasury in the Estimates submitted by the different departments, so as to form a very effectual control? – I have known very large reductions made by the Chancellor of the Exchequer; not merely suggested, but made in the Estimates.

92. And assented to by the departments to which they were returned? – In some instances they have been submitted to, in others they have shown good reason why the charge should be retained.

121. [Mr Henley to Spearman] Does the Treasury subsequently exercise any authority over the application of the money? – No doubt, in this way. Take the case of the Admiralty: they are bound by Act of Parliament to lay before the Commissioners of Audit a statement of the mode in which they have spent the grant; and if the Board of Audit find that they have exceeded the amount granted for any

particular head of service, it is the business of the Board of Audit to report that fact to the Treasury.

123. [Sir G. Clerk to Crafer] By a Treasury Minute every department of expenditure is bound to apply for the previous sanction of the Treasury before they can apply an excess of grant under one head to make up a deficiency under another? – Certainly.

124. [Dr Bowring] That sanction being obtained, the transfer may be made from one head to another? – Yes.

125. Are you aware that that state of things is altogether opposed to the system adopted in France? – I am not aware of the system in France.

[b] FROM The Report of the Select Committee on Public Monies (*PP* (1856) XV).

Evidence given by W. G. Anderson, Principal Clerk of the Treasury's Finance Division, 9 June and 10 July 1856.

Q.939 [Chairman] What, in your opinion, is the great object of the finance system? – It appears to me that the objects of such a system should be, the security of the public money, the utmost simplicity of management, and the greatest economy in the employment of the public balances.

940. How do you think that those three objects are to be best obtained, as a general principle? – I think that those objects will be best attained by placing the finances under one individual control and responsibility, consolidating all the public monies into one fund, and issuing them from that fund under one direct authority – the direct authority of the controlling department.

1021. [Mr Henley] Then, if I understand your opinion rightly upon this subject, it is this, that there ought to be no check whatever upon the Treasury as to any issue of money from the Exchequer, but that the only check, so far as the public is concerned, would be in the other departments, or parties to whom this money is issued? – I think that the Treasury should be the department of check and its control is far more efficient than any which the Exchequer can exercise; it has the control over the expending departments. The Treasury spends but little itself, but it can control those by whom the public money is applied.

1090. [Chairman] You stated that you thought that the Audit Office was the best check upon the expenditure of the public money, and that the control of the Exchequer was comparatively useless? – Yes.

1091. You were speaking, were you not, of the system of audit which exists under Sir James Graham's Bill? – Precisely.

1171. [Mr Wilson] I think the substance of your evidence is, that the functions of the Exchequer are, that the Comptroller of the Exchequer has no power whatever over the receipt of monies before they are brought to the Exchequer; that he has only power over the account in the Bank of England, which stands in his name, for the purpose of preventing any issue to the Paymaster's credit upon account of supply services, for which ways and means have not been provided, and seeing that the whole aggregate amount of the votes is not exceeded in the issues in the course of the year? – Those are the functions of the Comptroller, and that is the full extent to which they can be exercised.

1172. He neither knows anything of the monies before they come into the Exchequer, nor does he know anything of the monies after they pass to the credit of the Paymaster out of the Exchequer? – No, he has no control over the receipt. His duty there resolves itself into a simple matter of book-keeping, and as regards the issue, he has a control over the aggregate issue, but he has no control over the application of the different parts of the issue.

1173. Then, with regard to the Treasury, the functions of the Treasury are these, a central and general check, and not those of expenditure? – The Treasury is to a limited extent, but only to a limited extent, a department authorising expenditure upon some of the miscellaneous votes. It has no control over the application of any portion of the monies voted for Army services; it has no control over the application of any portion of the monies voted for the Navy services, or the Commissariat, or any other military services; but it is the department whose duty, according to its constitution, should be to control those departments through which the expenditure is conducted.

1174. But the whole of the functions of the Treasury are rather those of control than of expenditure? – Clearly, the Treasury has greater power of exercising control than the Exchequer, because it can call upon any department for explanation if it finds that the department is spending a larger proportion of their grants than the Treasury thinks they ought to have spent in a certain period, and it can call upon them to revise their accounts and their estimates, that they may satisfy the Treasury that they have made a sufficient provision for carrying on the public service for the year. This actually occurred last year, and the whole of those departments were brought before Parliament to demand supplemental estimates. The control of the Exchequer would have come too late ... and unless the Treasury had exercised its control in time they must have been in the predicament of not having sufficient monies to carry on those great services.

1179. [Mr Hankey] Is every estimate necessarily submitted to the Treasury before it is brought to Parliament? – It is done; I cannot say that they are minutely investigated, but those large estimates are principally settled in the Cabinet. The force is agreed upon, and that regulates in great measure all the rest of those great services. An estimate cannot be submitted to the House until it has received the sanction of the Treasury.

1181. Then it rests upon the responsibility of the Treasury to furnish ways and means from time to time, and to see that they have the means of meeting the demands which Parliament has granted for all those services? – The Treasury calculate their ways and means upon the amount of those estimates, and if those departments exceed them of course they disturb the whole of the financial arrangements of the Treasury; it is exceedingly inconvenient to the Government, and it is therefore necessary that the Treasury should exercise a control over those departments, because their own proceedings are very much dependent upon the due observance of the regulations laid down at the commencement of the Session.

1187. Then the general nature of the duties of the Treasury extending over the whole of the financial area of income and expenditure, places the Treasury in a much better situation than any other department can be of control over the whole? – I think the Treasury is a department of control; the responsibility for every variation ultimately rests with them.

1385. [Sir James Graham] I observe that you state in your memorandum that the best control is an effective audit after payment? – I think it is the only effectual control.

1386. You then go on to say, let your system be based on confidence in the Government, and let the controlling responsible department of the State have full freedom of action; does not Parliamentary control rather proceed on an opposite principle than great confidence in the Government? – No doubt. Parliamentary jealousy rather, we might say. I think that Parliament would act wisely to strengthen and place a little more confidence in the controlling department of the Government, because control through a Parliamentary officer before payment can only be carried out by placing restrictions and impediments in the way of business.

1885. [Chairman] I mean this: is not the Treasury responsible if they submit for a vote in Parliament a sum which is not required for any particular office which is contained in the Civil Service Estimate? – You cannot ascertain whether the sum for an establishment is too much, or whether the establishment is too large, without an investigation into the duties of the office itself; that would necessitate a revision of the whole duties of the department. As long as the establishment exists the money must be provided to pay it.

2161. [Mr Williams] Then the control exercised by the Treasury over the general expenditure is only partial under all circumstances? –

The great departments charged with the execution of the public business are the departments that really control the expenditure. The control of the Treasury is of a general character, to see that those departments keep within the limits of the sums appropriated by Parliament for their respective departments.

2196. [Mr Williams] Does the Treasury exercise any control over the preparation of the estimates for the different departments ? – Yes; all the estimates are submitted to the Treasury before they are laid on the Table of the House; the Army and Navy Estimates are prepared in the respective departments; of course, previous communications take place between the heads of those departments and the Government as to the extent of the force to be employed, and that having been determined, the estimates are prepared accordingly; and those estimates, before they are finally completed and laid on the Table of House, are submitted to the Treasury for their approval. All the Miscellaneous Estimates are prepared in the Treasury; returns are obtained from the various departments, and they are finally embodied in those classes which are known under the title of Miscellaneous Estimates for Civil Service.

2198. Does the Treasury exercise any authority over the amounts of the different items ? – The Treasury has the power of objecting to any items in those estimates; and if that occurred there would be a communication between the ministers at the head of the two departments, and the estimates would probably be withdrawn and presented afresh. There is a power in the Treasury of objecting to any items in those estimates.

2199. And that objection would be made effective, would it not ? – In my short experience at the Treasury I do not recollect any case in which the estimates have been reduced. It would be a serious responsibility for the Treasury to cut down war estimates.

2200. In time of peace do they exercise any more authority ? – Yes; those estimates undergo revision; I do not say that it is very minute; but the scale of expenditure is so agreed on before hand between the ministers at the head of the two departments, (between the Chancellor of the Exchequer and the ministers controlling those departments) that there is no chance of any rejection when the estimates come before the Treasury.

2201. Then it comes to a question of agreement amongst the Cabinet Ministers ? – Yes; those large questions are Cabinet questions.

10 July 1856

4179. [Graham] You presume a daily knowledge on the part of the Treasury, under the system suggested, of the exact state of the cash account under each vote; and also you presume the subordination of all the departments to the supreme authority of the Treasury? – Clearly so.

4180. Those are the two assumptions? – Yes, I apprehend that without subordination there can be no control at all.

4181. Upon these two assumptions of daily knowledge, and the effective control which should be exercised, you think, with concurrent audit, the system would be perfect? – I think it would be very stringent.

4182. You would also recommend early and frequent communications by the Audit department to Parliament? – As frequently as necessity might arise.

4183. [Sir Henry Willoughby] If the control of the Treasury breaks down, who is to carry into effect the powers given? – Parliament must be the last resort in all those cases.

4186. [Graham] Is not the object of the Legislature to concentrate and accumulate control in the Treasury? – I think it should be so, as the responsibility ultimately rests with the controlling department of the Government.

18. The Exchequer and Audit Departments Act of 1866.

This Act placed the coping stone on the structure of collaborative control of public expenditure by Treasury, Exchequer and Parliament. In clause 33 it looks beyond the mere checking of appropriation accounts to the prospect of checking on the efficiency, as well as the economy, of public spending.

FROM An Act to consolidate the Duties of the Exchequer and Audit Departments, to regulate the Receipt, Custody, and Issue of Public Moneys, and to provide for the Audit of the Accounts thereof (29 & 30 Vict. c. 39, *Public General Statutes*, London, 1866).

§ 27. Every appropriation account shall be examined by the Comptroller and Auditor General on behalf of the House of Commons; and in the examination of such accounts the Comptroller and Auditor General shall ascertain, first, whether the payments which the accounting Department has charged to the grant are supported by vouchers or proofs of payments, and second, whether the money expended has been applied to the purpose or purposes for which such grant was intended to provide: provided always, and it is hereby enacted, that whenever the said Comptroller and Auditor General shall be required by the Treasury to ascertain whether the expenditure included or to be included in an appropriation account, or any portion of such expenditure, is supported by the authority of the Treasury, the Comptroller and Auditor General shall examine such expenditure with that object, and shall report to the Treasury any expenditure which may appear, upon such examination, to have been incurred without such authority; and if the Treasury should not thereupon see fit to sanction such unauthorized expenditure, it shall be regarded as being not properly chargeable to a Parliamentary grant, and shall be reported to the House of Commons in the manner hereinafter provided.

§ 33. Besides the appropriation accounts of the grants of Parliament, the Comptroller and Auditor General shall examine and audit, if required so to do by the Treasury, and in accordance with any regulations that may be prescribed for his guidance in that behalf by the Treasury, the following accounts; *viz.*, the accounts of all principal accountants, the accounts of the receipt of revenue by the departments of Customs, Inland Revenue, and Post Office, the accounts of every receiver of money which is by law payable into Her Majesty's Exchequer, and any other public accounts which, though not relating directly to the receipt or expenditure of Imperial funds, the Treasury may by Minute, to be laid before Parliament, direct.

19. Treasury control re-defined: the Treasury Minute of April 1868.

This Minute marks the earliest stage in the long working relationship between the Treasury and the Comptroller and Auditor-General. It reveals the essentially negative character of Treasury control, which could be exerted only upon proposed increases of public expenditure; but in its last paragraph the Minute urges the Comptroller to use his discretion in applying the deceptively simple definition of Treasury control outlined above.

FROM Treasury Minute, April 1868; Appendix 1, No. 4, to the Report from the Committee of Public Accounts (*PP* (1867–8) XIII p. 607).

My Lords have before them Mr Ryan's[1] letters of 25 February and 28 March last, conveying the opinion of the Comptroller and Auditor General upon the subject of the provisions of the 27th section of the Exchequer and Audit Departments Act, and requesting the instructions of the Treasury thereon. State in reply, that my Lords, in their Minute of 28 February, deferred issuing directions upon the subject dealt with in the 27th section of the Exchequer and Audit Departments Act until the arrangements connected with the Appropriation Accounts were in a more forward state; but that directions regarding these accounts have now been issued, and my Lords have taken under their consideration the question as to how far the expenditure included in these Appropriation Accounts should be supported by the direct authority of the Treasury.

It appears to my Lords that it would be beyond the functions of this Board to control the ordinary expenditure placed under the charge of the several departments, within the limits of the sums set forth under the subheads of the several grants of Parliament, and that it is only in exceptional cases that the special sanction of the Treasury should be held to be necessary.

My Lords consider that such sanction should be required for any increase of establishment, of salary, or of cost of a service, or for any additional works or new services which have not been specially provided for in the grants of Parliament.

My Lords therefore desire that, in conducting the Appropriation Audit of the several Votes, the Comptroller and Auditor General will bring to their notice any excess of charge beyond the amount assigned to each subhead of such Votes, or any expenditure which, upon examination may, in any of the several cases referred to above, appear to

[1] The Assistant Comptroller and Auditor-General.

have been incurred without Treasury authority, in order that my Lords may determine whether they will sanction the admission of such unauthorized expenditure as a charge against the Parliamentary grant.

Add, that my Lords at the same time do not wish to limit the discretion of the Comptroller and Auditor General in reporting to this Board upon any item of expenditure which, in his opinion, should be the subject of special Treasury authority.

20. The Treasury and the City: a proposal to create an Assistant (Financial) Secretary, 1710.

This proposal, submitted to Robert Harley on his appointment as Chancellor of the Exchequer, is an interesting reflection of the demand for expert knowledge which the 'financial revolution' was imposing upon the Treasury.

A Proposal humbly offered for constituting an Assistant Secretary to the Right Honourable the Lords Commissioners of Her Majesty's Treasury – from Mr Slyford, August 17th, 1710 (BM Loan 29/45B 12/253).

The great business which the Treasury now has, more than in former times, and the continual increase which the war and the Union bring to it, do plainly show the occasion that there is for such an Assistant. But the usefulness of this constitution will farther and more particularly appear from the methods and services he is proposed to pursue.

This Assistant, at such times as he does not attend the sittings of the said Lords Commissioners, it is humbly proposed may employ his thoughts how to draw the several affairs of the Treasury into distinct and obvious schemes that may plainly and readily show, upon any occasion, the true state and course of any part thereof; as for instance, and in respect to the more immediate service, such a scheme may show:

– what payments are now instant on the Treasury and will become due, before new funds and methods can be settled by Parliament;

– what means are provided to answer those payments;

– what funds or securities there are to support them;

– what is raised upon them for those services and what remains to be raised;

– how those payments are to be made, and when the accounts are balanced.

Such schemes, it is humbly conceived, are as useful and necessary in great concerns of state, that have great accounts, as – it is well known – good and accurate maps are in the science of geography.

He is to get the soonest intelligence he can of any contrivances or practices on foot concerning any of the principal stocks in the City, and consider how their fall may be prevented or the public credit secured from any mischiefs by it, as it is believed may be effectually done by proper methods and such an authority from the Treasury.

He is to take all occasions and opportunities of enquiring into other matters that may be of service to the Government; as the prices current of those commodities which the Government takes considerable quantities of; what rates the Government pays for them, and several other occurrences that may be useful for the Government if timely known at the Treasury.

For these purposes, this Assistant should frequent the Royal Exchange at the usual Exchange hours, and have some known place to be at, where any persons may come to him that are willing to communicate any means or methods for improving the Government's revenues, raising proper funds, or for advancement of the public credit, or any other service for the Government.

He is to take minutes of what is so communicated, and is to examine the validity of what is proposed by considering all the reasons for and against that he either knows himself or can learn from others of the best skill and experience in such matters.

Such proposals as are valuable, he is to draw up in clear method and lay before the said Lords Commissioners, without troubling the proposers to attend and solicit about them, unless they are willing and until required by their Lordships.

In regard a method is considered for exerting the public credit after a better manner than has yet been done in Britain, and as beneficial for our Government – with respect to low interest and certainty of the supplies – as any state in Europe now does; and in regard the nature of this method requires its being settled by Parliament, and the public necessities seem to call for it the next session; and that the said Lords Commissioners may have timely and ample satisfaction about the merit and success of it; it is humbly suggested that this Assistant may take the proper opportunities he may have to get the opinion and testimony of the ablest and most knowing persons in the City, concerning the practicableness and great advantages to the nation of this important method, and an assurance of their readiness to assist in its favour whenever it may be requisite.

21. The eighteenth-century Treasury Establishment: Minutes on organization and reform, 1714–82.

These minutes reflect the Treasury's developing concern with the efficiency and professionalism of the clerical Establishment, and include the reorganization minutes of 1776 and 1782 which fundamentally influenced the character of the nineteenth-century Treasury.

(a)	18 November 1714	(i)	16 March 1722
(b)	28 August 1716	(j)	27 July 1757
(c)	14 May 1717	(k)	31 July 1759
(d)	17 December 1717	(l)	4 September 1759
(e)	22 July 1718	(m)	22 December 1761
(f)	3 April 1721	(n)	22 February 1776
(g)	20 April 1721	(o)	30 November 1782
(h)	6 September 1721		

FROM Treasury Minute Books, PRO T 29/22, pp. 29–32; T 29/23 pp. 24, 106, 179; T 29/24(i) p. 63; T 29/24(ii) pp. 43, 51, 92, 152; T 29/32 p. 475; T 29/33 pp. 218–19; T 29/34 p. 207; T 29/45 p. 54; T 29/52 pp. 516–24.

[a] 1714 November 18

The under-written paper being read and considered was approved by their Lordships, *vizt.*,

Orders for the more regular keeping of papers and despatch of business at the Treasury

The 4 Chief Clerks

Mr Glanville: To receive all petitions, and when they are read to enter the answers that shall be endorsed thereupon in a book to be kept for that purpose, and to prepare such letters or references as shall be directed. Also to lay up such petitions as shall have received final answers, and when a second petition shall be brought by any suitor, after one has been answered, he is to return it back or tear it; and likewise to enter in the said book the orders or resolutions of the Lords of the Treasury which shall be written or endorsed upon any reports, letters or memorials upon reading thereof before their Lordships.

Mr Tilson: To have the custody of all memorials, papers and reports coming from the Navy, Ordnance, Paymaster of the Land Forces, Secretary at War and other officers relating to military affairs and public funds (petitions excepted) as also from the Surveyor General and Surveyors of the Woods, the Auditors of Imprests and Auditors of the Revenues and Plantations, Remembrancers, Clerk of the Pipe or any other the offices belonging to the Court or Receipt of the Exchequer, and to draw the warrants or letters relating thereunto: and to receive and have the custody of all certificates of receipts and payments in public office; also to have the care and inspection of the making up quarterly and annual accounts and abstracts of the receipts and issues of his Majesty's revenues from the said certificates.

Mr Powys: To receive all reports and papers whatsoever (petitions excepted) relating to the Customs, Excise, Post Office, Stamp Duties, Hackney Coaches and Chairs, Hawkers and Pedlars, Alienation Office, Wine Licences, and First Fruits and Tenths, and to draw such warrants and orders as shall be directed thereupon; also to receive all memorials relating to the allowances to Ambassadors, Envoys, etc., from His Majesty to foreign Princes and States, and to prepare the warrants for them when directed, and to have the custody of all letters to the Lords of the Treasury concerning the public from the Secretaries of State, Ambassadors, Envoys, etc., from foreign Princes, Governors of the Plantations, and such like; and of the reports and papers (petitions excepted) relating to Ireland.

Mr Kelsey [i.e. Kelsall.]: To receive and have the custody of all memorials, papers and accounts from the Cofferer, Treasurer of the Chamber, Great Wardrobe, Works and Gardens, Stables, Jewel Office, and other offices relating to the civil government, and also of all papers concerning Scotland (certificates of the Receivers there and petitions excepted); and to prepare the warrants directed upon any of them; also to collect, make up, and (if need be) abstract the papers to be from time to time laid before the King.

All other casual papers and business not here enumerated [are] to be put into the hands of such of the four Chief Clerks as the Secretaries shall think most proper, who are immediately from time to time to make short entries or memorandums thereof, and keep them in such order as they may readily be laid before the Lords of the Treasury at any time when required.

And it is further ordered by their Lordships that the said Chief Clerks respectively do every day of their Lordships' sitting deliver to their Secretaries in the morning the respective papers and reports remaining in their several custodies, which according to the orders hung up in the Treasury . . . are to be considered as the business of the day, and that such of them as through their Lordships' want of time may not receive answers that day, be delivered back to the proper clerks to be kept till that day sevennight, unless any of them are called for sooner or contain matters of haste or importance.

[b] 1716 August 28

My Lords order that all drafts of Privy Seals and other warrants which are not things of course be brought to the Secretaries or one of them to be perused and examined before they are presented to the King for his signature or to the Lords [of the Treasury] for theirs.

[c] May 14

My Lords upon reading a letter from his Grace the Duke of Bolton, Lord Lieutenant of Ireland, in the words following, *vizt.*,

My Lords   6 May 1717

I have made choice of Mr Webster (one of your Lordships' clerks) for my secretary in the affairs of Ireland with a view to do him service and not to remove him from the settlement he hath in the Treasury to a preferment which though beneficial to him is but precarious in its duration. I therefore desire your Lordships will please to give him leave of absence and that he may enjoy his salary and not suffer in his pretensions in the office whilst he is in my service. This, my Lords, is but a reasonable request in behalf of a gentleman who hath served twenty-six years in the Treasury under very small encouragement and will be esteemed as a favour done,

My Lords, etc., etc., Bolton

Their Lordships do agree to the request of the said Duke made in Mr Webster's behalf and have ordered this minute to be made accordingly.

[d] December 17

The Clerks and Under Clerks are directed not to lay any warrants, orders, etc., upon their Lordships' table for their signing unless directions have been given for the same by three or more of their Lordships.

[e] 1718 July 22

My Lords being apprehensive that, in cases where officers under their power are allowed to resign their offices in order to the admittance of other particular persons, sums of money are given in consideration thereof do resolve not to consent to any such resignations for the future.

[f] 1721 April 3

My Lords dismiss Mr King from the office of Chamber Keeper of the Treasury and appoint Mr Thomas Mann to succeed him, but are pleased to declare they will give him an employment of equal value upon his acquainting my Lords with such a vacancy.

[g] April 20

Mr William Pitt, one of the Under Clerks of the Treasury, signifies by letter his resignation of that employment which my Lords accept of and do appoint Mr Peter Leheup to succeed him.

[h] September 6

Mr Christopher Lowe is appointed by the Secretaries to be a Clerk in the inner room, and my Lords agree that a salary of £50 p.a. be allowed him to commence from Midsummer last, and that the allowance of £100 p.a. be continued to Mr Webster.

[i] 1722 March 16

Whereas my Lords did on the 20th November last upon the humble petition of Mr Thomas Lowndes, a Clerk in the inner room at the salary of £50 p.a., give their consent that he should resign his said office to Mr Stephen Martin, Jr, he not being able to attend the duty thereof any longer upon account of his ill state of health, to which the Secretaries agreed and by my Lords' order the said Martin was to have the allowance of £50 p.a. as the youngest Clerk in the inner room; their Lordships, being better informed of the capacity of the said Mr Stephen Martin, Jr, do judge him not qualified to be a Clerk in the inner room of the Treasury and have therefore determined that he shall not be admitted, especially finding by the second application of the said Thomas Lowndes to them that he had contracted with the said Martin to resign his office to him for a pecuniary consideration with which my Lords were utterly unacquainted and do therefore in detestation of so vile and pernicious a practice revoke their first order of admittance.

[j] 1757 July 27

My Lords direct that Mr Burnaby succeed Mr Henry Fane as one of the Chief Clerks in the Treasury.

That the Under Clerks rise according to seniority as has been usual in the office, Mr Watkins filling up the vacancy.

That Mr Wilkins and Mr Speer, both good Clerks and Accomptants, having for a great number of years discharged their duty with industry and fidelity, be placed upon the Establishment.

That two of the Junior Clerks be appointed by the Secretaries to do business in the Accomptant's Office in order thoroughly to understand that branch of business.

That the Under Clerks do attend every day in the office from ten o'clock in the forenoon till four o'clock in the afternoon except Saturdays, and that the four junior Clerks do attend every Saturday at the same hours in rotation by two at a time.

[k] 1759 July 31

Ordered that Mr Postlethwayt be admitted this day a Principal Clerk of the Treasury in the room of Mr William Lowndes, and Mr Yeates, another Principal Clerk, in the room of Mr Burnaby; the Duke of Newcastle acquainting the Lords that the King had been pleased to promise a pension of £500 p.a. to Mr William Lowndes and Mr Burnaby.

The following disposition of the Treasury business is ordered by the Lords, *vizt.*,

Mr Kelsall is to read at the Board all petitions, memorials, etc.,

Mr Lowndes is to draw or examine (and correct when it may be necessary) all warrants, orders and contracts to be laid before the Lords of the Treasury for their signature.

Mr Postlethwayt is to enter the minutes of the Treasury and write the letters for issues to the Navy, Army and Ordnance, entering on the respective memorials the sums issued, and the times when issued, and carefully laying up the memorials when the issues thereupon shall be completed, and to examine all stated accounts, and also to make up the accounts of the office fees.

Mr Yeates is to write all letters (other than for the above-mentioned issues) and references according to the directions given by their Lordships' minutes, and to do all parliamentary business.

Each of the said Clerks at the end of every year is to deliver all papers of the preceding year, by schedules, to the officer for keeping the Treasury papers.

Though this be the general distribution proposed, yet each of the Principal Clerks is expected to be ready to undertake any business that the Lords or either of their Secretaries shall require.

[l] September 4

Mr Postlethwayt and Mr Yeates were called in and exhorted by the Duke of Newcastle to diligence and constant attendance and to live in harmony with their brethren.

[m] 1761 December 22

Read a paper written by Mr Martin [Junior Secretary to the Treasury] from Mr Pratt's mouth declining the office of a fifth Supernumerary [Chief] Clerk on account of his health.

Mr Martin acquaints my Lords that Mr Davis and Mr Tomkyns as well as Mr Pratt had each refused, though with great respect, to be the fifth Supernumerary Principal Clerk upon the terms intended by their Lordships, and Mr Rowe being asked the same question and agreeing to accept of the Lords' proposition in case the Duke of Newcastle, who hath been always his patron, shall command or desire it, is called in and acquainted by his Grace that he does expect it, and Mr Rowe agrees accordingly to accept.

My Lords order therefore that he be a fifth Supernumerary Clerk with a pension of neat £600 p.a. Mr Speer is called in and told that my Lords order him an increase of £160 p.a. to his salary in consideration of his particular merit, but his successor is to stand reduced to the salary which Mr Speer enjoyed at his entrance into his present office.

[n] 1776 February 22

Mr Davis, late one of the four Chief Clerks in this office, being dead, my Lords proposed to Mr Tompkyns, the Senior Clerk on the Establishment, to succeed to that office, but Mr Tompkyns desiring to decline my Lords direct the same to be offered to Sir John H. Mill, and he also desiring to decline my Lords are pleased to appoint Mr Reynolds to succeed Mr Davis as one of the four Chief Clerks of the Treasury.

My Lords on this occasion, taking into consideration the present state of the Clerks of the Treasury, are of opinion that the following regulations would be of great utility and tend much to the better conducting and carrying on the public business of the office. And as it is inconvenient to Mr Tomkyns, Sir John H. Mill, Mr Watkins and Mr Schutz from their situation and circumstances to attend the duties of their departments, my Lords direct that they be superannuated on the respective annuities following . . .

And that no persons be appointed in their room, my Lords being of opinion that the business may be effectually carried on without any new appointments. And in order to arrange the business of the office in such manner that in future every Clerk may from his entry into the office be regularly instructed, and go through every branch of business in succession as he shall be promoted, my Lords propose the following arrangement of the business to take place the 1st of March 1776, *vizt.*

[A detailed distribution among each of the Treasury Clerks follows, e.g.

John Martin Leake [a senior Under-Clerk] Army, Navy, Ordnance, Ordnance officers, America, American Customs, Treasurer of the Chamber, Gibraltar and Minorca, Stamp Office, Wine Licence officers, Cofferer.]

In respect to the Revenue Office, my Lords are of opinion that it should be kept as a distinct and separate department with Mr Speer at the head of it, at a salary of £100 on the Establishment and £700 p.a. from the Customs, and the several other Clerks with the respective salaries following [six clerks with salaries ranging from £100 *plus* £350 to £100 *plus* £100] as from 1st March 1776. And the persons named as Revenue Clerks to succeed in that office only.

And my Lords, in consideration of the very great encouragement now given to the several Clerks of the Treasury, do expect and are pleased to order that they shall daily and regularly attend in the office hours and personally transact the business assigned to them, as well as to execute a proportional share of the public business, and not leave the office during the sitting of the Board or when the public service requires their attendance, except dispensed with by order of the Board.

And if any Clerk shall absent himself without such authority and the business in his branch shall by that means be done by any other person, such persons shall be entitled to, and receive, the gratuity arising thereby.

And in case any other business shall arise which is not comprehended in this distribution, my Lords order that such business shall be executed by such Clerks as their Lordships or the Secretaries or either of them shall direct.

And my Lords think fit to declare that in all future regulations of this office and distributions of the business they shall regard the ability, attention, care and diligence of the respective Clerks, and not their seniority, and that in their opinion this rule at all times hereafter ought to be attended to, and pursued, in order the better to conduct and carry on the public business.

My Lords request Lord North that he will be pleased to lay this minute before his Majesty and humbly submit to his Majesty their Lordships' opinion thereon.[1]

[o] 1782 November 30

Mr Rowe and Sir Ferdinando Poole, two of the Chief Clerks of this office, having expressed a desire to resign, my Lords approve thereof and request the Earl of Shelburne will be pleased to take his Majesty's pleasure for granting pensions of £500 p.a. to each ...

My Lords upon this occasion taking into consideration the present state of this office, and having obtained full information hereupon, are of opinion it is highly important that new regulations should be established in order to the business being well and expeditiously done.

Read a minute of this Board of the 22nd February 1776 respecting the attendance of the Clerks and another of the same date declaring that in all future regulations in this office, and distribution of the business, the Lords will regard the ability, attention, care and diligence of the respective Clerks and not their seniority, expressing also their

---

[1] The King's approval was reported to the next Board meeting, 23 February 1776.

opinion that the said rule ought at all times hereafter to be attended to
and pursued . . .

My Lords are of opinion that it is adviseable to follow the spirit of
those minutes in the present arrangement and are pleased to appoint
Mr Cotton and Mr Leake to succeed Mr Rowe and Sir Ferdinando
Poole as Chief Clerks. [Other promotions are noted.]

Mr Webster having absented himself from the office for more than
two years without leave, and it being understood that he went long
since to the East Indies in the service of the Company, my Lords are
pleased to discontinue him as a Clerk in this office . . .

An account of the fees received by the Secretaries and Chief Clerks
during three years of peace from 1769 to 1771 inclusive and three
years of war from 1779 to 1781 inclusive being laid before the Board,
it appeared that on an average in the former period thereof, the
Secretaries amounted to £3414 p.a. each and the Chief Clerks to £853
p.a. each; and in the latter the Secretaries to £5114 and the Chief
Clerks to £1278. And an account of the produce of each branch of
business and of the profits arising therefrom to the several Clerks of
the Establishment according to the present distribution being also
produced, it appears the income of the Clerks of the Establishment
differ likewise in peace and war, as well as those of the Secretaries and
Chief Clerks, and that the profits of several of the branches of business
are very disproportionate to the trouble and responsibility.

My Lords are therefore pleased to direct that out of the common
stock of office fees the Secretaries shall receive a fixed allowance of
£3000 p.a. each, clear of all deductions, and the Chief Clerks £800 p.a.
each, in like manner clear of all deductions, and that in future the
several allowances following shall be annexed to the respective branches
of business to be paid also out of the common stock of the office fees . . .

[A detailed schedule follows]

And a new arrangement and distribution of the business being
rendered necessary by the promotions now made, my Lords are of
opinion it will conduce much to the several branches being well
understood and conducted with correctness that a Senior and a Junior
Clerk in the office shall be appointed to each Division and therefore
determine on the following distribution:

Six Divisions are specified, e.g.

1st Division   Mr Royer and Mr Brummell

Contracts & Commission business for furnishing
  provisions, clothing, necessaries, etc., and for   } £300
  remitting money and all references and letters
  to the Comptrollers of Army Accounts

Surveyor General and Auditors of the Land Revenue, Crown Leases, Duchy of Cornwall, Woods & Parks }	£200
Post Office	£20
Out of which Mr Royer is to receive £400 and Mr Brummell £120.	£520.

My Lords taking further into their consideration that it is of the highest importance to the public service to prevent so far as it is possible any fees, gratuities or perquisites being taken but such as are [known and][1] proper, revise the schedule of fees which have been taken for the use of the Secretaries, Chief Clerks and the other Clerks on the Establishment, and on mature deliberation do direct and most strictly enjoin that no fees of any kind or nature whatsoever under any description or pretence shall be taken or received hereafter but such as are contained in the schedule hereunto annexed, and that the following regulations shall hereafter be faithfully and punctually adhered to.

That all fees payable in the office for whose benefit soever they are due shall be paid only to a Clerk to be appointed by the Board for that purpose, whose sole business shall be the receiving of and accounting for the fees ... And any gentleman in the office who shall hereafter receive any fee, gift, gratuity or perquisite from any person or persons for or respecting business in the office (except according to the schedule through the Receiving Clerk) shall be immediately dismissed and be excluded from a possibility of re-admission; and any person after due notice given of these regulations, who shall offer any fee, gift, gratuity or perquisite to any Clerk or other person in this office, other than the Receiving Clerk, shall be considered as attempting corrupt practices and be dealt with accordingly.

[Arrangements for recording the fees due upon items of business, depositing them in an iron chest and distributing them monthly.]

That it shall be the business of another of the Chief Clerks, to be named for that purpose, to circulate all papers which are proper to be communicated to the Lords, who shall keep an accurate account of the time they are sent to and received from each Lord, and that one of the Junior Clerks be appointed by the Board to copy all such papers as are judged necessary for circulation.

That no deputy or person not belonging to the office shall be permitted to attend for any Clerk in the office, but every gentleman shall execute his own business and assist in copying papers whenever it shall be found necessary, except in cases of sickess or leave of absence

---

[1] MS. illegible.

obtained, care being taken that no papers are on any account suffered to be carried out of the office to be copied; and as nothing will tend more to accelerate business than any early and punctual attendance, it is expected that gentlemen shall in future absent themselves as little as possible during the office-hours which shall be considered as beginning every day at ten o'clock ...

It is further to be understood that as an encouragement to merit my Lords are positively determined that on all opportunities of preferment in the office they will continue to bring forward those who have distinguished themselves most by their diligence, attention and acquirement of the knowledge of business without regard to seniority.

22. The duties of Treasury officials, 1786:

[a] a Parliamentary Secretary; [b] a Chief Clerk;
[c] a Senior Clerk; [d] the Chief Clerk of the Revenue Room.

All members of the Treasury Establishment were called upon to give evidence of their duties and remuneration to the Commission appointed to inquire into fees. These selections illustrate some typical characteristics of the department.

FROM The Second Report of the Commissioners appointed to enquire into the Fees, Gratuities, Perquisites and Emoluments of Public Offices (*P.P.* 1806 vol. VII. Appendix).

(a) George Rose, esq.; 1st May 1786

This examinant saith, that he is one of the joint Secretaries to the Treasury; ...

His duty is to attend the Treasury Board and see all their directions carried into execution, and to superintend the conduct of the business in the various departments of the office.

His attendance on this duty is constant and unremitting.

... He is also Surveyor of the Green Wax, and Master of the Pleas in the Court of Exchequer (which last he executes by deputy); also Keeper of the Records in the Receipt of the Exchequer ... He has also the reversion of the office of Clerk of the Parliament ... He is likewise Provincial Agent to the Island of Dominica ...

(b) William Mitford, esq.; 12 Jan. 1786

This examinant saith, that he is one of the Chief Clerks in the Treasury; he has been in this Office near twenty-four years, and one of the Chief Clerks since December 1783.

There are four Chief Clerks in the Treasury; but one of them seldom attending, the duty is generally executed by three.

This examinant considers it as his duty to attend the Board and read the papers, or search for papers or precedents that may be wanted during the sitting of the Board, and occasionally in the absence of one of the Secretaries to take the Minutes; but no particular department being allotted, he holds it his duty to execute or superintend the execution of every part of the business that may be required by the Board or the Secretaries, or that arises in the Office.

His attendance is daily from eleven in the morning or sooner, till the business of the day is finished.

... He is also Receiver General of the Land Tax ... He is also by Treasury constitution and letter Agent for the Barons of the Exchequer in Scotland at the Treasury in London, ... He is also Agent for the Commissioners of the Customs and Salt Duties in Scotland ... also to the Commissioners of the Excise in the same kingdom ...

(c) William Beldam, esq.; 16 Jan. 1786

This examinant saith, that he is the first of the six Senior Clerks of the Treasury, and has been a clerk in this Office near twenty-eight years.

His particular department is to execute, or see to the execution of all business relative to contracts and commissions, furnishing provisions, clothing, necessaries, etc., or for remitting money abroad for public services; all references and letters to the Comptrollers of Army Accounts Surveyor General, and Auditors of the Land Revenue; all business relative to Crown leases, the Duchy of Cornwall, Woods, Forests and Parks, and all business relative to the Post Office.

He has one of the six Junior Clerks for his assistant in this department, and his attendance is daily, either of himself or his assistant. He has been given to understand, that on account of his long services, his constant attendance is not required; but that he is expected to give as much assistance not only to the specific branches of business which are allotted to him, but also to the general business of the office, as his long experience enables him to do.

(Since 1782 he has also been a Deputy Teller of the Exchequer.)

(d) William Speer, esq.; 2 March 1786

This examinant saith, that he is Principal Clerk of the Revenue Office in the Treasury; he has been employed in the Treasury since the month of August 1742, and has had his present office since the 5th January 1758.

The business of this office is to make up books containing the accounts of the income and issues of the Customs, and the other duties and revenues payable at the Receipt of the Exchequer.

Ever week a certificate is transmitted to him from the Auditor of the Receipt of the Exchequer, containing an account of all the monies received and issued there during the foregoing week; and a like certificate from the Clerk of the Pells, containing not only the receipts and issues of all monies, but also an account of the issues of Exchequer Bills during the same period.

He also receives a weekly certificate from the Exchequer Bill Office, containing a general account of the Exchequer Bills which have been issued, together with a particular account of those issued during the preceding week; also of those cancelled during the same period, and lastly of all those still outstanding.

He likewise receives from the Receiver General of His Majesty's Customs, Excise, and Post Office, weekly certificates of their receipts and payments, by which he checks the Exchequer certificates, and is enabled to make out his account of the Civil List cash.

He also receives certificates from the Stamp Office, Hackney Coach Office, Hawkers and Pedlars Office, and Alienation Office, of their receipts and payments, but these last certificates are not transmitted to him at any regular period.

From the above weekly certificates he prepares, for the Treasury Board, what is called a Cash Paper, containing an account of disposable money in the Exchequer for the uses of his Majesty's Civil Government, and for the public service of the current year, shewing the balance remaining on both.

He also prepares two half-yearly accounts of the surplus monies and other revenues of the Sinking Fund to be laid before Parliament, and an account shewing the monies granted by Parliament for the service of the year, and how the same have been disposed of, with the surplus or deficiency thereof.

An account is prepared every month of the receipts and payments of the Civil List, which, as he understands, is presented to his Majesty by the First Lord of the Treasury.

It is also his duty to prepare or cause to be prepared such other accounts as the Lords of the Treasury and Secretaries shall from time to time direct, many of which are frequently intricate, occasion him much trouble, and employ a great part of his time out of office hours.

He keeps an account in certain books, according to a list and description thereof now delivered and signed by him.

His attendance at the Treasury is in general daily, from about ten in the morning to four in the afternoon.

23. 'What's wrong with the Treasury': A Treasury Clerk proposes reforms, 1828.

This is a unique instance of a comparatively junior Treasury Clerk putting before his superiors recommendations to improve the efficiency and morale of the department. Martin Leake anticipates the concept (associated with Trevelyan) of a proper division of labour between intellectual and mechanical duties, and, in probing the discontents of his colleagues, shows a much better human understanding of their malaise than the Treasury Board.

FROM 'Mr Leakes Observations', miscellaneous Treasury papers (PRO T 1/4306).

No. 1

July 1828. The apparent inefficiency of the Establishment of the Treasury may be traced to the following causes.

1st   A want of a defined system of individual responsibility.

2nd   A want of that gradual official education which will alone qualify the persons employed to fill the highest situations in the office.

3rd   A want of classification of the cases coming before the Board, which is necessary to prevent the confusion in which the business is now sometimes involved, and to render it clear and simple.

The consequences of these defects in the system will appear in the following statement.

Neither the Chief Clerks nor the Senior Clerks are now entirely responsible for the execution of the business ordered by the Board, but both are responsible in part; this divided responsibility has the worst effect, the care and attention required in the execution of the business is thrown from one to the other. The following remedies are proposed for this defect.

The Chief Clerks to be entirely exempted from the responsibility of executing the business after it has passed the Board, but to be employed in preparing Minutes for the Board. Two Chief Clerks also to be Auditors; one Cashier; and one Clerk of the Minutes, and to be entirely responsible for the execution of those duties. Two officers only to be responsible in each department; a Senior [Clerk] to be solely and entirely responsible for the execution of the business in his department, unless when absent on leave; and an Assistant [Clerk] to be in the same manner responsible, *but only* when the Senior is absent. If the writing of the fair Minutes, and all copies and entries were taken from the department, two men in general would be sufficient to execute the business, but if further assistance were required in any department a Junior [Clerk] might be added, who however should not be at all responsible for the execution of the business.

The responsibility for the expeditious and accurate execution of the business being thrown entirely on one person only at the same time in each department would be a more effectual security for regular attendance than any positive regulation to that effect; it would also produce what no positive regulation could, an interest in the business during attendance. The Senior must see that the Assistant attends, or do all the business himself; and if the Senior absents himself without leave, he will always be liable to be called for, and his absence immediately discovered.

All the copies and entries should be done by Extra Clerks; for which they should be paid according to the work done. The work would thus be done much more economically than by Clerks on the Establishment as at present,[1] and the expense being precisely in proportion to the work done, no unnecessary expense could be incurred by increasing the number of Extra Clerks. At the same time, if the scale of allowances for Extra work were liberal, the industrious Extra Clerk would earn more than he receives in the shape of salary at present.[2] No Extra Clerk should be allowed to assist in the departments, all the original warrants and letters must therefore be drawn by the Clerks on the Establishment, who would in consequence[3] begin to learn their business immediately on their appointment, would in a few years be placed in a responsible situation, and must, unless very deficient in understanding, be fitted for the higher situations in the office after having served some time as Senior [Clerk]; and considering the varied and extensive nature of the business of the Treasury, many would be qualified for filling superior situations in any department of Government. At present a man of good abilities may be obliged to spend 20 or 25 years of his life in duties but little superior to copying, and thus become at the end of that time incapable of filling any responsible situation in the Treasury or any other department.[4]

The Minutes should be drawn with great care by a Minute Department under the superintendence of the Chief Clerk of the Minutes, who should also have the direction of the Register Department and the papers. The Minutes at present are written by different persons who

Marginal comments pencilled by the Hon. J. H. K. Stewart, Assistant Secretary July 1828–January 1836:

[1] I decidedly object to this as much importance is often reposed in an entering as in a writing Clerk, and the Clerk who enters by the entry acquires a knowledge useful if not essential to the discharge of other duties.

[2] I altogether object to Extra Clerks being employed except for strictly speaking Extra business.

[3] Entering letters does this.

[4] Not if he is fit for anything else.

have no communication with each other; the consequence is that no
system or uniformity is observed, many papers are stated more than
once and many not at all, and the statements are from necessity so
loose and inaccurate that it may be questioned whether they serve any
purpose but to increase the number of volumes of Minutes. The
Minutes have in consequence become so voluminous that it is scarcely
possible to find any case in them but by means of the Register Book;
and then the paper and the rough minute[5] is a better authority than
the Minute Book. To remedy this evil and at the same time to classify
the whole business of the office, it is proposed in the first place to
throw out of the Minute Book all orders of the nature of references
which do not involve any final directions of the Board,[6] all directions
for transmitting papers for information and giving information, all
papers on which for obvious reasons no directions are given (or *Nils*);
in all these cases the Minute might be written on the back of the paper,
and it might be delivered to the department to be executed or deposited,
but it would not be necessary to enter it in the Minute Book. Of the
directions of the Board which would remain, at least one half are not
original decisions, but are merely directions given according to precedent. In these instances it would be only necessary to enter one case in
the Minute Book, which should be done with care, stating the leading
facts which distinguish cases of that nature, and it should be followed
by a General Minute notifying that in that and all similar cases certain
specified directions should be given. All future cases of the same nature
might then be excluded from the Minutes, but on the back of the
papers a note might be made referring to the precedent for the directions
to be given upon them. The Minutes would then contain nothing but
original decisions[7] which should be stated clearly with all the facts
leading to them, and precedents, the distinguishing features of which
should also be clearly stated.

The advantages to be derived from this arrangement would be, first,
that the Minutes would be greatly reduced in quantity, and a propor-
tionate reduction would be made in labour and expense;

secondly, the smaller the compass to which the Minute Book is
reduced,[8] the easier it will be to find any particular case in it;

thirdly, instead of an immense mass of insulated and unconnected
directions we should have in the Minute Book a complete code of
precedents, by referring to which the whole of the routine business of
the office might be regulated, and an undeviating uniformity in the

[5] The Minutes ought to be indexed.
[6] The record may be shortened but it cannot be dispensed with.
[7] This would introduce complication and confusion. What is an original
decision?
[8] Not if properly indexed.

decisions would more effectually be established than by the present method under which errors and deviations from precedents are most likely to occur. The main features of the precedents being clearly stated, any deviation or variation of the circumstances in any new case would be immediately discovered and the attention of the Board called to it. The real business of the Board would remain in the Minute Book, namely, new precedents, cases which in some respects vary from the old precedents and special and distinct cases which are to be decided upon, on considering the peculiar circumstances attending them . . .

[After concluding his case for the revision of Treasury Minutes, Martin Leake proceeds to amplify all these points in paper No. 2, dated 3 December 1828, pp. 18–107. The following passage is an interesting anticipation of the diagnosis associated with Sir Charles Trevelyan:]

It becomes therefore necessary to make a distinction between the business and the labour to be executed in the office; such a distinction is required in justice to the Government, the Established Clerks and the Extra Clerks. In consequence of neglecting it the Government pay high salaries to Established Clerks for doing work which might be done at the market price by Extra Clerks; the Established Clerks are deprived of the official information and habits of business which are necessary to qualify them to succeed to the higher situations held out to them on their appointment; and the Extra Clerks are obliged to undertake very responsible duties at salaries much below a fair remuneration for those duties, while they are deprived of the extra work by means of which they might add to their fixed salaries the just reward due to their extraordinary diligence. The copying and entering would probably be performed more accurately and expeditiously by the Extra Clerks than by the Junior Clerks on the Establishment. They should be separated from the departments in order to put an end to the practice of throwing the more responsible duties upon them and to ensure the observance of that distinction between business and labour which is above recommended.

[The last thirty pages of Martin Leake's 'Observations' are devoted to an historical survey, designed to show that his proposals are not innovations 'but merely a recurrence to the ancient practice of the Treasury'. He notes the simplicity and efficiency of the traditional procedures under which the Chief Clerks 'appear to have had the general superintendence of the business both before and after it passed the Board', but traces the gradual loss of authenticity in Treasury Minutes during the reign of George III as the practice of reading and approving the Minutes at the next Board fell into disuse. The reorganization of 30 November 1782 marked a further weakening of interest in the accuracy of business; but 'from 19 August 1805, when the office of Assistant Secretary was established, an entirely new system was adopted' and 'in course of time new evils arose which probably were not foreseen and which all the zeal and diligence of the Assistant Secretary could not prevent'. The responsibility placed upon the Assistant Secretary for the preparation of Treasury Minutes was too heavy to be accurately discharged and decisions were increasingly clothed in fictitious forms designed to preserve the appearance of emanating immediately from the Board.]

The consequence of this principle may be further traced through every part of the Establishment. As the Minutes were supposed to issue from the Board in a perfect state, the employment of the Chief Clerks in preparing the business and in the general superintendence of the office was therefore confined to the execution of the orders of the Board, and the authority of each was restricted to a particular department, thus the weight and consequence of the whole body were lost, and the discipline of the office thereby relaxed. If the Chief Clerk neglected the superintendence of his Division, which was the best course he could pursue for the public service, his office became nearly a sinecure; if on the other hand he was determined to do his duty, his superintendence could go little further than the verbal comparison of the letters and warrants with the Minutes, as he was kept entirely ignorant of the intentions of the Board; and the Senior [Clerk] being completely relieved from his responsibility was not distinguished from the other clerks in his department but by the amount of his salary. Thus all personal responsibility was dissolved, orders were addressed to departments and not to individuals, and if any neglect occurred the department was blamed while each individual in it escaped ... An Extra Clerk who had the charge of the Indexes and the Department Book frequently took the lead in each department and possessed all the information while the Established Clerks were employed in copying the orders of the Board into the Minutes and the letters written from the Minutes literally and without venturing to make the smallest alteration in them, as these orders were supposed to come perfect from the Board and no one could presume to question even their grammatical construction, much less the correctness of the decisions and opinions which they contained. Thus a habit was acquired of writing these Minutes and letters mechanically in perfect ignorance of their meaning and intention; and this habit, which is so decidedly opposed to habits of business, was probably acquired with the greatest ease by those young men who possessed the best abilities ...

It being quite impossible for the Assistant Secretary to prepare Minutes at length on the vast multitude of papers, each to be taken up individually, and it being incompatible with the principle of the system to entrust any part of that duty to the Established Clerks in the office or to any responsible officers, it fell into the hands of private secretaries and other irresponsible persons, and the authenticity of the Minutes were thus further weakened. At last the office of Principal Clerk Assistant to the Secretaries was created,[1] care being taken however in conformity with the above principle, that neither his responsibility nor his authority should be very distinctly defined by the title of his office or the Minute of his appointment.

Part of the duty of preparing Minutes for the Board was, notwithstanding this appointment, still left to the private secretaries, and part fell into the hands of the Principal and Senior Clerks of the Commissariat. The premature death of the late Assistant Secretary[2] has however proved that even with those aids no man, whatever may be his memory and his talents for business, can attempt with impunity to cope with the immense multitude of insulated facts, decisions and opinions of which the business of the Treasury at present consists, unless he can contrive some plan for condensing and classifying that business and reducing it to a manageable shape.

The creation of the new appointment above alluded to opened a new and shorter road to promotion quite distinct from the regular line of succession in the office. It, however, soon became evident that no diligence in the execution of the duties of the department could ever lead to, or indeed qualify a man for these new offices, and it was equally evident that no want of diligence could exclude him from or disqualify him for the offices in the regular line. The only alternative left, therefore, was through favour to procure admission into the new line, or to wait in idleness for promotion in the old line. The indifference and supineness which this discouraging state of things produced were still further increased by the reduction of salaries in 1822 by which the promotion to the old offices was rendered of no value. If the reduction of salaries had been immediate, an immediate saving would have been made, and the effect of the measure, though more unpalatable at the time, would soon have been forgotten; but contrived as it was it tended permanently to paralyse the little zeal still remaining in the office by making every man more cautious than ever in confining his exertions strictly within the letter of his duty lest he should encroach upon the duties of his superior, who was enjoying a salary he could never aspire to.

It is confidently trusted that any impartial person, on considering all the facts above stated, will be satisfied that the apparent inefficiency of

[1] Set up in 1815, when William Hill was appointed, it was to be abolished in 1856.

[2] William Hill, appointed April 1826, died June 1828.

the present Establishment of the Treasury cannot be attributed to any defects in the dispositions or understandings of the persons composing it, but that it is to be traced to the inevitable operation of a system instituted probably with the best intentions but the remote effects of which were not sufficiently considered.

24. Gentlemen or experts?: Qualifications for clerkships in the Treasury, 1831.

Brooksbank's memorandum is the most cogent of those submitted by the Chief Clerks at the request of the Treasury Board, and although its views on the educational equipment of gentlemen are conventional it does look more carefully at the moral and intellectual requirements of Treasury recruits.

FROM Memorandum upon the subject of qualification for Clerkships in the Treasury, by T. C. Brooksbank, Chief Clerk of the Revenue Branch, 2nd February 1831 (PRO T 1/4306).

In expressing my opinion on the very important question of the qualification necessary for the situation of a Clerk in the Treasury, either for the duties generally, or for those of the Revenue Branch in particular, it becomes necessary for me to take a view of the nature of the duties which are to be performed – not merely the executive duties of a Junior, but those of the Senior and Chief Clerks, in superintending and advising upon the subjects and questions which they or the Secretaries have to submit for the decision of the Board: and as these higher offices are filled by selection from the inferior, the question for immediate consideration is what qualification, on his entrance, is the most likely to render the individual ultimately suited to *all the duties* he may afterwards have to perform.

To judge of the nature and measure of such qualifications it is necessary to bear in mind, first, what the business of the Treasury is generally, and secondly, what are the peculiar duties attaching to the Revenue Department.

The Treasury is not, like most of the inferior departments, a ministerial Board only. Its most important duties are those of superintending, directing and controlling all the civil departments of the State, and particularly those Departments (the Customs, Excise, Taxes and Stamps) immediately concerned in the collection of the public revenue.

In a more general manner, it also forms a check and control over the departments of the public expenditure.

In the exercise of these functions the Treasury Board is constantly engaged in sitting in judgment and in equity on cases in which the rights of the Crown and of the public are to be upheld on the one hand, and the appeals of individuals attentively and impartially considered on the other. Transgressions of the revenue laws are of daily occurrence, bearing various shades of guilt between the extreme limits of perfect innocence and wilful fraud, and a power of relief and mitigation of penalty beyond that of the Court of Exchequer is vested in the Crown and entrusted to the discretionary consideration of the Board of Treasury. Escheated property forms another important subject of investigation with a view to the maintenance of the rights of the Crown and the fair and liberal consideration due to the equitable claims of individuals.

In order to arrive at a sound judgment upon these and other matters, it is indispensable that their Lordships or the Secretaries should have always persons at hand competent to assist them in the evidence to be collected either from the officers of the Crown or the individuals appealing – to digest it when collected, divest it of extraneous matter, and bring, in a clear point of view, the several questions involved in the subject for the decision of the Secretaries or the Board.

The mental qualifications for this purpose must be those of analysing and combining; of readily comprehending a subject and of seeing all its ramifications; of descending from general principles into detail in carrying existing laws and regulations into effect; and on the other hand, of forming from extensive detail, general principles, in providing new laws or regulations to meet a variety of contingencies.

Without digressing further on the various duties of the Treasury, I may stop here and ask what kind of education or qualification is likely to be the best calculated for forming the mind for the exercise of these powers. Is it what is termed a liberal course of education, that is, the education of a gentleman, which up to the age of 18 or 19 has for its object the preparing the mind for every distinct branch of knowledge that may be afterwards taken up? Or is it one that from the beginning has in view only one particular object or pursuit? Is it that in which there is the greatest portion of general knowledge, or is it one of mere technicality? I at once unhesitatingly give my opinion that the general education of a gentleman is the best suited for all the purposes of the Treasury.

[Margin] The minimum and the test of such an education at 18 I consider to be

1. A sufficient knowledge of Classical literature to pass an examination for matriculation at Oxford – or for entrance at the Inner Temple.
2. Arithmetic, including vulgar and decimal fractions.
3. The five or six first books of Euclid.
4. Algebra, inclusive of quadratic equations.
Satisfactory certificates of these acquirements to be produced.

I will now look more particularly to the duties of the *Revenue Department*, the Clerks for which are usually selected from those engaged in the general business of the Treasury, with a view to the qualifications they may have shown as peculiarly adapted to the duties of the Branch.

The individual who enters this Department must, in order to understand its duties and to render himself useful, not merely possess some technical knowledge of the principles of accounts and of book-keeping, but he must make himself acquainted with the history of all the most important financial operations of the country for the last forty or fifty years – that is, from the General Consolidation Act in 1787 – and he should also be well informed of all the various inquiries by Committees and Commissions into the state of the public revenue and expenditure which have taken place during that period of time. With reference to his ordinary daily duties . . . he must be conversant with the forms of Parliament on all money matters, he must watch the daily progress of the Committees of Supply and of Ways and Means during each session and see that the Votes and the Money and Appropriation Bills are correctly made, and after they are passed it is the duty of the principal officers of this Department to attend cautiously and carefully to the manner of carrying the respective grants and other financial measures into effect – keeping a constant watch on the balances in the Exchequer that the reservation of revenue there be adequate to the daily wants for the military and other services, and also that all available surplus be used without delay for redeeming the Quarterly Deficiency Bills and saving the interest payable thereon.

For these objects the officers of this Department are in constant communication with the parties requiring payments on the one hand and with the Exchequer on the other, cautiously adjusting the accom-modation due to each; and if unforeseen pressure or difficulties should arise, as was of frequent occurrence during the late war, the chief of this Department has to submit the case without delay to the Chancellor of the Exchequer together with the measures which may appear to him to be the best for preventing any interruption of the public service.

The qualifications required for these important duties, by which a considerable portion of the whole business of the Treasury is regulated and kept in order, as well as the intentions of Parliament fulfilled, cannot be expected to be found in a mere stationer's copying clerk, nor even in any class of persons, however high and distinguished for talent, not formed by time and experience for the duties in question. Upon two occasions within my recollection (in 1802, when numerous calculations of compound interest respecting the Sinking Fund were laid by the Treasury before Parliament; and in 1808, when the Treasury framed the tables for the first Government Life Annuity Act), two of the most distinguished mathematicians in the country were severally called upon for their aid and assistance, and though deeply skilled in Algebra and in all the formulae of the questions to be solved, so utterly unacquainted were they with the financial measures of the country, with the nature of the Sinking Fund, the difference of the nominal and actual value of the Funded Debt and various other matters, that it was not without much time and labour that they gained the necessary information on those subjects.

It is easier for a mind of general information to acquire a branch of knowledge which is technical than for a mind which has been confined to one branch to extend itself to a multiplicity of objects. It is not therefore from any technical knowledge, high or low, that I should be desirous of selecting a Clerk for the Treasury, but from those usual general acquirements by which the mental powers are prepared for a more extensive range of information and judgment than is found in a counting house or within the limited circle of mathematical rules: and having in view the higher duties which I have stated, I should consider it as erroneous to select the Clerks for the Treasury upon the qualifications of mere manual or technical ability, as it would be to consider the Clerks of the House of Commons as the most competent from their technical knowledge for the duties of the members.

From what I have stated of the duties of the Revenue Department it must be obvious that they are occasionally of a very confidential nature when likely to affect the money market, as in the cases of loans, of funding Exchequer Bills, or of taxes to be imposed or repealed, and that the necessary degree of forbearance is not confined to that which prohibits one individual from imparting a transaction to another, but extends to his own conduct towards himself even, and restrains him from making any use for his own profit or advantage of the confidence reposed in him.

That individuals, duly prepared and qualified at the age of 18 for the Treasury or any other path of life, may not continue to advance and make themselves duly qualified for higher situations, must sometimes occur. We see in every profession or class of society that various causes, not always a lack of zeal, but mental or bodily infirmity and other contingencies, arise to retard the progress of some whilst others advance gradually in attainments and become eligible for the highest offices. It is not always that an efficient counsellor makes a good judge, nor an active officer an able General, and it must unavoidably occur in the official departments that an excellent Junior Clerk is eventually found to be unqualified for the duty of general superintendence.

It is, however, scarcely necessary to advert to this fact, as it cannot be clearly foreseen at an early age; and as regulations are established for making the promotion from the lower to the higher classes by selection on the ground of competence and seniority rather than of seniority alone, an opportunity is thereby afforded in every case of reconsidering the qualifications of the individuals and of estimating from their actual services their eligibility for promotion.

The interests of the public service require that the course of business in the Treasury should never stop or suffer interruption, that the knowledge of all its transactions, the uses of all the apparatus of books and records it contains, and its powers, usages and practice should be transmitted from one generation to another; and the principal means by which this unexpiring knowledge is kept alive must be by and through the *permanent officers* of the Department. The members of the Board are frequently changing; the two Parliamentary Secretaries, however able and experienced, cannot on retiring impart their knowledge to their successors; the Assistant Secretary, it is true, is a more permanent officer, but he is equally unable to bequeath his knowledge as a light and guide for the new officer who might be appointed in his place; and it is therefore necessary for all these new members and officers to learn their duties* from those who in their official characters never die, and though their names may change their knowledge continues in succession and in perpetuity.

This consideration is important to be borne in mind in estimating the qualifications for the superintending duties of the Treasury. It does not apply to the officers under the subordinate revenue Boards, where no such sudden and entire changes take place as in the chief political departments of Government, of which the Treasury is the most extensive and comprehensive in the various duties to be performed, and in its relative position as a centre power round which the other departments revolve and by which they are kept in continual motion, and it has doubtless been with this impression that the Chief Clerks of the Treasury have been always considered of equal official rank with the members of the highest of the permanent revenue Boards.

* I have heard the late Earl of Liverpool (than whom from his long official life, no better authority can be quoted) voluntarily, candidly and gratefully make this acknowledgment.

25. Trevelyan on the Treasury, 1848.

Trevelyan, comparatively isolated within the department, airs his views on Treasury reform before the Select Committee. His severely logical prescription was to be rejected by their report.

FROM Evidence given by C. E. Trevelyan (Assistant Secretary to the Treasury) to the Select Committee on Miscellaneous Expenditure, 28 March and 4 April, 1848 (*PP* (1847–8) XVIII (Part 1)).

Question 1352 [Chairman] Before we go through the items of the Treasury establishment, will you state to the Committee whether in your opinion the establishment of the Treasury is redundant in any way, or whether you consider it perfect as it is? – I will take this paper, giving a list of the establishment according to the duties performed by each person: the principal responsible officers upon the first page, who prepare minutes for the Board, are generally overtasked; they can overcome the press of business which is continually flowing in upon them only by the most incessant and painful exertions. All that department of the Treasury is decidedly stinted and undermanned. The business is done, and I hope it is well done; but it is done with such a sacrifice of personal comfort and health as ought not to be required from any public officers as the ordinary condition of their service ...

1372 ... Now I come to that branch of the Treasury business which consists in what is called the execution of the minutes; that is, turning the minutes into letters, preparing the warrants, and recording the minutes, letters and warrants; which duties are almost entirely performed by clerks on the regular establishment of the Treasury, who enter at £90 a year, as junior clerks, and rise, through the gradations of assistant and senior, to be chief clerks. I am bound to say that these gentlemen do their duty in a regular and exact manner; and I believe the business is done as well as it could reasonably be expected to be done, according to the present constitution of the office. But there cannot be a doubt that this portion of the Treasury establishment is overpaid, as compared with the nature of the business done by them. The business is principally of a mechanical kind, such as copying the minutes, letters and warrants, which would more properly be done by the class of extra clerks ... who are trained to this kind of work, and to whom a much lower rate of remuneration affords a sufficient motive for exertion. I consider it to be a great waste of public money, that gentlemen rising from £300 to £1000 a year, are employed on what could be done equally well, and if anything better, by persons whose business it is, on a much lower rate of salary. I must except from this

Mr [T. C.] Brooksbank, in the Fifth or Financial Department, who performs duties of a very superior order, in connexion with the Chancellor of the Exchequer, in the management of the financial business of the Board; and the gentlemen acting as his assistants also have duties of more or less importance to perform.

1373. Do your observations apply to the whole of the clerks in the divisions, or only to the seniors? – They apply to all except the juniors; and even as regards the juniors, I conceive that the mere copying is better done by persons who enter upon it as their profession for life, and who are paid accordingly, than by young gentlemen whose expectations and position in society leads them to look to something better, and to expect to have business of a superior order given to them.

1374. Is the business done in those divisions merely copying? – The clerks turn the minutes into letters, which calls for some little exercise of judgment and good taste.

1375. [Dr Bowring] Requiring no intellectual superiority? – Very slight. They also enter the letters, that is, copy them into books; and draw warrants according to the directions contained in the minutes, and copy the warrants into books; and they prepare what are called the 'Fair Minutes', that is, the minutes with an abstract of the papers upon which they are founded. All these duties require care and precision; but they do not call for the exercise of any superior intellectual qualities.

1376. [Chairman] Is it out of this body that the other clerks are taken afterwards, the principal clerks of whom you have recently spoken? – Not generally speaking. For instance, neither myself, nor Mr Pennington, nor Mr Brande, nor Mr Hankins were taken from that body. Mr Leake and Mr Crafer do belong to the regular establishment.

1391. [Mr Rice] With regard to all the chief clerks in each of the four divisions, those gentlemen receiving £100 a year, a great portion of their time is employed in mere copying? – Yes; it is a great anomaly. In order to make myself better understood, I will explain how it happened: originally these gentlemen were employed in the actual transaction of the business; they used to assist the Secretaries in attending upon the Board, and preparing the minutes; and they performed other important public functions; but owing to a want of proper regulations and organization in the office, the business fell into confusion during the pressure of the French war. An Assistant Secretary, Sir George Harrison, was then appointed, in 1805; and the officers on the regular establishment then had their duties fixed in this way, merely to attend to the execution of the business after it had been settled by the secretaries and the assistant secretary; and in later time other officers such as Mr Brande, Mr Leake, and Mr Hankins, have been called to the assistance of the secretaries.

1399. The chief clerk is a sort of honourable distinction? – Yes, for the most part; the business done by him is of the same kind as that done by the senior; sometimes it is not so important. What I would aim at would be to bring into active employment all those members of the present establishment who are equal to superior work; and to appoint the necessary number of copyists as vacancies occur. So that, in the course of ten or fifteen years, there would be a limited staff of well-paid officers employed on duties of a superior kind, and the rest would be copyists on an inferior rate of salary suited to that employment. And I believe that the office would cost several thousand pounds a year less, and would be in a more efficient state than it is at present; that there would be more work done, and a more general and thorough superintendence over our financial system in all its departments of revenue and expenditure.

(Further evidence on 4 April 1848.)

1664. [Chairman] The scheme that you have laid down supposes that for the future there should be a difference of qualification between the upper part of the department and the lower; and therefore you could not continue, as at present, to draw men up to the top of the establishment, commencing at the bottom, but you must select men for the superior offices who have not served in the inferior part of the department? – Yes.

1665. Then where would you select those officers for the heads of the departments? – For many years to come it would not be necessary to make any alteration either in the present men or in the present scale of salaries. Every person now on the establishment would rise through the successive gradations of assistant and senior, to be chief clerk. A very important point of justice would thus be provided for. It is not only an act of justice, but it is most important for the well-being of the public service, that the expectation with which public officers first entered the service should be adhered to as far as possible. But in the course of years, as no new persons would be appointed to the superior establishment on the present footing, that superior establishment would be very much diminished, and it would at last come to this, that we should have a few persons employed on the really important business of the office, and the rest would be employed in superintending the remaining four executive divisions. The time would then have arrived for appointing new persons to the superior establishment; but instead of taking very young men, whose education is not finished, and of whose qualifications we have no experience, I would take young men who had completed their education at the universities or elsewhere; and in

particular cases I would even go beyond that, and take young men who
have had some experience and success in life; for I conceive that no
test of fitness for public service is equal to that of a person having
succeeded in some other line of life.

1670. Do you consider that such a scheme would add much to the
economy as well as to the efficiency of the public service? – I consider
that it would add greatly to both. There is one point of view which it
is necessary to state for a proper understanding of this subject. The
higher duties of the Treasury are extremely important. The duties
performed by the Secretaries, and by Mr Brande, Mr Leake, and Mr
Hankins, are of the highest importance; but the training which the
young men on the superior establishment get is not at all such as to fit
them for those higher duties. A young man comes from a public school
full of energy, intelligence, and excited hopes, but after two or three
years' incessant copying he becomes disappointed and disgusted.
Feeling that he is employed on work of an inferior kind, he learns to
do it in a mechanical manner; and instead of following the public
service in the spirit of a profession, in the way the lawyers in Westminster Hall, or the active members of the mercantile, banking,
manufacturing and other professions follow theirs, he regards his
business as a tax upon his time, and executes it as a task which he
must get through. He acquires none of that description of experience
which is required to fit him for the performance of higher duties, and
when, after many years, he rises to a position in the office where he
may be called upon to perform higher duties, he is often not fit for
them. He acquires a knowledge of official forms, and to a certain
extent he becomes acquainted with the nature of the business by
having to record it and to convert minutes into letters, but he has no
experience of the actual transaction of the business, which is indis-
pensably necessary to give aptitude and self-confidence. I consider that
it would be greatly to the advantage of the gentlemen on the superior
establishment of the Treasury, especially to the young men among
them, that they should be employed from the first in superior duties;
they would then acquire an interest in their business, and would enter
into the spirit of their profession, and they would become better
qualified for rendering useful service to the public, either in the
Treasury or anywhere else.

26. The reorganization of 1856: the Treasury Minute of 4 July 1856.

As Assistant Secretary, Trevelyan was largely involved in the preparation of this reorganization, but although it is concerned to improve the scope for intelligence by a proper division of labour it falls very short of his vision of a reformed Treasury, and the credit for this measure was usually accorded to James Wilson, the Financial Secretary.

FROM Treasury Minute, July 4, 1856 (PRO Treasury Minute Books, T 29/564).

The First Lord and the Chancellor of the Exchequer suggest to the Board that advantage should be taken of the occurrence of the under-mentioned vacancies in the Treasury Establishment, to make arrangements whereby the Office would be rendered more efficient for the proper performance of the highly important duties intrusted to it:

Law Clerkship,
One of the two Chief Clerkships,
Two Senior Clerkships,
One Junior Clerkship.

The objects to be provided for by the proposed revision of the office are:

To secure, by a proper training in suitable duties, a succession of able officers for the highest posts on the permanent establishment;

To secure the prompt and exact execution of the decisions of the Treasury; and

To prevent the waste of intellectual power and of money at present caused by an imperfect division of labour.

With these objects in view, the First Lord and the Chancellor of the Exchequer recommend the adoption of the following arrangements:

1. That the whole business of the office should be apportioned according to the most convenient arrangement that can be devised, among Six Divisions; one Division being placed under the immediate control of the Assistant Secretary, and the others under that of the Auditor of the Civil List and four Principal Clerks.

2. That a First Class Clerk should be appointed under each of the Principal Officers, who, besides assisting in the preparation of the decisions, should be specially responsible for the dispatch of the business; and that the remainder of the establishment of each Division should ordinarily consist of two Clerks of the Second and one of the

Third Class, with the exception of the Financial Division, the number to be assigned to which will depend upon the result of inquiries now in progress.

3. That the minutes should be prepared and converted into letters and fair minutes in the respective Divisions.

4. That a separate department should be formed in connection with the Registry, in which all copies should be made, and the letters and warrants should be entered and made up for transmission by messenger or post, with the copies or original documents to accompany them, and in which the letter and fair minute books should be indexed.

5. That such arrangements should be made as will admit of all the officers of each Division transacting their business in immediate personal communication with each other; and,

6. That every part of the system of the office should be reduced to fixed rules, for the exact execution of which, under the general superintendence of the Assistant Secretary, and, when necessary, after reference to the Secretaries, the Principal Officers will be severally responsible.

My Lords entirely concur in the measures recommended by the First Lord and the Chancellor of the Exchequer; and they are accordingly pleased to fix the establishment of the office as follows:

1 Assistant Secretary, as at present.

1 Auditor of the Civil List, as at present.

4 Principal Clerks, £1,000 a-year, increasing by £50 a-year to £1,200.

10 First Class Clerks, £700 a-year, increasing by £25 a-year to £900.

16 Second Class Clerks, £350 a-year, increasing by £20 a-year to £600.

7 Third Class Clerks, £100 a-year, increasing by £15 a-year to £250.

27. The reorganization of 1870: the Treasury Minute of 25 May 1870.

On the eve of the introduction of Open Competition for entry to the Civil Service, the Treasury prepared itself to give a greater share of responsibility to the duties of its junior members. It freed their work of much mechanical labour and streamlined the upper establishment from thirty-three to twenty-five, *vizt.* Permanent Secretary, Assistant Secretary, 4 Principal Clerks, 7 First Class Clerks and 12 Second Class Clerks. This modest structure was to serve, virtually unaltered, until the First World War.

FROM Treasury Minute of 25 May 1870 (PRO T 1/7032 B/22719).

As regards the allotment of the duties, it may be generally stated that the *First Class Clerk* is, under the Principal Officer, responsible for the discipline of the division and for the despatch of its business. He minutes many of the less important papers, or prepares statements to assist the Principal Officer and Secretaries. He keeps the Departmental Register, and usually examines the fair minutes after execution. In the absence of the Principal Officer, he takes his place and performs all his duties. This description does not apply to the *Parliamentary Clerk*, whose position is necessarily more independent.

The duties of the *Second Class* and of the *Third Class Clerks* cannot be exactly distinguished. Between them, they prepare the fair minutes, write letters from the rough minutes for the signature of the Secretaries, and collect and prepare the papers for the consideration of the Principal Clerk, making précis and statements if desired. The more responsible of these duties of course devolve upon the Second Class Clerks.

An examination of the working of the office, – looking to the subjects dealt with, and to the responsibility of the Treasury as a check upon the public expenditure – leads to the conclusion that no transfer of the duties performed by the superior officers (that is, the five Principal Clerks), and no diminution of their number, can be entertained.

The same observation applies generally, although with some qualification, to the First Class Clerks. It does not appear that their present number is capable of reduction. But there are some portions of their duties which may advantageously be either dispensed with, or entrusted to other less highly-salaried officers.

The duties referred to are (1) the examination of the fair minutes; (2) the charge of the 'Department book'.

As regards the first, by the adoption of an arrangement which involves a discontinuance to a great extent, if not altogether, of the system of fair minutes, decided relief may be afforded.

As regards the charge of the 'Department book', it has been held that, because the First Class Clerk is responsible for the correct and prompt passage of business through the Department, he can only inform himself properly by making the entries in the book with his own hand – a duty involving a great deal of time and trouble, and causing constant interruption. Apart from the inexpediency of compelling a senior officer, with a salary of £900 a-year, whose time ought to be, and could be, much more profitably employed, to devote a considerable portion of his working-day to work of so mechanical a description, his acquirement of the necessary knowledge as to the state of the business can be sufficiently well attained by entrusting the actual keeping of the book to a Clerk of a lower class, subject to the inspection of the First Class Clerk. Indeed this arrangement is actually, and has been for several years, in operation in the Finance Division, and, for some time, in the Second Division. And my Lords desire that it may be introduced into the other Divisions of the office.

It is, however, in the lower classes that the greatest opportunity is afforded for economy and improvement, and there appears to be a double reform easy of application, which would secure both these objects:

1. The system of record in the Treasury, is indeed complete, but it is unnecessarily repeated. For purposes of reference, (a) the original paper accompanied by the Minute can be procured from the Registry, and this is the usual mode of reference. (b) All letters written in pursuance of Minutes are copied *verbatim* into ledgers, divided according to the nature of their contents, and constant reference is made to them. (c) When a paper is done with, and the order upon it has been executed, it is, if of importance, placed upon the 'Fair Minutes', – i.e. a précis is made of the paper and the Minute is recorded *verbatim*. This is done in each Division. Thus it follows that, in the case of nearly all important papers, a threefold record is kept of the Treasury decision. The system of fair Minutes appears, if not to be superfluous, at least to offer no advantage adequate to the labour which it imposes, and my Lords desire that it may be discontinued.

Those Minutes of the Treasury which are general in their character, or are of sufficient importance as precedents, should from time to time be printed. The Principal Clerk of each division will indicate such Minutes to the Secretary, who will decide whether or not to print them. The Principal Clerk will direct the preparation of copy for the printer, and will himself correct the proof. Copies will at once be furnished to the division, and a sufficient number kept on hand to bind into volumes for each of the Clerks at convenient intervals. By this plan, and by the elaborate indexes which are now kept in the Paper Room, materials will gradually collect in a form available for ultimately compiling a Digest of the more important parts of Treasury practice.

2. At present nearly the whole of the time of the Third Class Clerks is occupied in transforming Minutes into letters for despatch. In consequence of the manner in which, as a general rule, the Minute is drawn, a superior degree of intelligence is no doubt required in the Clerks charged with the duty of writing the letters; but by adopting a somewhat different system of writing the Minutes, the preparation of the letters could be reduced nearly to transcription, and could be entrusted to ordinary Writers.

My Lords desire, therefore, that in future the Principal Clerk shall send forward to the Secretaries the draft instructions which he considers necessary on the papers in the shape of a draft letter. In the case of an important decision, this will, in cases, be written by the Principal Clerk himself. Where the decision is simple, the draft will be prepared under his instructions, by his First or, perhaps, by his Second Class Clerk.

Their Lordships intend, by this part of their Minute, that the First and Second Class Clerks of each division, into whose hands its letters first come from the Registry Room, shall themselves write the draft replies, or other necessary directions, on all letters about which they feel no doubt before they transmit them to the Principal Clerk. The latter will thus receive only the more important letters for himself to deal with; while, as to the rest, his Clerks will primarily bear the responsibility of whatever draft reply or direction they have not specially referred to him. The Principal Clerk will retain the power of unquestioned alteration; but it is assumed by their Lordships that he will, as a general rule, initial the draft replies, &c., written by his Clerks, just as his own drafts are now initialed by the Secretaries, as often as the case appears to be *prima facie* ordinary, and the draft replies, &c., to be *prima facie* right. By this plan, the Principal Clerk's own time and attention will be reserved for the more important cases, and despatch will be promoted by the simultaneous disposal of each day's work. The First and Second Class Clerks will continue, as now, at the absolute disposal of the Principal Clerk in regard to the share which he may see fit to assign them in the disposal of any particular case. These provisions are in furtherance of the objects proposed by their Lordships' Minute of the 4th July, 1856, viz., to secure a succession of able officers by a proper training in suitable duties, and to economize labour by rightly dividing it.

The draft letter, ultimately returned by the Secretary, will be fair copied for signature, and for despatch by a Writer.

By the adoption of these arrangements the whole of the Third Class of Clerks may be abolished.

Looking to the nature of the duties which are imposed upon the Principal Clerks, and to the importance of securing for the discharge of them a succession of properly qualified officers, as well as to the fact that, under the altered organization of the Department, the Clerk, on first appointment, will at once be put to more responsible work, and will receive a higher salary than heretofore, my Lords are of opinion that a high order of examination, which shall test at once the general intelligence and the educational acquirements of the candidates is necessary for admission to the superior establishment of the Treasury.

The scheme of examination, which they consider should be similar to that for the Indian Civil Service, will be settled in communication with the Civil Service Commissioners.

My Lords further decide that the age of the candidates shall be not less than 20 nor more than 25 years.

INDEX

INDEX

Abbott, Lawrence, Treasury clerk 78
Accountability, definition of 47, 48, 73; *see also* Parliament
Accounts, public, *see* Parliament
Admiralty 71, 159, 161, 162
Albemarle, George Monck, Duke of, First Lord of 1667 Treasury Commission 20, 39n.
Anderson, William George, Principal Clerk of Finance 71, 99, 100; evidence on Treasury control 166–70
Anne, Queen 43, 46, 57, 58, 60, 81
Anson, G. E., Treasury clerk 97n.
Appropriation, *see* Parliament
Aram, Thomas, Treasury clerk 78
Arbuthnot, George, Treasury clerk, currency expert 98–9, 100
Arlington, Henry Bennet, Earl of, Secretary of State 20, 27; desire to be Lord Treasurer 41
Ashley, Anthony (Ashley Cooper) Lord; (later Earl of Shaftesbury), Chancellor of the Exchequer 20, 39n., 124, 127
Audit, *see* Exchequer; Parliament

Baillie-Hamilton, C. R., Treasury clerk 101n.
Baker, Eric, Treasury clerk 95
Bank of England 62, 63, 70, 72
Bankers, goldsmith 25, 39, 53
Barré, Colonel Isaac 61
Bates, Edward, Treasury clerk 97n.
Beldam, William, Treasury clerk 187
Bertie, Charles, Secretary to the Treasury 43, 77
Board of Trade 98
Book-keeping 53, 69, 70, 72, 96
Boyd, George, Treasury clerk 97n.
Bradshaw, Thomas, Secretary to the Treasury 78n., 83
Brande, George, Principal Clerk for Colonial Business, Treasury 97n., 98n., 202–3, 204
Brooksbank, Thomas C., Chief Clerk of Revenue Room 94, 95, 99; views on Treasury recruitment 196–200
Brummell, Benjamin, Treasury clerk 84n.

Brummell, William, Treasury clerk 84n.
Bullock, Edward C., Treasury clerk 94
Bulteel, Thomas, Treasury clerk 95
Burghley, Lord, Lord Treasurer 18
Burke, Edmund, on Treasury control 61–3, 65, 69
Burnaby, Edward, Treasury clerk 82, 179, 180
Business done in the Treasury, The, manuscript guide 86, 89

Carteret, Sir George, Treasurer of the Navy 52, 53, 54, 127
Cecil, Robert, Earl of Salisbury, Lord Treasurer 18
Chamberlayne, Edward, Treasury clerk, appointed Secretary to the Treasury 78n.
Chancery, Court of, rebuked by Treasury 49
Charles II, and the Treasury 18, 19, 20, 21, 28, 29, 32, 36, 38; reign of 18, 22, 45, 46, 51, 55, 56, 61
Charnock, Roger, Treasury clerk 78, 129–30
Civil List 60, 61, 68
Civil Service, Treasury control 68; pensions 66, 157, 162; salaries 68, 157; Open Competition 105
Civil Service Commission 98
Clarendon, Edward Hyde, Earl of 20, 23n., 24n.
Clay, F. E., Treasury clerk 101n.
Clifford, Sir Thomas (later Lord), Treasury Lord 20, 43, 124, 127; Lord Treasurer 39n.
Cole, J. H., Treasury clerk 103
Colonial Office 67, 161
Commission of Inquiry into Fees 86
Compton, P. A., Treasury clerk 95
Comptrollers of Army Accounts 58
Consolidated Fund 28, 64, 69
Cotterell, H., Treasury clerk 95
Cotton, Thomas, Treasury clerk 183
Cotton, William, Treasury clerk 87n., 94
Coventry, Sir William, Treasury